Here is what the critics say about Merriam-Webster:

"It is the closest we can get, in America, to the Voice of Authority."—*The New York Times*
WEBSTER'S THIRD NEW INTERNATIONAL DICTIONARY, UNABRIDGED

"It is the most up-to-the-minute dictionary in America today, one that keeps up with the headlines."—John Barkham
WEBSTER'S NINTH NEW COLLEGIATE DICTIONARY

"It is so ample and easy to use that for many it will largely supersede Roget ..."—*The Wall Street Journal*
WEBSTER'S COLLEGIATE THESAURUS

"... one of the great books on language in this generation ..."
—William Safire, *The New York Times*
WEBSTER'S DICTIONARY OF ENGLISH USAGE

"A must for every writer's library."—*The Boston Globe*
WEBSTER'S NEW DICTIONARY OF SYNONYMS

The
Merriam-Webster
Concise
Handbook
for Writers

A Merriam-Webster®

Merriam-Webster Inc., Publishers
Springfield, Massachusetts

A GENUINE MERRIAM-WEBSTER

The name *Webster* alone is no guarantee of excellence. It is used by a number of publishers and may serve mainly to mislead an unwary buyer.

A Merriam-Webster® is the registered trademark you should look for when you consider the purchases of dictionaries and other fine reference books. It carries the reputation of a company that has been doing business since 1831 and is your assurance of quality and authority.

Library of Congress Cataloging in Publication Data
Main entry under title:

The Merriam-Webster concise handbook for writers.
   p.   cm.
   Includes index.
   ISBN 0-87779-602-5
   1. English language—Rhetoric—Handbooks, manuals, etc.
2. English language—Grammar—1950–   —Handbooks,
manuals, etc.   I. Merriam-Webster, Inc.   II. Title: Concise
handbook for writers.
PE1408.M517   1991
428.2—dc20   91-27326
                                                      CIP

Printed and bound in the United States of America

12345RRD939291

Index/Eileen M. Haraty

Contents

Preface

THE MERRIAM-WEBSTER CONCISE HANDBOOK FOR WRITERS is designed to be a practical guide to the conventions of the English language in its written form. These conventions, generally referred to by writers and editors as *style,* include such day-to-day matters as punctuating sentences, capitalizing names and terms, using italics or underlining, spelling compound words and the plural and possessive forms of words, and deciding when to use abbreviations and numerals. This book also offers information and advice on composition and grammar and on a selection of other editing- and publishing-related topics. For each topic, the manual offers concise and comprehensive descriptions of the rules and conventions that writers and editors have developed for themselves to help them prepare copy that is clear, consistent, and attractive. Where the rules and conventions have exceptions, variations, and fine points that readers need to know of, these are also presented.

In many cases, the conventions discussed in this book offer choices rather than a single rule, as over the years writers and editors have developed differing sets of rules to guide them in their writing. One writer may favor a particular way of deciding when to use numerals and when to spell out numbers or how to form possessives of proper names ending in *s,* while another writer may favor other ways. Neither of these writers is necessarily wrong; each may simply be following a different style.

There are, of course, limits on the range of acceptable uses available to writers. And within that acceptable range, most writers and editors try to be consistent in the choices they make. This handbook is designed to help writers and editors make those acceptable and consistent choices.

The Merriam-Webster Concise Handbook for Writers was written and edited by working editors, the editors at Merriam-Webster Inc., and it reflects their experience in writing and editing for publication. However, the conventions of writing described in this book are by no means meant to be exhaustive of or limited to the style rules followed in Merriam-Webster® publications. Instead, this manual is based on Merriam-Webster's continuous study of the ways that Americans use their language. It draws on our extensive citation files, which include more than 14 million examples of English words used in context gathered from books by respected authors, major metropolitan newspapers, widely circulated general-interest magazines, and other publications, such as newsletters, annual reports, and special mailings by corporations and other institutions. Working from these sources, Merriam-Webster editors have been able to establish which practices are most commonly followed in standard American prose.

Based as it is on real-life source material, this handbook offers readers information about both the consensus and the variety that are apparent in standard American writing. The consensus in this book is recorded with simple descriptive statements, such as "A period terminates a sentence or a sentence fragment that is neither interrogative nor exclamatory."

In some cases, these statements have to be qualified, as in "The abbreviations A.D. and B.C. are usually styled in typeset matter as punctuated, unspaced, small capitals ...." The term *usually* is used throughout this handbook to indicate that we have evidence that some writers and editors follow a practice that is different from the one we are describing. However, *usually* appears only in statements describing a practice that is clearly the prevalent practice. Hence, the writer who prefers AD or A.D. or AD knows that he or she is departing from the prevalent practice but that such departures are not unprecedented in standard writing.

In describing practices that are clearly not prevalent, we have used the word *sometimes* to qualify the descriptive statement, as in "Commas are sometimes used to separate main clauses that are not joined by conjunctions." In most cases, a descriptive statement qualified with *sometimes* is also accompanied by an additional explanation that tells the reader what the circumstances are under which this use is most likely to occur and what the common alternatives to it are. In the case of the example just cited, the reader is told that this styling is likely to be used if the main clauses are short and feature obvious parallelism. The reader is also told that using a comma to join clauses that are not short or obviously parallel is usually considered an error, that most writers avoid it, and that clauses not joined by conjunctions are usually separated with a semicolon.

The qualifiers *often* and *frequently* are used throughout this book without meaning to suggest anything about the prevalence of the practice being described except that it is not universally followed. We say, for instance, that "a comma is often used to set off the word *Incorporated* or the abbreviation *Inc.* from the rest of a corporate name; however, many companies elect to omit this comma from their names." This statement is not meant to indicate whether most companies do or do not favor using a comma in this position. We are saying that both practices are so well-established within standard style that their relative frequency is fundamentally irrelevant.

Finally, some practices raise questions that demand explanations that go beyond the use of a simple qualifier. In these cases we have appended a note to the description. Notes are introduced by the all-capitalized designation "NOTE," and they serve to explain, in as much detail as needed, variations, exceptions, and fine points that relate to or qualify the descriptive statement that precedes them.

The Merriam-Webster Concise Handbook for Writers is adapted from *Webster's Standard American Style Manual* and various other Merriam-Webster® publications and, as such, is based on work done by the writers and editors of those books. The adaptation was carried out by Madeline L. Novak and John M. Morse with the assistance of Jennifer S. Goss, René P. Houle, and Anne Louise Kerr. The index was prepared by Eileen M. Haraty. Additional proofreading assistance was provided by Daniel J. Hopkins.

Chapter 1

Punctuation

CONTENTS

Punctuation marks are used in the English writing system to help clarify the structure and meaning of sentences. To some degree, they achieve this end by corresponding to certain elements of the spoken language, such as pitch, volume, pause, and stress. To an even greater degree, however, punctuation marks serve to clarify structure and meaning by virtue of the fact that they conventionally accompany certain grammatical elements in a sentence, no matter how those elements might be spoken. In many cases, the relationship between punctuation and grammatical structure is such that the choice of which mark of punctuation to use in a sentence is clear and unambiguous. In other cases, however, the structure of a sentence may be such that it allows for several patterns of punctuation. In cases like these, varying notions of correctness have grown up, and two writers might, with equal correctness and with equal clarity, punctuate the same sentence quite differently.

2 Punctuation

This chapter is designed to help writers and editors make decisions about which mark of punctuation to use. In situations where more than one pattern of punctuation may be used, each is explained; if there are reasons to prefer one over another, the reasons are presented, but there are many instances in which one styling is no more preferable or common than another. Therefore, even after having read this chapter, writers and editors will find that they still encounter questions requiring them to exercise their judgment and taste.

The descriptions in this chapter focus on the ways in which punctuation marks are used to convey grammatical structure. The chapter does not explain in any detailed way the use of some punctuation marks to style individual words and compounds. Specifically, this chapter does not discuss the use of quotation marks to style titles and other kinds of proper nouns, the use of apostrophes to form plurals and possessives, the use of hyphens to form compounds, or the use of periods to punctuate abbreviations. For a discussion of these topics, see Chapter 2, "Capitals, Italics, and Quotation Marks"; Chapter 3, "Plurals, Possessives, and Compounds"; and Chapter 4, "Abbreviations."

General Principles

In addition to the rules that have been developed for individual marks of punctuation, there are also conventions and principles that apply to marks of punctuation in general, and these are explained in the paragraphs that follow.

Open and Close Punctuation

Two terms frequently used to describe patterns of punctuation, especially in regard to commas, are *open* and *close*. An open punctuation pattern is one in which commas and other marks of punctuation are used sparingly, usually only to separate major syntactical units, such as main clauses, or to prevent misreading. A close punctuation pattern, on the other hand, makes liberal use of punctuation marks, often putting one wherever the grammatical structure of the sentence will allow it. Close punctuation is often considered old-fashioned, and open punctuation more modern; however, contemporary writing displays a wide range of practices in regard to commas, and some grammatical constructions are still punctuated in ways traditionally associated with close punctuation (see paragraphs 8 and 22 under Comma in this chapter).

Multiple Punctuation

The term *multiple punctuation* describes the use of two or more marks of punctuation following the same word in a sentence. A conventional rule says that multiple punctuation is to be avoided except in cases involving brackets, parentheses, quotation marks, and sometimes dashes. Unfortunately, it is not possible to formulate any simple general instructions that would allow writers and editors to apply this rule. This book addresses the question of multiple punctuation by including a section entitled "With Other Marks of Punctuation" at the end of the treatment of each mark of punctuation for which there is a specific convention regarding multiple punctuation.

Boldface and Italic Punctuation

In general, marks of punctuation are set in the same typeface (lightface or boldface, italic or roman) as the word that precedes them, but most writers and editors allow themselves a number of exceptions to this rule. Brackets and parentheses are nearly always set in the font of the surrounding text, usually lightface roman, regardless of the text they enclose. Quotation marks are usually handled in the same manner; however, if the text they enclose is entirely in a contrasting typeface, they are set in a typeface to match. Some writers and editors base decisions regarding the typeface of exclamation points and question marks on the context in which they are used. If the exclamation point or question mark is clearly associated with the word or words that precede it, it is set in a matching typeface. If, on the other hand, it punctuates the sentence as a whole, it is set in the same typeface as the rest of the sentence.

> **Summary:** Recently completed surveys tend to confirm the theory that . . .
>
> He lived up to his reputation as an *homme d'esprit*; only once did he fail to come up with a witty reply.
>
> You did *that!*
>
> We were talking with the author of the book *Who Did That?*
>
> Have you seen the latest issue of *Saturday Review*?

Spacing

The conventions regarding the amount of space that precedes or follows a mark of punctuation vary from mark to mark. In general, the usual spacing around each mark of punctuation should be clear from the example sentences included for each mark of punctuation. In cases where additional explanation is needed, it is included at the end of the discussion, often under the heading "Spacing."

Ampersand

An ampersand is typically written &, although it has other forms, as *&*, *&*, and &. The character represents the word *and*; its function is to replace the word when a shorter form is desirable. However, the ampersand is an acceptable substitute for *and* only in a few constructions.

1. The ampersand is used in the names of companies but not in the names of agencies that are part of the federal government.

   > American Telephone & Telegraph Co.
   > Gulf & Western Corporation
   > Occupational Safety and Health Administration
   > Securities and Exchange Commission

   NOTE: In styling corporate names, writers and editors often try to reproduce the form of the name preferred by the company (taken from an annual report or company letterhead). However, this information may not be available and, even if it is available, following the different preferences of different companies can lead to apparent inconsistencies in the text. Publications that include very many corporate names usually choose one styling, usually the one with the ampersand, and use it in all corporate names that include *and*.

2. Ampersands are frequently used in abbreviations. Style varies regarding the spacing around the ampersand. Publications that make heavy use of abbreviations, such as business or technical publications, most often omit the spaces. In general-interest publications, both the spaced and the unspaced stylings are common.

   > The R&D budget looks adequate for the next fiscal year.
   > Apply for a loan at your bank or S & L.

3. The ampersand is often used in cases where a condensed text is necessary, as in tabular material. While bibliographies, indexes, and most other listings use *and*, some systems of parenthetical documentation do use the ampersand. For more on parenthetical documentation, see Chapter 7, "Notes and Bibliographies."

   > (Carter, Good & Robertson 1984)

4. When an ampersand is used between the last two elements in a series, the comma is omitted.

   > the law firm of Shilliday, Fraser & French

Apostrophe

1. The apostrophe is used to indicate the possessive case of nouns and indefinite pronouns. For details regarding this use, see the section on Possessives, beginning on page 88, in Chapter 3, "Plurals, Possessives, and Compounds."

2. Apostrophes are sometimes used to form plurals of letters, numerals, abbreviations, symbols, and words referred to as words. For details regarding this use, see the section on Plurals, beginning on page 82, in Chapter 3, "Plurals, Possessives, and Compounds."

3. Apostrophes mark omissions in contractions made of two or more words that are pronounced as one word.

didn't	o'clock
you're	shouldn't've

4. The apostrophe is used to indicate that letters have been intentionally omitted from the spelling of a word in order to reproduce a perceived pronunciation or to give a highly informal flavor to a piece of writing.

   "Head back to N'Orleans," the man said.

   Get 'em while they're hot.

   dancin' till three

   NOTE: Sometimes words are so consistently spelled with an apostrophe that the spelling with the apostrophe becomes an accepted variant.

   fo'c'sle for *forecastle*
   bos'n for *boatswain*
   rock 'n' roll for *rock and roll*

5. Apostrophes mark the omission of numerals.

   class of '91
   politics in the '90s

   NOTE: Writers who use the apostrophe for styling the plurals of words expressed in numerals usually avoid the use of the apostrophe illustrated in the second example above. Either they omit the apostrophe that stands for the missing figures, or they spell the word out.

   90's *or* nineties *but not* '90's

6. Apostrophes are used to produce the inflected forms of verbs that are made of numerals or individually pronounced letters. Hyphens are sometimes used for this purpose also.

> 86'ed our proposal
> OK'ing the manuscript
> TKO'd his opponent

7. An apostrophe is often used to add an *-er* ending to an abbreviation, especially if some confusion might result from its absence. Hyphens are sometimes used for this purpose also. If no confusion is likely, the apostrophe is usually omitted.

> 4-H'er   CBer
> AA'er   DXer

8. The use of apostrophes to form abbreviations (as *ass'n* for *association* or *sec'y* for *secretary*) is avoided in most formal writing.

Brackets

Brackets work like parentheses to set off inserted material, but their functions are more specialized. Several of their principal uses occur with quoted material, as illustrated below. For other aspects of styling quotations, see Chapter 8, "The Treatment of Quotations."

With Editorial Insertions

1. Brackets enclose editorial comments, corrections, clarifications, or other material inserted into a text, especially into quoted matter.

> "Remember, this was the first time since it became law that the Twenty-first Amendment [outlining procedures for the replacement of a dead or incapacitated President or Vice President] had been invoked."
>
> "But there's one thing to be said for it [his apprenticeship with Samuels]: it started me thinking about architecture in a new way."
>
> He wrote, "I am just as cheerful as when you was [sic] here."

NOTE: While the text into which such editorial insertions are made is almost always quoted material, they are sometimes also used in nonquoted material, particularly in cases where an editor wishes to add material to an author's text without disturbing the author's original wording.

> Furthermore the Committee anticipates additional expenses in the coming fiscal year [October 1985–September 1986] and seeks revenues to meet these expenses.

2. Brackets set off insertions that supply missing letters.

> "If you can't persuade D[israeli], I'm sure no one can."

3. Brackets enclose insertions that take the place of words or phrases that were used in the original version of a quoted passage.

> The report, entitled "A Decade of Progress," begins with a short message from President Stevens in which she notes that "the loving portraits and revealing accounts of [this report] are not intended to constitute a complete history of the decade. . . . Rather [they] impart the flavor of the events, developments, and achievements of this vibrant period."

4. Brackets enclose insertions that slightly alter the form of a word used in an original text.

> The magazine reported that thousands of the country's children were "go[ing] to bed hungry every night."

5. Brackets are used to indicate that the capitalization or typeface of the original passage has been altered in some way.

> As we point out on pages 234–235, "The length of a quotation usually determines whether it is run into the text or set as a block quotation. . . . [L]ength can be assessed in terms of the number of words, the number of typewritten or typeset lines, or the number of sentences in the passage."

> They agreed with and were encouraged by her next point: "In the past, many secretaries have been placed in positions of responsibility *without being delegated enough authority to carry out the responsibility.* [Italics added.] The current pressures affecting managers have caused them to rethink the secretarial function and to delegate more responsibility and authority to their secretaries."

NOTE: The use of brackets to indicate altered capitalization is optional in many situations. For more on this use of brackets, see the section on Alterations, Omissions, and Interpolations, beginning on page 238, in Chapter 8, "The Treatment of Quotations."

As a Mechanical Device

6. Brackets function as parentheses within parentheses.

> The company was incinerating high concentrations of pollutants (such as polychlorinated biphenyls [PCBs]) in a power boiler.

7. Brackets set off phonetic symbols or transcriptions.

> [t] in British *duty*

8. Brackets are used in combination with parentheses to set off units in mathematical expressions. They are also used in chemical formulas.

> $x + 5[(x + y)(2x - y)]$
> $Ag[Pt(NO_2)_4]$

With Other Marks of Punctuation

9. No punctuation mark (other than a period after an abbreviation) precedes bracketed material within a sentence. If punctuation is required, the mark is placed after the closing bracket.

> The report stated, "If we fail to find additional sources of supply [of oil and gas], our long-term growth will be limited."

10. When brackets enclose a complete sentence, the required punctuation should be placed within the brackets.

> [A pawprint photographed last month in the Quabbin area has finally verified the cougar's continued existence in the Northeast.]

NOTE: Unlike parentheses, brackets are rarely used to enclose complete sentences within other sentences.

Spacing

11. No space is left between brackets and the material they enclose or between brackets and any mark of punctuation immediately following.

12. In typewritten material, two spaces precede an opening bracket and follow a closing bracket when the brackets enclose a complete sentence. In typeset material, only one space is used.

> ```
> We welcome the return of the cougar.  [A paw
> print photographed last month has verified its
> existence locally.]  Its habitation in this area
> is a good sign for the whole environment.
> ```

> We welcome the return of the cougar. [A paw print photographed last month has verified its existence locally.] Its habitation in this area is a good sign for the whole environment.

Colon

The colon is a mark of introduction. It indicates that what follows it—whether a clause, a phrase, or even a single word—is linked with some element that precedes it. Many uses of the colon are similar to those of the dash. Like the dash, the colon gives special emphasis to whatever follows it; lengthy material introduced by a colon is often further emphasized by indention. (For information on the question of capitalizing the first word following a colon, see the section on Beginnings, starting on page 53, in Chapter 2, "Capitals, Italics, and Quotation Marks.")

With Phrases and Clauses

1. A colon introduces a clause or phrase that explains, illustrates, amplifies, or restates what has gone before.

> The sentence was poorly constructed: it lacked both unity and co-herence.
>
> Throughout its history, the organization has combined a tradition of excellence with a dedication to human service: educating the young, caring for the elderly, assisting in community-development programs.
>
> Disk cartridges provide high-density storage capacity: up to 16 megabytes of information on some cartridges.
>
> Time was running out: a decision had to be made.

2. A colon directs attention to an appositive.

> The question is this: where will we get the money?
>
> He had only one pleasure: eating.

3. A colon is used to introduce a series. The introductory statement often includes a phrase such as *the following* or *as follows*.

> The conference was attended by representatives of five nations: England, France, Belgium, Spain, and Portugal.
>
> Anyone planning to participate should be prepared to do the following: hike five miles with a backpack, sleep on the ground without a tent, and paddle a canoe through rough water.

NOTE: Opinion varies regarding whether a colon should interrupt the grammatical continuity of a clause (as by coming between a verb and its objects). Although most style manuals and composition handbooks advise against this practice and recommend that a full independent clause precede the colon, the interrupting colon is common. It is especially likely to be used before a lengthy and complex list, in which case the colon serves to set the list distinctly apart from the normal flow of running text. With shorter or less complex lists, the colon is usually not used.

> Our programs to increase profitability include: continued modernization of our manufacturing facilities; consolidation of distribution terminals; discontinuation of unprofitable retail outlets; and reorganization of our personnel structure, along with across-the-board staff reductions.
>
> Our programs to increase profitability include plant modernization, improved distribution and retailing procedures, and staff reductions.
>
> Our programs to increase profitability include the following: continued modernization of our manufacturing facilities; consolidation of distribution terminals; discontinuation of unprofitable retail outlets; and reorganization of our personnel structure, along with across-the-board staff reductions.

4. A colon is used like a dash to introduce a summary statement following a series.

> Physics, biology, sociology, anthropology: he discusses them all.

With Quotations

5. A colon introduces lengthy quoted material that is set off from the rest of a text by indentation but not by quotation marks. For more on the treatment of lengthy quoted material, see Chapter 8, "The Treatment of Quotations."

> He took the title for his biography of Thoreau from a passage in *Walden*:
>> I long ago lost a hound, a bay horse, and a turtle-dove, and am still on their trail. . . . I have met one or two who had heard the hound, and the tramp of the horse, and even seen the dove disappear behind a cloud, and they seemed as anxious to recover them as if they had lost them themselves.
>
> However, the title *A Hound, a Bay Horse, and a Turtle-Dove* probably puzzled some readers.

6. A colon may be used before a quotation in running text, especially when (1) the quotation is lengthy, (2) the quotation is a formal statement or is being given special emphasis, or (3) the quotation is an appositive.

> Said Murdoch: "The key to the success of this project is good planning. We need to know precisely all of the steps that we will need to go through, what kind of staff we will require to accomplish each step, what the entire project will cost, and when we can expect completion."
>
> The inscription reads: "Here lies one whose name was writ in water."
>
> In response, he had this to say: "No one knows better than I do that changes will have to be made soon."

As a Mechanical Device

7. In transcriptions of dialogue, a colon follows the speaker's name.

> Robert: You still haven't heard from her?
> Michael: No, and I'm beginning to worry.

8. A colon follows a brief heading or introductory term.

> NOTE: The library will be closed on the 17th while repairs are being made to the heating system.
>
> 1977: New developments in microchip technology lead to less-expensive manufacturing.

9. A colon separates elements in page references, bibliographical and biblical citations, and fixed formulas used to express ratios and time.

Journal of the American Medical Association 48:356
Springfield, Mass.: Merriam-Webster Inc.
John 4:10
8:30 a.m.
a ratio of 3:5

10. A colon separates titles and subtitles (as of books).

The Tragic Dynasty: A History of the Romanovs

11. A colon is used to join terms that are being contrasted or compared.

Seventeenth-century rhymes include *prayer* : *afar* and
brass : *was* : *ass*.

12. A colon follows the salutation in formal correspondence.

Dear General Smith:
Dear Mr. Jiménez:
Dear Product Manager:
Ladies and Gentlemen:

13. A colon punctuates memorandum and government correspondence headings and subject lines in general business
letters.

TO:
SUBJECT:
VIA:
REFERENCE:

14. A colon separates writer/dictator/typist initials in the identification lines of business letters.

WAL:jml
WAL:WEB:jml

15. A colon separates carbon-copy or blind carbon-copy abbreviations from the initials or names of copy recipients in business
letters.

cc:RWP
　JES

bcc:MWK
　FCM

With Other Marks of Punctuation

16. A colon is placed outside quotation marks and parentheses.

There's only one thing wrong with "Harold's Indiscretion": it's
not funny.

I quote from the first edition of *Springtime in Savannah* (published
in 1952):

Spacing

17. In typewritten material, two spaces follow a colon used in running text, bibliographical references, publication titles, and letter or memorandum headings. In typeset material, only one space follows.

```
The answer is simple:  don't go.
SUBJECT:  Project X
```
New York: Macmillan, 1980.
Typewriting: A Guide

18. When a colon is being used between two correlated terms (see paragraph 11), it is centered with equal spacing on each side.

The stature of the two sexes shows the same female : male proportions.

19. No space precedes or follows a colon when it is used between numerals.

9:30 a.m.
a ratio of 2:4

20. No space precedes or follows a colon in a business-letter identification line or in a carbon-copy notation that indicates a recipient designated by initials.

FCM:hg
cc:FCM

21. Two spaces follow a colon in a carbon-copy notation that indicates a recipient designated by a full name.

cc: Mr. Johnson

Comma

The comma is the most frequently used punctuation mark in the English writing system. Its most common uses are to separate items in a series and to set off syntactical elements within sentences. Within these two broad categories, there are a great many specific uses to which commas can be put. This section explains the most common aspects of the comma, listed under the following headings.

Between Main Clauses
With Compound Predicates
With Subordinate Clauses and Phrases
With Appositives
With Introductory and Interrupting Elements

With Contrasting Expressions
With Items in a Series
With Compound Modifiers
In Quotations, Questions, and Indirect Discourse
With Omitted Words
With Addresses, Dates, and Numbers
With Names, Degrees, and Titles
In Correspondence
Other Uses
With Other Marks of Punctuation

Between Main Clauses

1. A comma separates main clauses joined by a coordinating conjunction (as *and, but, or, nor,* and *for*). For use of commas with clauses joined by correlative conjunctions, see paragraph 24 below.

> She knew very little about him, and he volunteered nothing.
>
> We will not respond to any more questions on that topic this afternoon, nor will we respond to similar questions at any time in the future.
>
> His face showed disappointment, for he knew that he had failed.

NOTE: Some reference books still insist that *so* and *yet* are adverbs rather than conjunctions and that therefore they should be preceded by a semicolon when they join main clauses. However, our evidence indicates that the use of *so* and *yet* as conjunctions preceded by a comma is standard.

> The acoustics in this hall are good, so every note is clear.
>
> We have requested this information many times before, yet we have never gotten a satisfactory reply.

2. When one or both of the clauses are short or when they are closely related in meaning, the comma is often omitted.

> The sun was shining and the birds were singing.
>
> We didn't realize it at the time but the spot we had picked for our home was the same spot one of our ancestors had picked for his home.
>
> Six thousand years ago, the top of the volcano blew off in a series of powerful eruptions and the sides collapsed into the middle.
>
> Many people want to take their vacations in August so it may be difficult for some of them to find good accommodations.

NOTE: In punctuating sentences such as the ones illustrated above, writers have to use their own judgment regarding whether clauses are short enough or closely related enough to warrant omitting the comma. There are no clear-cut rules to follow; however, factors such as the rhythm, parallelism, or logic of the sentence often influence how clearly or smoothly it will read with or without the comma.

3. Commas are sometimes used to separate main clauses that are not joined by conjunctions. This styling is especially likely to be used if the clauses are short and feature obvious parallelism.

> One day you are a successful corporate lawyer, the next day you are out of work.
>
> The city has suffered terribly in the interim. Bombs have destroyed most of the buildings, disease has ravaged the population.

NOTE: Using a comma to join clauses that are neither short nor obviously parallel is usually called *comma fault* or *comma splice* and most writers and editors avoid such a construction. In general, clauses not joined by conjunctions are separated by semicolons.

4. If a sentence is composed of three or more clauses, the clauses may be separated by either commas or semicolons. Clauses that are short and relatively free of commas can be separated by commas even if they are not joined by a conjunction. If the clauses are long or heavily punctuated, they are separated with semicolons, except for the last two clauses which may be separated by either a comma or a semicolon. Usually a comma will be used between the last two clauses only if those clauses are joined by a conjunction. For more examples of clauses separated with commas and semicolons, see paragraph 5 under Semicolon in this chapter.

> The pace of change seems to have quickened, the economy is uncertain, the technology seems sometimes liberating and sometimes hostile.
>
> Small fish fed among the marsh weed, ducks paddled along the surface, and a muskrat ate greens along the bank.
>
> The policy is a complex one to explain; defending it against its critics is not easy, nor is it clear the defense is always necessary.

With Compound Predicates

5. Commas are not usually used to separate the parts of a compound predicate.

> The firefighter tried to enter the burning building but was turned back by the thick smoke.

NOTE: Despite the fact that most style manuals and composition handbooks warn against separating the parts of compound predicates with commas, many authors and editors use commas in just this way. They are particularly likely to do so if the predicate is especially long and complicated, if they want to stress one part of the predicate, or if the absence of a comma could cause even a momentary misreading of the sentence.

The board helps to develop the financing, new product planning, and marketing strategies for new corporate divisions, and issues periodic reports on expenditures, revenues, and personnel appointments.

This is an unworkable plan, and has been from the start.

I try to explain to him what I want him to do, and get nowhere.

With Subordinate Clauses and Phrases

6. Adverbial clauses and phrases that precede a main clause are usually set off with commas.

> As cars age, they depreciate.
>
> Having made that decision, we turned our attention to other matters.
>
> To understand the situation, you must be familiar with the background.
>
> From the top of this rugged and isolated plateau, I could see the road stretching out for miles across the desert.
>
> In 1919, his family left Russia and moved to this country.
>
> In addition, staff members respond to queries, take new orders, and initiate billing.

7. If a sentence begins with an adverbial clause or phrase and can be easily read without a comma following it, writers will often omit the comma. In most cases where the comma is omitted, the phrase will be short—four words or less. But some writers will omit the comma even after a longer phrase if the sentence can be easily read or seems more forceful that way.

> In January the company will introduce a new line of entirely redesigned products.
>
> On the map the town appeared as a small dot in the midst of vast emptiness.
>
> If the project cannot be done profitably perhaps it should not be done at all.

8. Adverbial clauses and phrases that introduce a main clause other than the first main clause are usually set off with commas. However, if the adverbial clause or phrase follows a conjunction, style varies regarding how many commas are required to set it off. In most cases, two commas are used: one before the conjunction and one following the clause or phrase. Writers who prefer close punctuation usually use three commas: one before the conjunction and two more to enclose the clause or phrase. If the writer prefers open punctuation, the phrase may not be set off at all. In this case, only one comma that separates the main clauses is used. For more on open and close punctuation, see page 2.

His parents were against the match, and had the couple not eloped, their plans for marriage would have come to nothing.

They have redecorated the entire store, but, to the delight of their customers, the store retains much of its original flavor. [close]

We haven't left Springfield yet, but when we get to Boston we'll call you. [open]

9. A comma is not used after an introductory phrase if the phrase immediately precedes the main verb.

In the road lay a dead rabbit.

10. Subordinate clauses and phrases that follow a main clause or that fall within a main clause are usually not set off by commas if they are restrictive. A clause or phrase is considered restrictive if its removal from the sentence would alter the meaning of the main clause. If the meaning of the main clause would not be altered by removing the subordinate clause or phrase, the clause or phrase is considered nonrestrictive and usually is set off by commas.

We will be delighted if she decides to stay. [restrictive]

Anyone who wants his or her copy of the book autographed by the author should get in line. [restrictive]

Her new book, *Fortune's Passage,* was well received. [nonrestrictive]

That was a good meal, although I didn't particularly like the broccoli in cream sauce. [nonrestrictive]

11. Commas are used to set off an adverbial clause or phrase that falls between the subject and the verb.

The weather, fluctuating from very hot to downright chilly, necessitated a variety of clothing.

12. Commas enclose modifying phrases that do not immediately precede the word or phrase they modify.

Hungry and tired, the soldiers marched back to camp.

We could see the importance, both long-term and short-term, of her proposal.

The two children, equally happy with their lunches, set off for school.

13. Absolute phrases are set off with commas, whether they fall at the beginning, middle, or end of the sentence.

Our business being concluded, we adjourned for refreshments.

We headed southward, the wind freshening behind us, to meet the rest of the fleet in the morning.

I still remember my first car, its bumpers sagging, its tires worn, its body rusting.

With Appositives

14. Commas are used to set off a word, phrase, or clause that is in apposition to a noun and that is nonrestrictive.

> My husband, Larry, is in charge of ticket sales for the fair.
>
> The highboy, or tallboy, is a tall chest of drawers typically made between 1690 and 1780.
>
> George Washington, first president of the United States, has been the subject of countless biographies.
>
> We were most impressed by the third candidate, the one who brought a writing sample and asked so many questions.

NOTE: A nonrestrictive appositive sometimes precedes the word with which it is in apposition. It is set off by commas in this position also.

> A cherished landmark in the city, the Hotel Sandburg has managed once again to escape the wrecking ball.

15. Restrictive appositives are not set off by commas.

> My daughter Andrea had the lead in the school play.
>
> Alfred Hitchcock's thriller "Psycho" will be screened tonight.

With Introductory and Interrupting Elements

16. Commas set off transitional words and phrases (as *finally, meanwhile,* and *after all*).

> Indeed, close coordination between departments can minimize confusion during this period of expansion.
>
> We are eager to begin construction; however, the necessary materials have not yet arrived.
>
> The most recent report, on the other hand, makes clear why the management avoids such agreements.

NOTE: Adverbs that can serve as transitional words can often serve in other ways as well. When these adverbs are not used to make a transition, no comma is necessary.

> The materials had finally arrived.

17. Commas set off parenthetical elements, such as authorial asides and supplementary information, that are closely related to the rest of the sentence.

> All of us, to tell the truth, were completely amazed by his suggestion.
>
> The headmaster, now in his sixth year at the school, was responsible for the changes in the curriculum.

NOTE: When the parenthetical element is digressive or otherwise not closely related to the rest of the sentence, it is often set off by dashes or parentheses. For contrasting examples, see paragraph 3 under Dash and paragraphs 1 and 9 under Parentheses in this chapter.

18. Commas are used to set off words or phrases that introduce examples or explanations.

> He expects to visit three countries this summer, namely, France, Spain, and Germany.
>
> I would like to develop a good, workable plan, i.e., one that would outline our goals and set a timetable for their accomplishment.

NOTE: Words and phrases such as *i.e., e.g., namely, for example,* and *that is* are often preceded by a dash, open parenthesis, or semicolon, depending on the magnitude of the break in continuity represented by the examples or explanations that they introduce; however, regardless of the punctuation that precedes the word or phrase, a comma always follows it. For contrasting examples of dashes, parentheses, and semicolons with these words and phrases, see paragraph 6 under Dash, paragraph 2 under Parentheses, and paragraph 6 under Semicolon in this chapter.

19. Commas are used to set off words in direct address.

> We would like to discuss your account, Mrs. Reid.
>
> The answer, my friends, lies within us.

20. Commas set off mild interjections or exclamations such as *ah* or *oh*.

> Ah, summer—season of sunshine and goodwill.
>
> Oh, what a beautiful baby.

NOTE: The vocative *O* is not set off by commas.

> O Time! O Death!
>
> Have mercy, O Lord.

With Contrasting Expressions

21. A comma is used to set off contrasting expressions within a sentence.

> This project will take six months, not six weeks.
>
> He has merely changed his style, not his ethics.

22. Style varies regarding use of the comma to set off two or more contrasting phrases used to describe a single word that follows immediately. In open punctuation, a comma follows the first modifier but is not used between the final modifier and the word modified. In close punctuation, the contrasting phrase is treated as a nonrestrictive modifier and is, therefore, both preceded and followed by a comma. For more on open and close punctuation, see page 2.

The harsh, although eminently realistic critique is not going to make you popular. [open]

The harsh, although eminently realistic, critique is not going to make you popular. [close]

This street takes you away from, not toward the capitol building. [open]

This street takes you away from, not toward, the capitol building. [close]

23. Adjectives and adverbs that modify the same word or phrase and that are joined by *but* or some other coordinating conjunction are not separated by a comma.

    a bicycle with a light but sturdy frame
    a multicolored but subdued rag rug
    errors caused by working carelessly or too quickly

24. A comma does not usually separate elements that are contrasted through the use of a pair of correlative conjunctions (as *either . . . or, neither . . . nor,* and *not only . . . but also*).

    The cost is either $69.95 or $79.95.

    Neither my brother nor I noticed the mistake.

    He was given the post not only because of his diplomatic connections but also because of his great tact and charm.

    NOTE: Correlative conjunctions are sometimes used to join main clauses. If the clauses are short, a comma is not added; however, if the clauses are long, a comma usually separates them.

    Either you do it my way or we don't do it at all.

    Not only did she have to see three salesmen and a visiting reporter during the course of the day, but she also had to prepare for the next day's meeting with the president.

25. Long parallel contrasting and comparing clauses are separated by commas; short parallel phrases are not.

    The more I heard about this new project, the greater was my desire to volunteer.

    "The sooner the better," I said.

With Items in a Series

26. Words, phrases, and clauses joined in a series are separated by commas. If main clauses are joined in a series, they may be separated by either semicolons or commas. For more on the use of commas and semicolons to separate main clauses, see paragraphs 1, 3, and 4 above and paragraph 5 under Semicolon in this chapter.

Men, women, and children crowded aboard the train.

Her job required her to pack quickly, to travel often, and to have no personal life.

He responded patiently while reporters shouted questions, flash-bulbs popped, and the crowd pushed closer.

NOTE: Style varies regarding the use of the comma between the last two items in a series if those items are also joined by a conjunction. In some cases, as in the example below, omitting the final comma (often called the serial comma) can result in ambiguity. Some writers feel that in most sentences the use of the conjunction makes the comma superfluous, and they favor using the comma only when a misreading could result from omitting it. Others feel that it is easier to include the final comma routinely rather than try to consider each sentence separately to decide whether a misreading is possible without the comma. Most reference books, including this one, and most other book-length works of nonfiction use the serial comma. In all other categories of publishing, according to our evidence, usage is evenly or nearly evenly divided on the use or omission of this comma.

We are looking for a house with a big yard, a view of the harbor, and beach and docking privileges. [with serial comma]

We are looking for a house with a big yard, a view of the harbor and beach and docking privileges. [without serial comma]

27. A comma is not used to separate items in a series that are joined with conjunctions.

I don't understand what this policy covers or doesn't cover or only partially covers.

I have talked to the president and the vice president and three other executives.

28. When the elements in a series are long or complex or consist of clauses that themselves contain commas, the elements are usually separated by semicolons, not commas. For more on this use of the semicolon, see paragraphs 7 and 8 under Semicolon in this chapter.

With Compound Modifiers

29. A comma is used to separate two or more adjectives, adverbs, or phrases that modify the same word or phrase. For the use of commas with contrasting modifiers, see paragraphs 22 and 23 above.

She spoke in a calm, reflective manner.

We watched the skier move smoothly, gracefully through the turns.

His story was too fantastic, too undersupported by facts for us to take seriously.

30. A comma is not used between two adjectives when the first modifies the combination of the second adjective plus the word or phrase it modifies.

    a little brown jug
    a modern concrete-and-glass building

31. A comma is not used to separate an adverb from the adjective or adverb that it modifies.

    a truly distinctive manner
    running very quickly down the street

In Quotations, Questions, and Indirect Discourse

32. A comma separates a direct quotation from a phrase identifying its source or speaker. If the quotation is a question or an exclamation and the identifying phrase follows the quotation, the comma is replaced by a question mark or an exclamation point.

    Mary said, "I am leaving."
    "I am leaving," Mary said.
    Mary asked, "Where are you going?"
    "Where are you going?" Mary asked.
    "I am leaving," Mary said, "even if you want me to stay."
    "Don't do that!" Mary shouted.

    NOTE: In some cases, a colon can replace a comma preceding a quotation. For more on this use of the colon, see paragraph 6 under Colon in this chapter.

33. A comma does not set off a quotation that is tightly incorporated into the sentence in which it appears.

    Throughout the session his only responses were "No comment" and "I don't think so."

    Just because he said he was "about to leave this minute" doesn't mean he actually left.

34. Style varies regarding the use of commas to set off shorter sentences that fall within longer sentences and that do not constitute actual dialogue. These shorter sentences may be mottoes or maxims, unspoken or imaginary dialogue, or sentences referred to as sentences; and they may or may not be enclosed in quotation marks. (For more on the use of quotation marks with sentences like these, see paragraph 6 under Quotation Marks, Double, in this chapter.) Typically the shorter sentence functions as a subject, object, or complement

within the larger sentence and does not require a comma. Sometimes the structure of the larger sentence will be styled like actual quoted dialogue, and in such cases a comma is used to separate the shorter sentence from the text that introduces or identifies it. In some cases, where an author decides not to use quotation marks, a comma may be inserted simply to mark the beginning of the shorter sentence clearly.

> "The computer is down" was the response she dreaded.
>
> Another confusing idiom is "How do you do?"
>
> He spoke with a candor that seemed to insist, This actually happened to me and in just this way.
>
> The first rule is, When in doubt, spell it out.

When the shorter sentence functions as an appositive in the larger sentence, it is set off with a comma when nonrestrictive and not when restrictive. (For more on restrictive modifiers and appositives, see paragraphs 10, 14, and 15 above.)

> He was fond of the slogan "Every man a king, but no man wears a crown."
>
> We had the club's motto, "We make waves," printed on our T-shirts.

35. A comma introduces a direct question regardless of whether it is enclosed in quotation marks or if its first word is capitalized.

> I wondered, what is going on here?
>
> The question is, How do we get out of here?
>
> What bothered her was, who had eaten all of the cookies?

36. The comma is omitted before quotations that are very short exclamations or representations of sounds.

> He jumped up suddenly and cried "Yow!"
>
> When she was done, she let out a loud "Whew!"

37. A comma is not used to set off indirect discourse or indirect questions introduced by a conjunction (such as *that* or *what*).

> Mary said that she was leaving.
>
> I wondered what was going on there.
>
> The clerk told me that the book I had ordered had just come in.

With Omitted Words

38. A comma indicates the omission of a word or phrase, especially in parallel constructions where the omitted word or phrase appears earlier in the sentence.

> Common stocks are preferred by some investors; bonds, by others.

39. A comma often replaces the conjunction *that*.

> The road was so steep and winding, we thought for sure that we would go over the edge.
>
> The problem is, we don't know how to fix it.

With Addresses, Dates, and Numbers

40. A comma is used to set off the individual elements of an address except for zip codes. In current practice, no punctuation appears between a state name and the zip code that follows it. If prepositions are used between the elements of the address, commas are not needed.

> Mrs. Bryant may be reached at 52 Kiowa Circle, Mesa, Arizona.
>
> Mr. Briscoe was born in Liverpool, England.
>
> The collection will be displayed at the Wilmington, Delaware, Museum of Art.
>
> Write to the Bureau of the Census, Washington, DC 20233.
>
> The White House is located at 1600 Pennsylvania Avenue in Washington, D.C.

NOTE: Some writers omit the comma that follows the name of a state when no other element of an address follows it. This is most likely to happen when a city name and state name are being used in combination to modify a noun that follows; however, our evidence indicates that retaining this comma is still the more common practice.

> We visited their Enid, Oklahoma plant.
>   *but more commonly*
> We visited their Enid, Oklahoma, plant.

41. Commas are used to set off the year from the day of the month. When only the month and the year are given, the comma is usually omitted.

> On October 26, 1947, the newly hired employees began work on the project.
>
> In December 1903, the Wright brothers finally succeeded in keeping an airplane aloft for a few seconds.

42. A comma groups numerals into units of three to separate thousands, millions, and so on; however, this comma is generally not used in page numbers, street numbers, or numbers within dates. For more on the styling of numbers, see Chapter 5, "The Treatment of Numbers."

> a population of 350,000
> 4509 South Pleasant Street
> the year 1986
> page 1419

24   Punctuation

With Names, Degrees, and Titles

43. A comma punctuates an inverted name.

> Sagan, Deborah J.

44. A comma is often used between a surname and *Junior, Senior,* or their abbreviations. For more on the use of *Jr.* and *Sr.,* see paragraph 45 in the section on Specific Styling Conventions, beginning on page 112, in Chapter 4, "Abbreviations."

> Morton A. Williams, Jr.
> Douglas Fairbanks, Senior

45. A comma is often used to set off the word *Incorporated* or the abbreviation *Inc.* from the rest of a corporate name; however, many companies elect to omit this comma from their names.

> Leedy Manufacturing Company, Incorporated
> Tektronics, Inc.
> Merz-Fortunata Inc.

46. A comma separates a surname from a following academic, honorary, military, or religious degree or title.

> Amelia P. Artandi, D.V.M.
> John L. Farber, Esq.
> Sister Mary Catherine, S.C.
> Robert Menard, M.A., Ph.D.
> Admiral Herman Washington, USN

In Correspondence

47. The comma follows the salutation in informal correspondence and follows the complimentary close in both informal and formal correspondence. In formal correspondence, a colon follows the salutation. For examples of this use of the colon, see paragraph 12 under Colon in this chapter.

> Dear Rachel,
> Affectionately,
> Very truly yours,

Other Uses

48. The comma is used to avoid ambiguity when the juxtaposition of two words or expressions could cause confusion.

> Whatever will be, will be.
> To John, Marshall was someone special.
> I repaired the lamp that my brother had broken, and replaced the bulb.

49. A comma often follows a direct object or a predicate nominative or predicate adjective when they precede the subject and verb in the sentence. If the meaning of the sentence is clear without this comma, it is often omitted.

> That we would soon have to raise prices, no one disputed.
>
> Critical about the current state of affairs, we might have been.
>
> A disaster it certainly was.

With Other Marks of Punctuation

50. Commas are used in conjunction with brackets, ellipsis points, parentheses, and quotation marks. Commas are not used in conjunction with colons, dashes, exclamation points, question marks, or semicolons. If one of these latter marks falls at the same point in a sentence at which a comma would fall, the comma is dropped and the other mark is retained. For more on the use of commas with other marks of punctuation, see the heading With Other Marks of Punctuation in the sections of this chapter covering those marks of punctuation.

Dash

In many of its uses, the dash functions like a comma, a colon, or a pair of parentheses. Like commas and parentheses, dashes set off parenthetic material such as examples, supplemental facts, or appositional, explanatory, or descriptive phrases. Like colons, dashes introduce clauses that explain or expand upon some element of the material that precedes them. The dash is sometimes considered to be a less formal equivalent of the colon and parenthesis, and it does frequently take their place in advertising and other informal contexts. However, dashes are prevalent in all kinds of writing, including the most formal, and the choice of which mark to use is usually a matter of personal preference.

The dash exists in a number of different lengths. The dash in most general use is the em dash, which is approximately the width of an uppercase M in typeset material. In typewritten material, it is represented by two hyphens. The en dash and the two- and three-em dashes have more limited uses which are explained in paragraphs 15–18 below.

Abrupt Change or Suspension

1. The dash marks an abrupt change in the flow of a writer's thought or in the structure of a sentence.

> The mountain that we climbed is higher than—well, never mind how high it is.
>
> The students seemed happy enough with the new plan, but the alumni—there was the problem.

2. Dashes mark a suspension in the writer's flow of thought or in the sentence structure. Such suspensions are frequently caused by an authorial aside.

> He was—how shall we put it?—a controversial character to say the least.

> If I had kept my notes—and I really wish that I had—I would be able to give you the exact date of the sale.

Parenthetic and Amplifying Elements

3. Dashes are used in place of other punctuation (such as commas or parentheses) to emphasize parenthetic or amplifying material or to make such material stand out more clearly from the rest of the sentence.

> She is willing to discuss all problems—those she has solved and those for which there is no immediate solution.

> In 1976, they asked for—and received—substantial grants from the federal government.

> The privately owned consulting firm—formerly known as Aborjaily and Associates—is now offering many new services.

NOTE: When dashes are used to set off parenthetic elements, they often indicate that the material is more digressive than elements set off with commas but less digressive than elements set off by parentheses. For contrasting examples see paragraph 17 under Comma and paragraphs 1 and 9 under Parentheses in this chapter.

4. Dashes are used to set off or to introduce defining and enumerating phrases.

> The fund sought to acquire controlling positions—a minimum of 25% of outstanding voting securities—in other companies.

> The essay dealt with our problems with waste—cans, bottles, discarded tires, and other trash.

5. A dash is often used in place of a colon or semicolon to link clauses, especially when the clause that follows the dash explains, summarizes, or expands upon the clause that precedes it.

> The test results were surprisingly good—none of the tested models displayed serious problems.

> The deterioration of our bridges and roads has been apparent for many years—parts of the interstate highway system are 30 years old, after all, and most of our bridges are older than that.

6. A dash or a pair of dashes often sets off parenthetic or amplifying material introduced by such phrases as *for example, namely, that is, e.g.,* and *i.e.*

After some discussion the motion was tabled—that is, it was removed indefinitely from the board's consideration.

Sports develop two valuable traits—namely, self-control and the ability to make quick decisions.

Not all "prime" windows—i.e., the ones installed when a house is built—are equal in quality.

NOTE: Commas, parentheses, and semicolons are often used for the same purpose. For contrasting examples, see paragraph 18 under Comma, paragraph 2 under Parentheses, and paragraph 6 under Semicolon in this chapter.

7. A dash introduces a summary statement that follows a series of words or phrases.

Unemployment, inflation, stock prices, mortgage rates—all are part of the economy.

Once into bankruptcy, the company would have to pay cash for its supplies, defer maintenance, and lay off workers—moves that could threaten its long-term profitability.

As a Mechanical Device

8. A dash precedes the name of an author or source at the end of a quoted passage.

Winter tames man, woman and beast.
—William Shakespeare

"A comprehensive, authoritative, and beautifully written biography."—*National Review*

NOTE: This method of attribution is most often used when the quoted material is not part of the main text. Examples of such situations are quotations set as epigraphs and quotations set as extracts. The attribution may appear immediately after the quotation, or it may appear on the next line.

9. A dash is used to indicate interrupted speech or a speaker's confusion or hesitation.

"The next point I'd like to bring up—" the speaker started to say. "I'm sorry. I'll have to stop you there," the moderator broke in.

"Yes," he went on, "yes—that is—I guess I agree."

NOTE: There is some disagreement among style manuals regarding the use of a comma between a quotation ending with a dash and its attribution. Our evidence indicates that the comma is usually omitted in such circumstances. This follows the general practice regarding the use of commas with dashes described in paragraph 11 below.

10. Dashes are used variously as elements in page design. They may, for example, precede items in a vertical enumeration, set off elements in the dateline of a newspaper report, or separate words from their definitions in a glossary. The use of dashes in such circumstances is usually determined by the editor or designer of the publication.

Required skills are:
— Shorthand
— Typing
— Transcription

With Other Marks of Punctuation

11. If a dash appears at a point in a sentence where a comma could also appear, the dash is retained and the comma is dropped. For one situation in which this practice is not always followed, see paragraph 9 above.

> If we don't succeed—and the critics say we won't—then the whole project is in jeopardy.
>
> Our lawyer has read the transcript—all 1200 pages of it—and he has decided that an appeal would not be useful.
>
> Some of the other departments, however—particularly Accounting, Sales, and Credit Collection—have expanded their computer operations.

12. If the second of a pair of dashes appears at a point in a sentence where a period or semicolon would also appear, the period or semicolon is retained and the dash is dropped.

> His conduct has always been exemplary—near-perfect attendance, excellent productivity, a good attitude; nevertheless, his termination cannot be avoided.

13. Dashes are used with exclamation points and question marks. When a pair of dashes sets off parenthetic material calling for either of these marks of punctuation, the exclamation point or the question mark is placed inside the second dash. If the parenthetic material falls at the end of a sentence ending with an exclamation point or question mark, the closing dash is not required.

> His hobby was getting on people's nerves—especially mine!—and he was extremely good at it.
>
> When the committee meets next week—are you going to be there?—I will present all of the final figures.
>
> Is there any way to predict the future course of this case—one which we really cannot afford to lose?

14. Dashes and parentheses are used in combination to indicate parenthetic material appearing within parenthetic material. Our evidence indicates that dashes within parentheses and parentheses within dashes occur with about equal frequency.

We were looking for a narrator (or narrators—sometimes a script calls for more than one) who could handle a variety of assignments.

On our trip south we crossed a number of major rivers—the Hudson, the Delaware, and the Patapsco (which flows through Baltimore)—without paying a single toll.

NOTE: If the inner parenthetic element begins with a dash and its closing dash would fall in the same position as the closing parenthesis, the closing dash is omitted and the parenthesis is retained, as in the first example above. If the inner phrase begins with a parenthesis and its closing parenthesis would coincide with the closing dash, the closing parenthesis and the closing dash are both retained, as in the second example above.

En Dash

15. En dashes appear only in typeset material. The en dash is shorter than the em dash but slightly longer than the hyphen, and it is used in place of the hyphen in some situations. The most common use of the en dash is as an equivalent to "(up) to and including" when used between numbers, dates, or other notations that indicate range.

1984–85	Monday–Friday
$20–$40	35–40 years
levels D–G	ages 10–15
8:30 a.m.–4:30 p.m.	pages 128–34

    NOTE: The use of the en dash to replace the hyphen in such cases, although urged by most style manuals, is by no means universal. Writers and editors who wish to have en dashes set in their copy need to indicate on their manuscripts which hyphens should be set as en dashes (see Chapter 9, "Copyediting and Proofreading," page 268), and this need to mark en dashes can obviously be an inconvenience and an invitation to errors. However, many writers and editors prefer to use en dashes because of the visual clarity they provide between numbers and because of the distinction they make between en dashes used to mean "to" and hyphens used to connect elements in compound words.

16. Publishers make various uses of the en dash, and no one set of rules can be said to be standard. Some common uses of the en dash include using it as a replacement for the hyphen following a prefix that is added to an open compound, as a replacement for the word *to* between capitalized names, and to indicate linkages, such as boundaries, treaties, or oppositions.

    pre–Civil War architecture
    the New York–Connecticut area

Chicago–Memphis train
Washington–Moscow diplomacy
the Dempsey–Tunney fight

Long Dashes

17. A two-em dash is used to indicate missing letters in a word and, less frequently, to indicate a missing word.

Mr. P—— of Baltimore
That's b——t and you know it.

18. A three-em dash indicates that a word has been left out or that an unknown word or figure is to be supplied. For the use of this dash in bibliography listings, see Chapter 7, "Notes and Bibliographies," page 227.

The study was carried out in ——, a fast-growing Sunbelt city.
We'll leave New York City on the —— of August.

Spacing

19. Style varies as to spacing around the dash. Some publications insert a space before and after the dash, others do not. Our evidence indicates that the majority of publishers style the dash without spaces.

Ellipsis Points

Ellipsis points is the name most often given to periods when they are used, usually in groups of three, to signal an omission from quoted material or to indicate a pause or trailing off of speech. Other names for periods used in this way include *ellipses, points of ellipsis,* and *suspension points.* Ellipsis points are often used in conjunction with other marks of punctuation, including periods used to mark the ends of sentences. When ellipsis points are used in this way with a terminal period, the omission is sometimes thought of as being marked by four periods. This discussion of ellipsis points is illustrated with examples of ellipsis points used with quoted material enclosed in quotation marks. For examples of ellipsis points used to indicate omissions from quoted material set as extracts, see Chapter 8, "The Treatment of Quotations," especially the section on Alterations, Omissions, and Interpolations, beginning on page 238.

NOTE: The examples given below present passages in which ellipsis points indicate omission of material. In most cases, the full text from which these omissions have been made is some portion of the headnote above.

1. Ellipsis points indicate the omission of one or more words within a quoted sentence.

> One book said, "Other names . . . include *ellipses, points of ellipsis,* and *suspension points.*"

2. Ellipsis points are usually not used to indicate the omission of words that precede the quoted portion. However, style varies on this point, and in some formal contexts, especially those in which the quotation is introduced by a colon, ellipsis points are used.

> The book maintained that "the omission is sometimes thought of as being marked by four periods."
> The book maintained: ". . . the omission is sometimes thought of as being marked by four periods."

3. Punctuation used in the original that falls on either side of the ellipsis points is often omitted; however, it may be retained, especially if such retention helps clarify the sentence.

> According to the book, "*Ellipsis points* is the name most often given to periods when they are used . . . to signal an omission from quoted material or to indicate a pause or trailing off of speech."
> According to the book, "When ellipsis points are used in this way . . . , the omission is sometimes thought of as being marked by four periods."
> According to the book, "*Ellipsis points* is the name most often given to periods when they are used, usually in groups of three, . . . to indicate a pause or trailing off of speech."

4. If an omission comprises an entire sentence within a passage, the last part of a sentence within a passage, or the first part of a sentence other than the first quoted sentence, the end punctuation preceding or following the omission is retained and is followed by three periods.

> That book says, "Other names for periods used in this way include *ellipses, points of ellipsis,* and *suspension points.* . . . When ellipsis points are used in this way with a terminal period, the omission is sometimes thought of as being marked by four periods."
> That book says, "*Ellipsis points* is the name given to periods when they are used, usually in groups of three, to signal an omission from quoted material. . . . Other names for periods used in this way include *ellipses, points of ellipsis,* and *suspension points.*"
> That book says, "Ellipsis points are often used in conjunction with other marks of punctuation, including periods used to mark ends of sentences. . . . The omission is sometimes thought of as being marked by four periods."

NOTE: The capitalization of the word *The* in the third example is acceptable. For more on the capitalization of words in quotations, see the section on Alterations, Omissions, and Interpolations, beginning on page 238, in Chapter 8, "The Treatment of Quotations."

5. If the last words of a quoted sentence are omitted and if the original sentence ends with a period, that period is retained and three ellipsis points follow. However, if the original sentence ends with punctuation other than a period, the end punctuation often follows the ellipsis points, especially if it helps clarify the quotation.

> Their book said, "Ellipsis points are often used in conjunction with other marks of punctuation. . . ."
>
> He always ends his harangues with some variation on the question, "What could you have been thinking when you . . . ?"

NOTE: Many writers and editors, especially those writing in more informal contexts, choose to ignore the styling considerations presented in paragraphs 4 and 5. They use instead an alternative system in which all omissions are indicated by three periods and all terminal periods that may precede or follow an omission are dropped.

6. Ellipsis points are used to indicate that a quoted sentence has been intentionally left unfinished. In situations such as this the terminal period is not included.

> In that section, the introductory paragraph begins, *"Ellipsis points is the name most often given* . . ."

7. A line of ellipsis points indicates that one or more lines of poetry have been omitted from a text. For more on this use of ellipsis points, see the section on Quoting Verse, beginning on page 242, in Chapter 8, "The Treatment of Quotations."

8. Ellipsis points are used to indicate faltering speech, especially if the faltering involves a long pause between words or a sentence that trails off or is left intentionally unfinished. In these kinds of sentences most writers treat the ellipsis points as terminal punctuation, thus removing the need for any other punctuation; however, style does vary on this point, and some writers routinely use other punctuation in conjunction with ellipsis points.

> The speaker seemed uncertain how to answer the question. "Well, that's true . . . but even so . . . I think we can do better."
>
> "Despite these uncertainties, we believe we can do it, but . . ."
>
> "I mean . . ." he said, "like . . . How?"

9. Ellipsis points are sometimes used as a stylistic device to catch and hold a reader's attention.

> They think that nothing can go wrong . . . but it does.

10. Each ellipsis point is set off from other ellipsis points, from adjacent punctuation (except for quotation marks, which are closed up to the ellipsis points), and from surrounding text by a space. If a terminal period is used with ellipsis points, it precedes them with no space before it and one space after it.

Exclamation Point

The exclamation point is used to mark a forceful comment. Writers and editors usually try to avoid using the exclamation point too frequently, because its heavy use can weaken its effect.

1. An exclamation point can punctuate a sentence, phrase, or interjection.

> This is the fourth time in a row he's missed his cue!
> No one that I talked to—not even the accounting department!—seemed to know how the figures were calculated.
> Oh! you startled me.
> Ah, those eyes!

2. The exclamation point replaces the question mark when an ironic or emphatic tone is more important than the actual question.

> Aren't you finished yet!
> Do you realize what you've done!
> Why me!

3. Occasionally the exclamation point is used with a question mark to indicate a very forceful question.

> How much did you say?!
> You did what!?

NOTE: The interrobang, printed ‽, was created to punctuate the types of sentences described in paragraphs 2 and 3 above. However, the character is not available to most typesetters, and it is rarely used.

4. In mathematical expressions, the exclamation point indicates a factorial.

> $n! \cdot m \geq (n)(m!)$

5. The exclamation point is enclosed within brackets, dashes, parentheses, and quotation marks when it punctuates the material so enclosed rather than the sentence as a whole. It should be placed outside them when it punctuates the entire sentence.

> He expressed his feelings in a letter to his wife: "Such a long delay would be a catastrophie [sic]!"
>
> All of this proves—at long last!—that we were right from the start.
>
> Somehow the dog got the gate open (for the third time!) and ran into the street.
>
> He shouted, "Wait!" and sprinted toward the train.
>
> The correct word is "mousse," not "moose"!

6. Exclamatory phrases that occur within a sentence are set off by dashes or parentheses.

> And now our competition—get this!—wants to start sharing secrets.
>
> The board accepted most of the recommendations, but ours (alas!) was not even considered.

7. If an exclamation point falls at a place in a sentence where a comma or a terminal period could also go, the comma or period is dropped and the exclamation point is retained.

> "Absolutely not!" he snapped.
>
> She has written about sixty pages so far—and with no help!

NOTE: If the exclamation point is part of a title, as of a play, book, or movie, it may be followed by a comma. If the title falls at the end of a sentence, the terminal period is usually dropped.

> Marshall and Susan went to see the musical *Oklahoma!*, and they enjoyed it very much.
>
> They enjoyed seeing the musical *Oklahoma!*

8. In typewritten material, two spaces follow an exclamation point that ends a sentence. If the exclamation point is followed by a closing bracket, closing parenthesis, or closing quotation marks, the two spaces follow the second mark. In typeset material, only one space follows the exclamation point.

> `The time is now!  Decide what you are going to do.`
>
> `She said, "The time is now!"  That meant we had to decide what to do.`
>
> The time is now! Decide what you are going to do.
>
> She said, "The time is now!" That meant we had to decide what to do.

Hyphen

1. Hyphens are used to link elements in compound words. For more on the styling of compound words, see the section on Compounds, beginning on page 92, in Chapter 3, "Plurals, Possessives, and Compounds."

2. A hyphen marks an end-of-line division of a word when part of the word is to be carried down to the next line.

   > We went to three different showrooms (it wasn't a pleasant experience; prices in this area have gone up) and asked every question we could think of.

3. A hyphen divides letters or syllables to give the effect of stuttering, sobbing, or halting speech.

   > S-s-sammy   ah-ah-ah   y-y-es

4. Hyphens indicate a word spelled out letter by letter.

   > p-r-o-b-a-t-i-o-n

5. A hyphen indicates that a word element is a prefix, suffix, or medial element.

   > anti-   -ship   -o-

6. A hyphen is used in typewritten material as an equivalent to the phrase "(up) to and including" when placed between numbers and dates. In typeset material this hyphen is very often replaced by an en dash. For more on the use of the en dash, see paragraphs 15 and 16 under Dash in this chapter.

7. Hyphens are sometimes used to produce inflected forms of verbs that are made of individually pronounced letters or to add an -*er* ending to an abbreviation; however, apostrophes are more commonly used for this purpose. For more on these uses of the apostrophe, see paragraphs 6 and 7 under Apostrophe in this chapter.

   > D.H.-ing for the White Sox
   > a loyal AA-er

Parentheses

Parentheses enclose supplementary elements that are inserted into a main statement but that are not intended to be part of the statement; in fact, parenthetic elements often interrupt the main structure of the sentence. For some of the cases described below, especially those listed under the heading "Parenthetic Elements," commas and dashes are frequently used instead of parentheses. (For contrasting examples, see paragraph 17 under Comma and paragraph 3 under Dash in this chapter.) In general, commas tend to be used when the inserted material is closely related, logically or grammatically, to the main clause; parentheses are more often used when the inserted material is incidental or digressive. Some newspapers and news magazines avoid the use of parentheses in straight news reporting and rely instead on the dash. In most cases, however, the choice of dashes or parentheses to enclose parenthetic material is a matter of personal preference.

Parenthetic Elements

1. Parentheses enclose phrases and clauses that provide examples, explanations, or supplementary facts. Supplementary numerical data may also be enclosed in parentheses.

   Nominations for the association's principal officers (president, vice president, treasurer, and secretary) were heard and approved at the last meeting.

   Although we liked the restaurant (their Italian food was the best), we seldom went there.

   Three old destroyers (all now out of commission) will be scrapped.

   Their first baseman was hitting well that season (.297, 84 RBIs), and their left fielder was doing well also (21 HRs, 78 RBIs).

2. Parentheses enclose phrases and clauses introduced by expressions such as *namely, that is, e.g.,* and *i.e.* Commas, dashes, and semicolons are also used to perform this function. (For contrasting examples, see paragraph 18 under Comma, paragraph 6 under Dash, and paragraph 6 under Semicolon in this chapter.)

   In writing to the manufacturer, be as specific as possible (i.e., list the missing or defective parts, describe the nature of the malfunction, and provide the name and address of the store where the unit was purchased).

3. Parentheses set off definitions, translations, or alternate names for words in the main part of a sentence.

   The company sold off all of its retail outlets and announced plans to sell off its houseware (small appliance) business as well.

   He has followed the fortunes of the modern renaissance (*al-Nahdad*) in the Arab-speaking world.

   The hotel was located just a few blocks from San Antonio's famous Paseo del Rio (river walk).

They were scheduled to play Beethoven's Trio in B-flat major, Opus 97 ("The Archduke").

4. Parentheses enclose abbreviations synonymous with spelled-out forms and occurring after those forms, or they may enclose the spelled-out form occurring after the abbreviation.

   She referred to a ruling by the Federal Communications Commission (FCC).

   They were involved with a study regarding the manufacture and disposal of PVC (polyvinyl chloride).

5. Parentheses are used in running text to set off bibliographical or historical data about books, articles, or other published or artistic works. (For full information regarding the use of parentheses with bibliographical references, see the section on Parenthetical References, beginning on page 211, in Chapter 7, "Notes and Bibliographies."

   His work was influenced by several of Freud's essays, including "Some Character Types Met with in Psychoanalytic Work" (1916).

   Ohio Impromptu (1981) was written for a special performance at Ohio State University.

   Another book in this category is Alice Schick's *Serengeti Cats* (Lippincott, $10.53).

6. Parentheses often set off cross-references.

   Telephone ordering service is also provided (refer to the list of stores at the end of this catalog).

   Textbooks are available at the bookstore for all on-campus courses. (See page 12 for hours.)

   The diagram (Fig. 3) illustrates the action of the pump.

7. Parentheses enclose Arabic numerals that confirm a spelled-out number in a text.

   Delivery will be made in thirty (30) days.

8. Parentheses enclose the name of a city or state that is inserted into a proper name for identification.

   the Norristown (Pa.) State Hospital
   the *Tulsa* (Okla.) *Tribune*

9. Some writers use parentheses to set off personal asides.

   It was largely as a result of this conference that the committee was formed (its subsequent growth in influence is another story).

10. Parentheses are used to set off quotations, either attributed or unattributed, that illustrate or support a statement made in the main text.

After he had had a few brushes with the police, his stepfather had him sent to jail as an incorrigible ("It will do him good").

As a Mechanical Device

11. Parentheses enclose unpunctuated numbers or letters in a series within running text.

    We must set forth (1) our long-term goals, (2) our immediate objectives, and (3) the means at our disposal.

    NOTE: Some writers and editors use only a single parenthesis following the number; however, most style books advise that parentheses be used both before and after, and most publications do follow that style.

12. Parentheses indicate alternative terms.

    Please indicate the lecture(s) you would like to attend.

13. Parentheses are used in combination with numbers for several mechanical purposes, such as setting off area codes in telephone numbers, grouping elements in mathematical expressions, and indicating losses in accounting.

    (413) 256-7899
    $3(a+b) + 4(a+b)$

    Operating Profits (in millions)
    Cosmetics.. 26.2
    Food products.................................... 47.7
    Food services..................................... 54.3
    Transportation................................. (17.7)
    Sporting goods............................... (11.2)
    _____
    Total   99.3

With Other Marks of Punctuation

14. If a parenthetic expression is an independent sentence, its first word is capitalized and a period is placed *inside* the last parenthesis. On the other hand, a parenthetic expression that occurs within a sentence—even if it could stand alone as a separate sentence—does not end with a period. It may, however, end with an exclamation point, a question mark, a period after an abbreviation, or a set of quotation marks. A parenthetic expression within a sentence does not require capitalization unless it is a quoted sentence. (For more on the use of capitals with parenthetic expressions, see the section on Beginnings, starting on page 53, in Chapter 2, "Capitals, Italics, and Quotation Marks.")

    The discussion was held in the boardroom. (The results are still confidential.)

    Although several trade organizations worked actively against the legislation (there were at least three paid lobbyists working on Capitol Hill at any one time), the bill passed easily.

After waiting in line for an hour (why do we do these things?), we finally left.

The conference was held in Vancouver (that's in B.C.).

He was totally confused ("What can we do?") and refused to see anyone.

15. If a parenthetic expression within a sentence is composed of two independent clauses, capitalization and periods are avoided. To separate the clauses within the parentheses, semicolons are usually used. If the parenthetic expression occurs outside of a sentence, normal patterns of capitalization and punctuation prevail.

We visited several showrooms, looked at the prices (it wasn't a pleasant experience; prices in this area have not gone down), and asked all the questions we could think of.

We visited several showrooms and looked at the prices. (It wasn't a pleasant experience. Prices in this area have not gone down.) If salespeople were available, we asked all of the questions we could think of.

16. No punctuation mark (other than a period after an abbreviation) is placed before parenthetic material within a sentence; if a break is required, the punctuation is placed after the final parenthesis.

I'll get back to you tomorrow (Friday), when I have more details.

17. Parentheses sometimes appear within parentheses, although the usual practice is to replace the inner pair of parentheses with a pair of brackets. (For an example of brackets within parentheses, see paragraph 6 under Brackets in this chapter.)

Checks must be drawn in U.S. dollars. (PLEASE NOTE: In accordance with U.S. Department of Treasury regulations, we cannot accept checks drawn on Canadian banks for amounts less than four U.S. dollars ($4.00). The same regulation applies to Canadian money orders.)

18. Dashes and parentheses are often used together to set off parenthetic material within a larger parenthetic element. For details and examples, see paragraph 14 under Dash in this chapter.

Spacing

19. In typewritten material, a parenthetic expression that is an independent sentence is followed by two spaces. In typeset material, the sentence is followed by one space. In typewritten or

typeset material, a parenthetic expression that falls within a sentence is followed by one space.

> ```
> We visited several showrooms and looked at the
> prices. (It wasn't a pleasant experience.  Prices
> in this area have gone up.)  We asked all the
> questions we could think of.
> ```

> We visited several showrooms and looked at the prices. (It wasn't a pleasant experience. Prices in this area have gone up.) We asked all the questions we could think of.

NOTE: Paragraphs 14 and 15 above are followed by examples that illustrate the appearance in typeset material of parenthetic expressions that are independent sentences.

Period

This section describes uses of the period in running text. For rules regarding use of the period in bibliographies, see Chapter 7, "Notes and Bibliographies." For the use of three periods to indicate a pause or omission, see the section on Ellipsis Points in this chapter.

1. A period terminates a sentence or a sentence fragment that is neither interrogative nor exclamatory.

> Do your best.
> I did my best.
> Total chaos. Nothing works.

2. A period punctuates some abbreviations. For more on the punctuation of abbreviations, see the section on Punctuation, beginning on page 109, in Chapter 4, "Abbreviations."

a.k.a.	U.S.	e.g.
fig.	Dr.	Co.
N.W.	No.	Ph.D.
Assn.	Inc.	ibid.
in.	Jr.	Corp.

3. A period is used with an individual's initials. If all of the person's initials are used instead of the name, however, the unspaced initials may be written without periods.

> F. Scott Fitzgerald
> F.D.R. *or* FDR
> Susan B. Anthony
> T. S. Eliot

4. A period follows Roman and Arabic numerals and also letters when they are used without parentheses in outlines and vertical enumerations.

> I. Objectives
>   A. Economy
>   1. Low initial cost
>   2. Low maintenance cost
>   B. Ease of operation
>
> Required skills are:
>   1. Shorthand
>   2. Typing
>   3. Transcription

5. A period is placed within quotation marks even when it does not punctuate the quoted material.

> The charismatic leader was known to his followers as "the guiding light."
>
> "I said I wanted to fire him," Henry went on, "but she said, 'I don't think you have the contractual privilege to do that.' "

6. When brackets or parentheses enclose a sentence that is independent of surrounding sentences, the period is placed inside the closing parenthesis or bracket. However, when brackets or parentheses enclose a sentence that is part of a surrounding sentence, the period for the enclosed sentence is omitted.

> On Friday the government ordered a 24-hour curfew and told all journalists and photographers to leave the area. (Authorities later confiscated the film of those who did not comply.)
>
> I took a good look at her (she was standing quite close to me at the time).

7. In typewritten material, two spaces follow a period that ends a sentence. If the period is followed by a closing bracket, closing parenthesis, or quotation marks, the two spaces follow the second mark. In typeset material, only one space follows this period.

> Here is the car.   Do you want to get in?
> He said, "Here is the car."   I asked if I should get in.
> Here is the car. Do you want to get in?

8. One space follows a period that comes after an initial in a name. If a name is composed entirely of initials, no space is required; however, the usual styling for such names is to omit the periods.

> Mr. H. C. Matthews
> F.D.R. *or* FDR

9. No space follows an internal period within a punctuated abbreviation.

f.o.b.	Ph.D.	p.m.
i.e.	A.D.	R.S.V.P.

Question Mark

1. The question mark terminates a direct question.

> What went wrong?
>
> "When do they arrive?" she asked.

NOTE: The intent of the writer, not the word order of the sentence, determines whether or not the sentence is a question. Polite requests that are worded as questions, for instance, usually take periods, because they are not really questions. Similarly, sentences whose word order is that of a statement but whose force is interrogatory are punctuated with question marks.

> Will you please sit down.
>
> He did that?

2. The question mark terminates an interrogative element that is part of a sentence. An indirect question is not followed by a question mark.

> The old arithmetic books were full of How-much-wallpaper-will-it-take-to-cover-a-room? questions.
>
> How did she do it? was the question on everybody's mind.
>
> She wondered, will it work?
>
> She wondered whether it would work.

3. The question mark punctuates each element of an interrogative series that is neither numbered nor lettered. When an interrogative series is numbered or lettered, only one question mark is used, and it is placed at the end of the series.

> Can you give us a reasonable forecast? back up your predictions? compare them with last year's earnings?
>
> Can you (1) give us a reasonable forecast, (2) back up your predictions, (3) compare them with last year's earnings?

4. The question mark indicates a writer's or editor's uncertainty about a fact.

> Geoffrey Chaucer, English poet (1340?–1400)

5. The question mark is placed inside a closing bracket, dash, parenthesis, or pair of quotation marks when it punctuates only the material enclosed by that mark and not the sentence as a whole. It is placed outside that mark when it punctuates the entire sentence.

> What did Andrew mean when he called the project "a fiasco from the start"?

> I had a vacation in 1975 (was it really that long ago?), but I haven't had time for one since.

> "She thought about it for a moment," Alice continued, "and finally she said, 'Can you guarantee this will work?' "

> He asked, "Do you realize the extent of the problem [the housing shortage]?"

6. In typewritten material, two spaces follow a question mark that ends a sentence. If the question mark is followed by a closing bracket, closing parenthesis, or quotation marks, the two spaces follow the second mark. In typeset material, only one space follows the question mark.

> `She wondered, will it work?    He said he thought`
> `it would.`
> `She asked, "Will it work?"    He said he thought it`
> `would.`

> She wondered, will it work? He said he thought it would.

7. One space follows a question mark that falls within a sentence.

> Are you coming today? tomorrow? the day after?

Quotation Marks, Double

This section describes the use of quotation marks to enclose quoted matter in running text. It also describes the mechanical uses of quotation marks, such as to set off translations of words or to enclose single letters within sentences. For the use of quotation marks to enclose titles of poems, paintings, or other works, see the section on Proper Nouns, Pronouns, and Adjectives, beginning on page 56, in Chapter 2, "Capitals, Italics, and Quotation Marks." For a discussion of extended quotations set off from the rest of the text by indention, see Chapter 8, "The Treatment of Quotations."

Basic Uses

1. Quotation marks enclose direct quotations but not indirect quotations.

> She said, "I am leaving."

> "I am leaving," she said, "and I'm not coming back."

"I am leaving," she said. "This has gone on long enough."

She said that she was leaving.

2. Quotation marks enclose fragments of quoted matter when they are reproduced exactly as originally stated.

The agreement makes it clear that he "will be paid only upon receipt of an acceptable manuscript."

As late as 1754, documents refer to him as "yeoman" and "husbandman."

3. Quotation marks enclose words or phrases borrowed from others, words used in a special way, or words of marked informality when they are introduced into formal writing.

That kind of corporation is referred to as "closed" or "privately held."

Be sure to send a copy of your résumé, or as some folks would say, your "biodata summary."

They were afraid the patient had "stroked out"—had had a cerebrovascular accident.

4. Quotation marks are sometimes used to enclose words referred to as words. Italic type is also frequently used for this purpose. For more on this use of italics, see the section on Other Uses of Italics, beginning on page 78, in Chapter 2, "Capitals, Italics, and Quotation Marks."

He went through the manuscript and changed every "he" to "she."

5. Quotation marks enclose short exclamations or representations of sounds. Representations of sounds are also frequently set in italic type. For more on this use of italics, see the section on Other Uses of Italics, beginning on page 78, in Chapter 2, "Capitals, Italics, and Quotation Marks."

"Ssshh!" she hissed.

They never say anything crude like "shaddap."

6. Quotation marks enclose short sentences that fall within longer sentences, especially when the shorter sentence is meant to suggest spoken dialogue. Kinds of sentences that may be treated in this way include mottoes and maxims, unspoken or imaginary dialogue, or sentences referred to as sentences.

Throughout the camp, the spirit was "We can do."

She never could get used to his "That's the way it goes" attitude.

In effect, the voters were saying "You blew it, and you don't get another chance."

Their attitude could only be described as "Kill the messenger."

Another example of a palindrome is "Madam, I'm Adam."

NOTE: Style varies regarding the punctuation of sentences such as these. In general, the force of the quotation marks is to set the shorter sentence off more distinctly from the surrounding sentence and to give the shorter sentence more of the feel of spoken dialogue; omitting the quotation marks diminishes the effect. (For a description of the use of commas in sentences like these, see paragraphs 33 and 34 under Comma in this chapter.)

The first rule is, When in doubt, spell it out.

They weren't happy with the impression she left: "Don't expect favors, because I don't have to give them."

7. Quotation marks are not used to enclose paraphrases.

Build a better mouse trap, Emerson says, and the world will beat a path to your door.

8. Direct questions are usually not enclosed in quotation marks unless they represent quoted dialogue.

The question is, What went wrong?

As we listened to him, we couldn't help wondering, Where's the plan?

She asked, "What went wrong?"

NOTE: As in the sentences presented in paragraph 6 above, style varies regarding the use of quotation marks with direct questions; and in many cases, writers will include the quotation marks.

As we listened to him, we couldn't help wondering, "Where's the plan?"

9. Quotation marks are used to enclose translations of foreign or borrowed terms.

The term *sesquipedalian* comes from the Latin word *sesquipedalis,* meaning "a foot and a half long."

While in Texas, he encountered the armadillo ("little armored one") and developed quite an interest in it.

10. Quotation marks are sometimes used to enclose single letters within a sentence.

The letter "m" is wider than the letter "i."

We started to work on the dictionary, beginning with the letter "A."

Put an "x" in the right spot.

The metal rod was shaped into a "V."

NOTE: Style varies on this point. Sans serif type is most often used when the shape of the letter is being stressed. Letters referred to as letters are commonly set in italic type. (For more on this use of italics, see the section on Other Uses of Italics, beginning on page 78, in Chapter 2, "Capitals, Italics, and Quotation Marks.") Finally, letters often appear in the same typeface as the surrounding text if no confusion would result from the styling.

> a "V"-shaped blade
> He was happy to get a B in the course.
> How many e's are in her name?

With Other Marks of Punctuation

11. When quotation marks follow a word in a sentence that is also followed by a period or comma, the period or comma is placed within the quotation marks.

    > He said, "I am leaving."
    > Her camera was described as "waterproof," but "moisture-resistant" would have been a better description.

    NOTE: Some writers draw a distinction between periods and commas that belong logically to the quoted material and those that belong to the whole sentence. If the period or comma belongs to the quoted material, they place it inside the quotation marks; if the period belongs logically to the sentence that surrounds the quoted matter, they place it outside the quotation marks. This distinction was previously observed in a wide range of publications, including U.S. Congressional publications and Merriam-Webster® dictionaries. In current practice, the distinction is made in relatively few publications, although the distinction is routinely made for dashes, exclamation points, and question marks used with quotation marks, as described in paragraph 13 below.

    > The package was labeled "Handle with Care".
    > The act was referred to as the "Army-Navy Medical Services Corps Act of 1947".
    > Her camera was described as "waterproof", but "moisture-resistant" would have been a better description.
    > He said, "I am leaving."

12. When quotation marks follow a word in a sentence that is also followed by a colon or semicolon, the colon or semicolon is placed outside the quotation marks.

    > There was only one thing to do when he said, "I may not run": promise him a larger campaign contribution.
    > She spoke of her "little cottage in the country"; she might better have called it a mansion.

13. The dash, question mark, and exclamation point are placed inside quotation marks when they punctuate the quoted matter only. They are placed outside the quotation marks when they punctuate the whole sentence.

> He asked, "When did she leave?"
> What is the meaning of "the open door"?
> Save us from his "mercy"!
> "I can't see how—" he started to say.
> He thought he knew where he was going—he remembered her saying, "Take two lefts, then stay to the right"—but the streets didn't look familiar.

14. One space follows a quotation mark that is followed by the rest of a sentence.

> "I am leaving," she said.

15. In typewritten material, two spaces follow a quotation mark that ends a sentence. In typeset material one space follows.

> He said, "Here is the car. "   I asked if I should get in.
>
> He said, "Here is the car." I asked if I should get in.

Quotation Marks, Single

1. Single quotation marks enclose a quotation within a quotation in conventional English.

> The witness said, "I distinctly heard him say, 'Don't be late,' and then I heard the door close."
> The witness said, "I distinctly heard him say, 'Don't be late.' "

NOTE: When both single and double quotation marks occur at the end of a sentence, the period typically falls *within* both sets of marks.

2. Single quotation marks are sometimes used in place of double quotation marks especially in British usage.

> The witness said, 'I distinctly heard him say, "Don't be late," and then I heard the door close.'

3. On rare occasions, authors face the question of how to style a quotation within a quotation within a quotation. Standard styling practice would be to enclose the innermost quotation in double marks; however, this construction can be confusing, and in many cases rewriting the sentence can remove the need for it.

The witness said, "I distinctly heard him say, 'Don't you say "Shut up" to me.' "

The witness said that she distinctly heard him say, "Don't you say 'Shut up' to me."

4. In some specialized fields, such as theology, philosophy, and linguistics, special terminology or words referred to as words are enclosed within single quotation marks. When single quotation marks are used in this way, any other punctuation following the word enclosed is placed outside the quotation marks.

She was interested in the development of the word 'humongous', especially during the 1960s.

Semicolon

The semicolon is used in ways that are similar to those in which periods and commas are used. Because of these similarities, the semicolon is often thought of as either a weak period or a strong comma. As a weak period, the semicolon marks the end of a complete clause and signals that the clause that follows it is closely related to the clause that precedes it. As a strong comma, the semicolon clarifies meaning usually by distinguishing major sentence divisions from the minor pauses that are represented by commas.

Between Clauses

1. A semicolon separates independent clauses that are joined together in one sentence without a coordinating conjunction.

He hemmed and hawed for over an hour; he couldn't make up his mind.

The river rose and overflowed its banks; roads became flooded and impassable; freshly plowed fields disappeared from sight.

Cream the shortening and sugar; add the eggs and beat well.

2. Ordinarily a comma separates main clauses joined with a coordinating conjunction. However, if the sentence might be confusing with a comma in this position, a semicolon is used in its place. Potentially confusing sentences include those with other commas in them or with particularly long clauses.

We fear that this situation may, in fact, occur; but we don't know when.

In a society that seeks to promote social goals, government will play a powerful role; and taxation, once simply a means of raising money, becomes, in addition, a way of furthering those goals.

As recently as 1988 the company felt the operation could be a successful one that would generate significant profits in several different markets; but in 1991 the management changed its mind and began a program of shutting down plants and reducing its product line.

3. A semicolon joins two statements when the grammatical construction of the second clause is elliptical and depends on that of the first.

The veal dishes were very good; the desserts, too.

In many cases the conference sessions, which were designed to allow for full discussions of topics, were much too long and tedious; the breaks between them, much too short.

4. A semicolon joins two clauses when the second begins with a conjunctive adverb, as *accordingly, also, besides, consequently, furthermore, hence, however, indeed, likewise, moreover, namely, nevertheless, otherwise, still, then, therefore,* and *thus.* Phrases such as *by the same token, in that case, as a result, on the other hand,* and *all the same* can also act as conjunctive adverbs.

Most people are covered by insurance of one kind or another; indeed, many people don't even see their medical bills.

It won't be easy to sort out the facts of this confusing situation; however, a decision must be made.

The case could take years to work its way through the court system; as a result, many plaintiffs will accept out-of-court settlements.

NOTE: Style varies regarding the treatment of clauses introduced by *so* and *yet.* Although many writers continue to treat *so* and *yet* as adverbs, it has become standard to treat these words as coordinating conjunctions that join clauses. In this treatment, a comma precedes *so* and *yet* and no punctuation follows them. (For examples, see paragraph 1 under Comma in this chapter.)

5. When three or more clauses are separated by semicolons, a coordinating conjunction may or may not precede the final clause. If a coordinating conjunction does precede the final clause, the final semicolon is often replaced with a comma. (For the use of commas to separate three or more clauses without conjunctions, see paragraph 4 under Comma in this chapter.)

Their report was one-sided and partial; it did not reflect the facts; it distorted them.

They don't understand; they grow bored; and they stop learning.

The report recounted events leading up to the incident; it included observations of eyewitnesses, but it drew no conclusions.

NOTE: The choices of whether to use a conjunction and whether to use a semicolon or comma with the conjunction are matters of personal preference. In general, the force of the semicolon is to make the transition to the final clause more abrupt, which often serves to place more emphasis on that clause. The comma and conjunction ease the transition and make the sentence seem less choppy.

With Phrases and Clauses Introduced by *for example, i.e.,* etc.

6. A semicolon is sometimes used before expressions (as *for example, for instance, that is, namely, e.g.,* or *i.e.*) that introduce expansions or series. Commas, dashes, and parentheses are also used in sentences like these. For contrasting examples, see paragraph 18 under Comma, paragraph 6 under Dash, and paragraph 2 under Parentheses in this chapter.

> On one point only did everyone agree; namely, that too much money had been spent already.

> We were fairly successful on that project; that is, we made our deadlines and met our budget.

> Most of the contestants had traveled great distances to participate; for example, three had come from Australia, one from Japan, and two from China.

In a Series

7. A semicolon is used in place of a comma to separate phrases in a series when the phrases themselves contain commas. A comma may replace the semicolon before the last item in a series if the last item is introduced with a conjunction.

> She flung open the door; raced up the stairs, taking them two at a time; locked herself in the bathroom; and, holding her sides, started to laugh uncontrollably.

> The visitor to Barndale was offered three sources of overnight accommodation: The Rose and Anchor, which housed Barndale's oldest pub; The Crawford, an American-style luxury hotel; and Ellen's Bed and Breakfast on Peabody Lane.

> We studied mathematics in the morning; English, French, and Spanish right after lunch, and science in the late afternoon.

8. When the individual items in an enumeration or series are long or are sentences themselves, they are usually separated by semicolons.

> Among the committee's recommendations: more hospital beds in urban areas where there are waiting lists for elective surgery; smaller staff size in half-empty rural hospitals; review procedures for all major purchases.

> There is a difference between them: she is cross and irritable; he is merely moody.

As a Mechanical Device

9. A semicolon separates items in a list in cases where a comma alone would not clearly separate the items or references.

   (Friedlander 1957; Ballas 1962)
   (Genesis 3:1–19; 4:1–16)

With Other Marks of Punctuation

10. A semicolon is placed outside quotation marks and parentheses.

    They referred to each other as "Mother" and "Father"; they were the archetypal happily married elderly couple.

    She accepted the situation with every appearance of equanimity (but with some inward qualms); however, all of that changed the next day.

Virgule

The virgule is known by many names, including *diagonal, solidus, oblique, slant, slash*, and *slash mark*. Most commonly, the virgule is used to represent a word that is not written out or to separate or set off certain adjacent elements of text.

In Place of Missing Words

1. A virgule represents the word *per* or *to* when used with units of measure or when used to indicate the terms of a ratio.

40,000 tons/year	price/earnings ratio
14 gm/100 cc	a 50/50 split
9 ft./sec.	risk/reward tradeoff

2. A virgule separates alternatives. In this context, the virgule usually represents the words *or* or *and/or*.

   alumni/ae
   his/her
   introductory/refresher courses
   oral/written tests

3. A virgule replaces the word *and* in some compound terms.

   molybdenum/vanadium steel
   in the May/June issue
   1973/74
   in the Falls Church/McLean, Va., area
   an innovative classroom/laboratory

4. A virgule is used, although less commonly, to replace a number of prepositions, such as *at, versus, with,* and *for.*

U.C./Berkeley   parent/child issues
table/mirror   Vice President/Editorial

With Abbreviations

5. A virgule punctuates some abbreviations.

c/o	w/	A/1C	d/b/a
A/R	A/V	V/STOL	S/Sgt

NOTE: In some cases the virgule may stand for a word that is not represented in the abbreviation (e.g., *in* in *W/O*, the abbreviation for *water in oil*).

To Separate Elements

6. The virgule is used in a number of mechanical ways to separate groups of numbers, such as elements in a date, numerators and denominators in fractions, and area codes in telephone numbers. For more on the use of virgules with numbers, see Chapter 5, "The Treatment of Numbers."

7. The virgule serves as a divider between lines of poetry that are run in with the text around them. This method of quoting poetry is usually limited to passages of no more than three or four lines. Longer passages are usually set off from the text as extract quotations, as shown in Chapter 8, "The Treatment of Quotations."

When Samuel Taylor Coleridge wrote in "Christabel" that "'Tis a month before the month of May, /And the Spring comes slowly up this way," he could have been describing New England.

8. The virgule sets off certain elements—such as the parts of an address that are normally placed on separate lines—when they appear run in with the surrounding text.

Mlle Christine Lagache/20, Passage des Écoliers/75051 Paris/France

9. The virgule sets off phonemes and phonemic transcriptions.

/b/ as in *but*
pronounced /ˌekə'nämik/ or /ˌēkə'nämik/

Spacing

10. In general, no space is used between the virgule and the words, letters, or figures separated by it. Some authors and editors prefer to place spaces around a virgule used to separate lines of poetry, but most omit the space. In the case of virgules used to set off phonemes and phonemic transcriptions, however, a space precedes the first virgule and follows the second virgule.

Chapter 2

Capitals, Italics, and Quotation Marks

CONTENTS

Words and phrases are capitalized, italicized, or enclosed in quotation marks in order to indicate that they have a special significance in a particular context. Some rules regarding capitals, italics, and quotation marks are backed by long tradition and are quite easy to apply ("The first word of a sentence or sentence fragment is capitalized"); others require arbitrary decisions or personal judgment ("Foreign words and phrases that have not been fully adopted into the English language are italicized"). Careful writers and editors usually make notes or keep a style sheet to record the decisions that they make so they can be consistent in their use of capitals, italics, and quotation marks. For more on keeping and using style sheets, see Chapter 9, "Copyediting and Proofreading," pages 256–260.

This chapter is divided into four sections. The first section explains the use of capitalized words to begin sentences and phrases. The second section explains the use of capitals, italics, and quotation marks to indicate that a word or phrase is a proper noun, pronoun, or adjective. The third and fourth sections explain other uses of capital letters and italics. For other uses of quotation marks, see the sections on Quotation Marks beginning on page 43, in Chapter 1, "Punctuation." For a discussion of the treatment of extended quotations, see Chapter 8, "The Treatment of Quotations."

Beginnings

---

1. The first word of a sentence or sentence fragment is capitalized.

The meeting was postponed.
No! I cannot do it.
Will you go?
Total chaos. Nothing works.

2. The first word of a sentence contained within parentheses is capitalized; however, a parenthetical sentence occurring inside another sentence is not capitalized unless it is a complete quoted sentence.

The discussion was held in the boardroom. (The results are still confidential.)

Although we liked the restaurant (their Italian food was the best), we could not afford to eat there often.

After waiting in line for an hour (why do we do these things?), we finally left.

He was totally demoralized ("There is just nothing we can do") and was contemplating resignation.

3. The first word of a direct quotation is capitalized; however, if the quotation is interrupted in midsentence, the second part does not begin with a capital.

The President said, "We have rejected this report entirely."

"We have rejected this report entirely," the President said, "and we will not comment on it further."

4. When a quotation, whether a sentence fragment or a complete sentence, is syntactically dependent on the sentence in which it occurs, the quotation does not begin with a capital.

The President made it clear that "there is no room for compromise."

5. The first word of a sentence within a sentence is usually capitalized. Examples of sentences within sentences include mottoes and rules, unspoken or imaginary dialogue, sentences referred to as sentences, and direct questions. (For an explanation of the use of commas and quotation marks with sentences such as these, see paragraphs 34 and 35 in the section on Comma, beginning on page 12, and paragraph 6 in the section on Quotation Marks, Double, beginning on page 43, in Chapter 1, "Punctuation."

You know the saying, "A stitch in time saves nine."

The first rule is, When in doubt, spell it out.

The clear message coming back from the audience was "We don't care."

My question is, When can we go?

She kept wondering, how did they get here so soon?

NOTE: In the cases of unspoken or imaginary dialogue and of direct questions, it is a matter of individual preference whether or not to capitalize the first word; however, the most common practice is to capitalize it.

6. The first word of a line of poetry is conventionally capitalized.

> The best lack all conviction, while the worst
> Are full of passionate intensity.
> —W. B. Yeats

7. The first word following a colon may be either lowercased or capitalized if it introduces a complete sentence. While the former is the usual styling, the latter is also quite common, especially when the sentence introduced by the colon is fairly lengthy and distinctly separate from the preceding clause.

> The advantage of this particular system is clear: it's inexpensive.
>
> The situation is critical: This company cannot hope to recoup the fourth-quarter losses that were sustained in five operating divisions.

NOTE: For the sake of consistency, many authors and editors prefer to use one style or the other in all cases, regardless of sentence length. The capitalized style is more common in newspapers, but overall the lowercased styling is more frequently used.

8. If a colon introduces a series of sentences, the first word of each sentence is capitalized.

> Consider the following steps that we have taken: A subcommittee has been formed to evaluate our past performance and to report its findings to the full organization. New sources of revenue are being explored, and relevant organizations are being contacted. And several candidates have been interviewed for the new post of executive director.

9. The first words of run-in enumerations that form complete sentences are capitalized, as are the first words of phrasal lists and enumerations arranged vertically beneath running texts. Phrasal enumerations run in with the introductory text, however, are lowercased.

> Do the following tasks at the end of the day: 1. Clean your typewriter. 2. Clear your desktop of papers. 3. Cover office machines. 4. Straighten the contents of your desk drawers, cabinets, and bookcases.
>
> This is the agenda:
> > Call to order
> > Roll call
> > Minutes of the previous meeting
> > Treasurer's report

On the agenda will be (1) call to order, (2) roll call, (3) minutes of the previous meeting, (4) treasurer's report . . .

10. The introductory words *Whereas* and *Resolved* are capitalized in minutes and legislation, as is the word *That* or an alternative word or expression which immediately follows either.

Resolved, That . . .
Whereas, Substantial benefits . . .

11. The first word in an outline heading is capitalized.

  I. Editorial tasks
 II. Production responsibilities
    A. Cost estimates
    B. Bids

12. The first word of the salutation of a letter and the first word of a complimentary close are capitalized.

Dear Mary,	Ladies and Gentlemen:
Gentlemen:	Sincerely yours,
Dear Sir or Madam:	Very truly yours,

13. The first word and each subsequent major word following a SUBJECT or TO heading (as in a memorandum) are capitalized.

SUBJECT: Pension Plans
TO: All Department Heads and Editors

Proper Nouns, Pronouns, and Adjectives

This section describes the ways in which a broad range of proper nouns, pronouns, and adjectives are styled—with capitals, italics, quotation marks, or some combination of these devices. In almost all cases, proper nouns, pronouns, and adjectives are capitalized. The essential distinction in the use of capitals and lowercase letters lies in the particularizing or individualizing significance of capitals as against the generalizing significance of lowercase. A capital is used with a proper noun because it distinguishes some individual person, place, or thing from others of the same class. A capital is used with a proper adjective because it takes its descriptive meaning from a proper noun.

In many cases, proper nouns are italicized or enclosed in quotation marks in addition to being capitalized. No clear distinctions can be drawn between the kinds of words that are capitalized and italicized, capitalized and enclosed in quotation marks, or simply capitalized, as styling on these points is governed almost wholly by tradition.

The paragraphs in this section are grouped under the following alphabetically arranged headings:

Abbreviations	Legal Material
Abstractions and	Medical Terms
Personifications	Military Terms
Academic Degrees	Numerical Designations
Animals and Plants	Organizations
Awards, Honors, and Prizes	People
Derivatives of Proper Names	Pronouns
Geographical and	Religious Terms
Topographical References	Scientific Terms
Governmental, Judicial, and	Time Periods and Zones
Political Bodies	Titles
Historical Periods and Events	Trademarks
Hyphenated Compounds	Transportation

Abbreviations

1. Abbreviated forms of proper nouns and adjectives are capitalized, just as the spelled-out forms would be. For more on the capitalization of abbreviations, see the section on Capitalization, beginning on page 110, in Chapter 4, "Abbreviations."

> Dec. for *December*
> Col. for *Colonel*
> Wed. for *Wednesday*
> Brit. for *British*

Abstractions and Personifications

2. Abstract terms, such as names of concepts or qualities, are usually not capitalized unless the concept or quality is being presented as if it were a person. If the term is simply being used in conjunction with other words that allude to human characteristics or qualities, it is usually not capitalized. For more on the capitalization of abstract terms, see the section on Other Uses of Capitals in this chapter.

> a time when Peace walked among us
> as Autumn paints each leaf in fiery colors
> an economy gripped by inflation
> hoping that fate would lend a hand

3. Fictitious names used as personifications are capitalized.

> Uncle Sam   John Bull
> Ma Bell   Jack Frost
> Big Oil squirmed under the new regulations.

Academic Degrees

4. The names of academic degrees are capitalized when they follow a person's name. The names of specific academic degrees not following a person's name are capitalized or not capitalized according to individual preference. General terms referring to degrees, such as *doctorate, master's degree,* or *bachelor's* are not capitalized. Abbreviations for academic degrees are always capitalized.

> Martin Bonkowski, Doctor of Divinity
> earned her Doctor of Laws degree
>   *or* earned her doctor of laws degree
> working for a bachelor's degree
> Susan Wycliff, M.S.W.
> received her Ph.D.

Animals and Plants

5. The common names of animals and plants are not capitalized unless they contain a proper noun as a separate element, in which case the proper noun is capitalized, but any element of the name following the proper noun is lowercased. Elements of the name preceding the proper noun are usually but not always capitalized. In some cases, the common name of the plant or animal contains a word that was once a proper noun but is no longer thought of as such. In these cases, the word is usually not capitalized. When in doubt about the capitalization of a plant or animal name, consult a dictionary. (For an explanation of the capitalization of genus names in binomial nomenclature or of New Latin names for groups above genera in zoology and botany, see paragraphs 67 and 68 below.)

cocker spaniel	Great Dane
great white shark	wandering Jew
Steller's jay	ponderosa pine
Rhode Island red	Kentucky bluegrass
black-eyed Susan	Japanese beetle
lily of the valley	Brown Swiss
Hampshire hog	holstein

NOTE: In references to specific breeds, as distinguished from the animals that belong to the breed, all elements of the name are capitalized.

Gordon Setter	Holstein
Rhode Island Red	

Awards, Honors, and Prizes

6. Names of awards, honors, and prizes are capitalized. Descriptive words and phrases that are not actually part of the award's name are lowercased. (For an explanation of capitaliz-

ing the names of military decorations, see paragraph 44 below.)

    Academy Award
    Nobel Prize
    Nobel Prize winner
    Rhodes Scholarship
    Emmy
    Nobel Prize in medicine
    Nobel Peace Prize
    Rhodes scholar
    New York Drama Critics' Circle Award

Brand Names—See **Trademarks** below.

Computer Terms—See **Scientific Terms** below.

Derivatives of Proper Names

7. Derivatives of proper names are capitalized when they are used in their primary sense. However, if the derived term has taken on a specialized meaning, it is usually not capitalized.

Roman architecture	pasteurized milk
an Americanism	manila envelope
Keynesian economics	french fries
Victorian customs	a quixotic undertaking
an Egyptologist	cesarean section

Geographical and Topographical References

8. Terms that identify divisions of the earth's surface and distinct areas, regions, places, or districts are capitalized, as are derivative nouns and adjectives.

    Chicago, Illinois
    the Middle Eastern situation
    the Southwest
    Tropic of Capricorn
    the Western Hemisphere
    the Sunbelt

9. Popular names of localities are capitalized.

the Big Apple	the Twin Cities
the Village	Hell's Kitchen
the Loop	the Valley

10. Compass points are capitalized when they refer to a geographical region or when they are part of a street name. They are lowercased when they refer to a simple direction.

    back East
    up North
    out West

West Columbus Avenue
South Pleasant Street
down South
east of the Mississippi
traveling north on I-91

11. Nouns and adjectives that are derived from compass points and that designate or refer to a specific geographical region are usually capitalized.

a Southern accent
Northerners
a Western crop
part of the Eastern establishment

12. Words designating global, national, regional, or local political divisions are capitalized when they are essential elements of specific names. However, they are usually lowercased when they precede a proper name or when they are not part of a specific name.

the British Empire
Washington State
Hampden County
New York City
Ward 1
Ohio's Ninth Congressional District
the fall of the empire
the state of Washington
the county of Hampden
the city of New York
fires in three wards
carried her district

NOTE: In legal documents, these words are often capitalized regardless of position.

the State of Washington
the County of Hampden
the City of New York

13. Generic geographical terms (as *lake, mountain, river, valley*) are capitalized if they are part of a specific proper name.

Crater Lake	Atlantic Ocean
the Columbia River	Strait of Gibraltar
Great Barrier Reef	Rocky Mountains
Hudson Bay	Long Island
Lake Como	Niagara Falls
Ohio Valley	Bering Strait

14. Generic geographical terms preceding names are usually capitalized.

Lakes Mead and Powell
Mounts Whitney and Shasta

NOTE: When *the* precedes the generic term, the generic term is lowercased.

the river Thames

15. Generic geographical terms that are not used as part of a proper name are not capitalized. These include plural generic geographical terms that follow two or more proper names and generic terms that are used descriptively or alone.

the Himalaya and Andes mountains
the Atlantic coast of Labrador
the Mississippi delta
the river valley
the Missouri and Platte rivers
the Arizona desert
the Caribbean islands
the valley

16. The names of streets, monuments, parks, landmarks, well-known buildings, and other public places are capitalized. However, generic terms that are part of these names (as *avenue, bridge,* or *tower*) are lowercased when they occur after multiple names or are used alone (but see paragraph 17 below).

Golden Gate Bridge	Coit Tower
Eddystone Lighthouse	the Statue of Liberty
the San Diego Zoo	Rock Creek Park
the Pyramids	Fanueil Hall
the Capitol	the Mall
the Dorset Hotel	Peachtree Street
the Dorset and Drake hotels	Fifth and Park avenues
on the bridge	walking through the park

17. Well-known informal or shortened forms of place-names are capitalized.

the Avenue for *Fifth Avenue*
the Street for *Wall Street*
the Exchange for the *New York Stock Exchange*

Governmental, Judicial, and Political Bodies

18. Full names of legislative, deliberative, executive, and administrative bodies are capitalized, as are easily recognizable short forms of these names. However, nonspecific noun and adjective references to them are usually lowercased.

United States Congress
the Congress
the Federal Bureau of Investigation

the Federal Reserve Board
the House
the Fed
a federal agency
congressional hearings

NOTE: Style varies regarding the capitalization of words such as *department, committee,* or *agency* when they are being used in place of the full name of a specific body. They are most often capitalized when the department or agency is referring to itself in print. In most other cases, these words are lowercased.

The Connecticut Department of Transportation is pleased to offer this new booklet on traffic safety. The Department hopes that it will be of use to all drivers.

We received a new booklet from the Connecticut Department of Transportation. This is the second pamphlet the department has issued this month.

19. The U.S. Supreme Court and the short forms *Supreme Court* and *Court* referring to it are capitalized.

the Supreme Court of the United States
the United States Supreme Court
the Supreme Court
the Court

20. Official and full names of higher courts and names of international courts are capitalized. Short forms of official higher court names are often capitalized in legal documents but lowercased in general writing.

The International Court of Arbitration
the United States Court of Appeals for the Second Circuit
the Virginia Supreme Court
the Court of Queen's Bench
a ruling by the court of appeals
the state supreme court

21. Names of city and county courts are usually lowercased.

the Lawton municipal court
the Owensville night court
small claims court
police court
the county court
juvenile court

22. The single designation *court,* when specifically applicable to a judge or a presiding officer, is capitalized.

It is the opinion of this Court that . . .
The Court found that . . .

23. The terms *federal* and *national* are capitalized only when they are essential elements of a name or title.

> Federal Trade Commission
> National Security Council
> federal court
> national security

24. The word *administration* is capitalized in some publications when it refers to the administration of a specific United States president; however, the word is more commonly lowercased in this situation. If the word does not refer to a specific presidential administration, it is not capitalized except when it is a part of an official name of a government agency.

> the Truman administration   *or*   the Truman Administration
> the administration   *or*   the Administration
> the Farmers Home Loan Administration
>
> The running of the White House varies considerably from one administration to another.

25. Names of political organizations and their adherents are capitalized, but the word *party* may or may not be capitalized, depending on the writer's or publication's preference.

> the Democratic National Committee
> Tories
> the Republican platform
> Nazis
> the Democratic party   *or*   the Democratic Party
> the Communist party   *or*   the Communist Party

26. Names of political groups other than parties are usually lowercased, as are their derivative forms.

> rightist   *but usually*
> right wing   the Left
> left winger   the Right

27. Terms describing political and economic philosophies and their derivative forms are usually capitalized only if they are derived from proper names.

> authoritarianism   civil libertarian
> isolationist   Marxist
> democracy   social Darwinism
> nationalism   fascism   *or*   Fascism
> supply-side economics

Historical Periods and Events

28. The names of conferences, councils, expositions, and specific sporting, historical, and cultural events are capitalized.

the Yalta Conference
the Minnesota State Fair
the World Series
the Boston Tea Party
the Bonus March of 1932
the Golden Gate International Exposition
the Congress of Vienna
the Games of the XXIII Olympiad
the Series
the San Francisco Earthquake
the Philadelphia Folk Festival

29. The names of some historical and cultural periods and movements are capitalized. When in doubt about such a name, consult a dictionary or encyclopedia.

Augustan Age	Stone Age
Prohibition	space age
Renaissance	fin de siècle
the Enlightenment	cold war *or* Cold War
the Great Depression	

30. Numerical designations of historical time periods are capitalized only when they are part of a proper name; otherwise they are lowercased.

the Third Reich	seventeenth century
Roaring Twenties	eighties

31. Full names of treaties, laws, and acts are capitalized.

Treaty of Versailles
The Controlled Substances Act of 1970

32. The full names of wars are capitalized; however, words such as *war, revolution, battle,* and *campaign* are capitalized only when they are part of a proper name. Descriptive terms such as *assault, siege,* and *engagement* are usually lowercased even when used in conjunction with the name of the place where the action occurred.

the French and Indian War
the War of the Roses
the American Revolution
the Revolution of 1688
the Battle of the Bulge
the Peninsular Campaign
the Spanish American War
the War of the Spanish Succession
the Whiskey Rebellion
the Battle of the Coral Sea
the second battle of Manassas
the Meuse-Argonne offensive

> the assault on Iwo Jima
> the naval battle of Guadalcanal
> the American and French revolutions
> the siege of Yorktown
> the winter campaign
> was in action throughout most of the war

Hyphenated Compounds

33. Elements of hyphenated compounds are capitalized if they are proper nouns or adjectives.

> Arab-Israeli negotiations
> East-West trade agreements
> Tay-Sachs disease
> U.S.-U.S.S.R. détente
> American-plan rates
> an eighteenth-century poet

NOTE: If the second element in a two-word compound is not a proper noun or adjective, it is lowercased.

> French-speaking peoples
> an A-frame house
> Thirty-second Street

34. Word elements (as prefixes and combining forms) may or may not be capitalized when joined to a proper noun or adjective. Common prefixes (as *pre-* or *anti-*) are usually not capitalized when so attached. Geographical and ethnic combining forms (as *Anglo-* or *Afro-*) are capitalized; *pan-* is usually capitalized when attached to a proper noun or adjective.

> the pro-Soviet faction
> un-American activities
> post–Civil War politics
> Sino-Soviet relations
> Pan-Slavic nationalism
> Afro-Americans
> Greco-Roman architecture
> the Pan-African Congress

Languages—See **People** below.

Legal Material—See also **Governmental, Judicial, and Political Bodies** above.

35. The names of both plaintiff and defendant in legal case titles are italicized. The *v.* for *versus* may be roman or italic. Cases that do not involve two opposing parties have titles such as *In re Watson* or *In the matter of John Watson;* these case titles are also italicized. When the person involved rather than the case itself is being discussed, the reference is not italicized.

Jones v. *Massachusetts*
In re Jones
Smith et al. v. Jones
She covered the Jones trial for the newspaper.

NOTE: In running text a case name involving two opposing parties may be shortened.

The judge based his ruling on a precedent set in the *Jones* decision.

Medical Terms

36. Proper names that are elements in terms designating diseases, symptoms, syndromes, and tests are capitalized. Common nouns are lowercased.

> Down's syndrome
> Duchenne-Erb paralysis
> German measles
> Parkinson's disease
> Rorschach test
> syndrome of Weber
> acquired immunodeficiency syndrome
> measles
> mumps
> herpes simplex

37. Taxonomic names of disease-causing organisms follow the rules established for binomial nomenclature discussed in paragraph 67 below. The names of diseases or pathological conditions derived from taxonomic names of organisms are lowercased and not italicized.

> a neurotoxin produced by *Clostridium botulinum*
> nearly died of botulism

38. Generic names of drugs are lowercased; trade names should be capitalized.

> a prescription for chlorpromazine
> had been taking Thorazine

Military Terms

39. The full titles of branches of the armed forces are capitalized, as are easily recognized short forms of full branch designations.

> U.S. Air Force
> the Navy
> U.S. Coast Guard
> the Marine Corps
> the Air Force
> U.S. Army
> the Coast Guard
> the Marines
> U.S. Navy
> the Army
> U.S. Marine Corps
> the Corps

40. The terms *air force, army, coast guard, marine(s)*, and *navy* are lowercased unless they form a part of an official name or refer back to a specific branch of the armed forces previously named. They are also lowercased when they are used collectively or in the plural.

> the combined air forces of the NATO nations
> the navies of the world
> the American army
>
> In some countries the duty of the coast guard may include ice-breaking in inland waterways.

41. The adjectives *naval* and *marine* are lowercased unless they are part of a proper name.

> naval battle   Naval Reserves
> marine barracks

42. The full titles of units and organizations of the armed forces are capitalized. Elements of full titles are lowercased when they stand alone.

> U.S. Army Corps of Engineers   the corps
> the Reserves   a reserve commission
> First Battalion   the battalion
> 4th Marine Regiment   the regiment
> Eighth Fleet   the fleet
> Cruiser Division   the division
> Fifth Army   the army

43. Military ranks are capitalized when they precede the names of their holders, and when they take the place of a person's name (as in direct address). Otherwise they are lowercased.

> Admiral Nimitz
> General Creighton W. Abrams
> I can't get this rifle any cleaner, Sergeant.
> The major arrived precisely on time.

44. The specific names of decorations, citations, and medals are capitalized.

> Medal of Honor   Distinguished Service Medal
> Navy Cross   Silver Star
> Purple Heart

Nicknames—See paragraphs 49, 51, and 52 below.

Numerical Designations

45. A noun introducing a reference number is usually capitalized.

> Order 704
> Flight 409

Form 2E
Policy 118-4-Y

46. Nouns used with numbers or letters to designate major reference headings (as in a literary work) are capitalized. However, nouns designating minor reference headings are typically lowercased.

Book II	page 101
Volume V	line 8
Division 4	note 10
Figure 1	paragraph 6.1
Table 3	question 21

Organizations

47. Names of firms, corporations, schools, and organizations and terms derived from those names to designate their members are capitalized. However, common nouns used descriptively or occurring after the names of two or more organizations are lowercased.

Merriam-Webster Inc.
University of Michigan
Smith College
Washington Huskies
played as a Pirate last year
Rotary International
Kiwanians
American and United airlines
Minnesota North Stars

NOTE: The word *the* at the beginning of such names is capitalized only when the full legal name is used.

48. Words such as *agency, department, division, group,* or *office* that designate corporate and organizational units are capitalized only when they are used with a specific name.

worked at the Criminal Division in the Department of Justice
a notice to all department heads

NOTE: Style varies regarding the capitalization of these words when they are used in place of the full name of a specific body. For more on this aspect of styling, see the note following paragraph 18 above.

49. Nicknames, epithets, or other alternate terms for organizations are capitalized.

referred to IBM as Big Blue
the Big Three automakers
trading stocks on the Big Board

People

50. The names and initials of persons are capitalized. If a name is hyphenated, both elements are capitalized. Particles forming the initial elements of surnames (as *de, della, der, du, la, ten, ter, van,* and *von*) may or may not be capitalized, depending on the styling of the individual name. However, if a name with a lowercase initial particle begins a sentence, the particle is capitalized.

> Thomas de Quincey
> Sir Arthur Thomas Quiller-Couch
> James Van Allen
> the paintings of de Kooning
> E. I. du Pont de Nemours
> Gerald ter Hoerst
> Heinrich Wilhelm Von Kleist
> De Kooning's paintings are . . .

51. The name of a person or thing can be added to or replaced entirely by a nickname or epithet, a characterizing word or phrase. Nicknames and epithets are capitalized.

Calamity Jane	Dusty Rhodes
Buffalo Bill	Bird Parker
Louis the Fat	Night Train Lane
Bubba Smith	Doctor J.
Goose Gossage	Attila the Hun
Big Mama Thornton	Dizzy Gillespie
the Golden Bear	Rusty Staub
Wilt the Stilt	Meadowlark Lemon
Murph the Surf	Lefty Grove

52. Nicknames and epithets are frequently used in conjunction with both the first and last names of a person. If it is placed between the first and last name, it will often be enclosed in quotation marks or parentheses; however, if the nickname is expected to be very well known to readers, the quotation marks or parentheses are often omitted. If the nickname precedes the first name, it is sometimes enclosed in quotation marks, but more often it is not.

> Thomas P. "Tip" O'Neill
> Earl ("Fatha") Hines
> Mary Harris ("Mother") Jones
> Joanne "Big Mama" Carner
> Dennis (Oil Can) Boyd
> Anna Mary Robertson "Grandma" Moses
> Kissin' Jim Folsom
> Slammin' Sammy Snead
> Blind Lemon Jefferson
> Mother Maybelle Carter

53. Words of family relationship preceding or used in place of a person's name are capitalized. However, these words are lowercased if they are part of a noun phrase that is being used in place of a name.

> Cousin Mercy
> Grandfather Barnes
> I know when Mother's birthday is.
> I know when my mother's birthday is.

54. Words designating languages, nationalities, peoples, races, religious groups, and tribes are capitalized. Descriptive terms used to refer to groups of people are variously capitalized or lowercased. Designations based on color are usually lowercased.

> | | |
> |---|---|
> | Latin | Ibo |
> | Caucasians | Christians |
> | Canadians | Afro-American |
> | Muslims | Navajo |
>
> Bushman (for a nomadic hunter of southern Africa)
> bushman (for an inhabitant of the Australian bush)
> the red man in America
> black, brown, and white people

55. Corporate, professional, and governmental titles are capitalized when they immediately precede a person's name, unless the name is being used as an appositive.

> | | |
> |---|---|
> | President Roosevelt | Professor Greenbaum |
> | Doctor Malatesta | Senator Henry Jackson |
> | Queen Elizabeth | Pastor Linda Jones |
>
> They wanted to meet the new pastor, Linda Jones.
> Almost everyone has heard of Chrysler's president, Lee Iacocca.

56. When corporate or governmental titles are used as part of a descriptive phrase to identify a person rather than as a person's official title, the title is lowercased.

> Senator Ted Stevens of Alaska
> *but* Ted Stevens, senator from Alaska
> Lee Iacocca, president of Chrysler Corporation

NOTE: Style varies when governmental titles are used in descriptive phrases that precede a name.

> Alaska senator Ted Stevens   *or*   Alaska Senator Ted Stevens

57. Specific governmental titles may be capitalized when they are used in place of particular individuals' names. In minutes and official records of proceedings, corporate titles are capitalized when they are used in place of individuals' names.

The Secretary of State gave a news conference.
The Judge will respond to questions in her chambers.
The Treasurer then stated his misgivings about the project.

58. Some publications always capitalize the word *president* when it refers to the United States presidency. However, the more common practice is to capitalize the word *president* only when it refers to a specific individual.

It is one of the duties of the President to submit a budget to Congress.
It is one of the duties of the president to submit a budget to Congress.

59. Titles are capitalized when they are used in direct address.

Tell me the truth, Doctor.
Where are we headed, Captain?

Personifications—See **Abstractions and Personifications** above.

Prefixes—See **Hyphenated Compounds** above.

Pronouns

60. The pronoun *I* is capitalized. For pronouns referring to the Deity, see rule 62 below.

He and I will attend the meeting.

Religious Terms

61. Words designating the Deity are capitalized.

Allah	Yahweh
Jehovah	Christ
God Almighty	the Holy Spirit

62. Personal pronouns referring to the Deity are usually capitalized. Relative pronouns (as *who, whom,* and *whose*) usually are not.

God in His mercy
when God asks us to do His bidding
believing that it was God who created the universe

NOTE: Some style manuals maintain that the pronoun does not need to be capitalized if it is closely preceded by its antecedent; however, in current practice, most writers capitalize the pronoun regardless of its position.

63. Traditional designations of apostles, prophets, and saints are capitalized.

our Lady	the Lawgiver
the Prophet	

64. Names of religions, denominations, creeds and confessions, and religious orders are capitalized, as are adjectives derived from these names. The word *church* is capitalized only when it is used as part of the name of a specific body or edifice or, in some publications, when it refers to organized Christianity in general.

> Judaism
> the Church of Christ
> Apostles' Creed
> the Poor Clares
> Hunt Memorial Church
> Islamic
> the Thirty-nine Articles of the Church of England
> Catholicism
> the Southern Baptist Convention
> the Society of Jesus
> Franciscans
> a Buddhist monastery
> the Baptist church on the corner

65. Names of the Bible or its books, parts, versions, or editions of it and other sacred books are capitalized but not italicized. Adjectives derived from the names of sacred books are variously capitalized and lowercased. When in doubt, consult a dictionary.

> Authorized Version   Apocrypha
> Koran   Pentateuch
> Talmud   talmudic
> Gospel of Saint Mark biblical
> Old Testament   Vedic
> Genesis   Koranic

66. The names of prayers and well-known passages of the Bible are capitalized.

> Ave Maria
> Ten Commandments
> the Lord's Prayer
> the Sermon on the Mount
> the Beatitudes
> the Our Father

Scientific Terms

67. Genus names in biological binomial nomenclature are capitalized; species names are lowercased, even when derived from a proper name. Both genus and species names are italicized.

> Both the wolf and the domestic dog are included in the genus *Canis*.

> The California condor (*Gymnogyps californianus*) is facing extinction.

Trailing arbutus (*Epigaea repens*) and rue anemone (*Anemonella thalictroides*) are among the earliest wildflowers to bloom in the spring.

NOTE: When used, the names of races, varieties, or subspecies are lowercased. Like genus and species names, they are italicized.

Hyla versicolor chrysoscelis
Otis asio naevius

68. The New Latin names of classes, families, and all groups above the genus level in zoology and botany are capitalized but not italicized. Their derivative adjectives and nouns in English are neither capitalized nor italicized.

Gastropoda	gastropod
Thallophyta	thallophyte

69. The names, both scientific and informal, of planets and their satellites, asteroids, stars, constellations, groups of stars, and other unique celestial objects are capitalized. However, the words *sun, earth,* and *moon* are usually lowercased unless they occur with other astronomical names. Generic terms that are the final element in the name of a celestial object are usually lowercased.

Ganymede	Venus
the Milky Way	Big Dipper
Pleiades	Great Bear
studying the Moon and Mars	Ursa Major
Sirius	Barnard's star

70. Names of meteorological phenomena are lowercased.

aurora australis	northern lights
aurora borealis	parhelic circle

71. Terms that identify geological eras, periods, epochs, and strata are capitalized. The generic terms that follow them are lowercased. The words *upper, middle,* and *lower* are capitalized when they are used to designate an epoch or series within a period; in most other cases, they are lowercased. The word *age* is capitalized in names such as *Age of Reptiles* or *Age of Fishes.*

Mesozoic era	Middle Ordovician
Oligocene epoch	Upper Cretaceous
Quaternary period	Lower Silurian

72. Proper names forming essential elements of scientific laws, theorems, and principles are capitalized. However, the common nouns *law, theorem, theory,* and the like are lowercased.

Boyle's law
the Pythagorean theorem
Planck's constant
Einstein's theory of relativity

NOTE: In terms referring to popular or fanciful theories or observations, descriptive words are usually capitalized as well.

Murphy's Law
the Peter Principle

73. The names of chemical elements and compounds are lowercased.

hydrogen fluoride
ferric ammonium citrate

74. The names of computer services and data bases are usually trademarks and should always be capitalized. The names of computer languages are irregularly styled either with an initial capital letter or with all letters capitalized. The names of some computer languages are commonly written either way. When in doubt, consult a dictionary.

CompuServe	COBOL *or* Cobol
Atek	PL/1
BASIC	APL
PENTA	FORTRAN *or* Fortran
TeleTransfer	Dow Jones News Retrieval
Pascal	Service

Time Periods and Zones

75. The names of days of the week, months of the year, and holidays and holy days are capitalized.

Easter	Yom Kippur
Passover	June
Tuesday	Thanksgiving
Independence Day	Ramadan
Memorial Day	

76. The names of time zones are capitalized when abbreviated but usually lowercased when written out except for words that are themselves proper names.

CST
central standard time
mountain time
Pacific standard time

77. Names of the seasons are lowercased if they simply declare the time of year; however, they are capitalized if they are personified.

My new book is scheduled to appear this spring.
the sweet breath of Spring

Titles—For titles of people, see **People** above.

78. Words in titles of books, long poems, magazines, newspapers, plays, movies, novellas that are separately published, and works of art such as paintings and sculpture are capitalized except for internal articles, conjunctions, prepositions, and the *to* of infinitives. The entire title is italicized. For the styling of the Bible and other sacred works, see paragraph 65 above.

> *The Lives of a Cell*
> *Saturday Review*
> Shakespeare's *Othello*
> Gainsborough's *Blue Boy*
> *Of Mice and Men*
> *Christian Science Monitor*
> *The Old Man and the Sea*
> the movie *Wait until Dark*

NOTE: Some publications also capitalize prepositions of five or more letters (as *about* or *toward*).

79. An initial article that is part of a title is often omitted if it would be awkward in context. However, when it is included it is capitalized and italicized. A common exception to this style regards books that are referred to by an abbreviation. In this case, the initial article is neither capitalized nor italicized.

> *The Oxford English Dictionary*
> the 13-volume *Oxford English Dictionary*
> the *OED*

80. Style varies widely regarding the capitalization and italicization of initial articles and city names in the titles of newspapers. One style rule that can be followed is to capitalize and italicize any word that is part of the official title of the paper as shown on its masthead. However, this information is not always available, and even if it is available it can lead to apparent inconsistencies in styling. Because of this, many publications choose one way of styling newspaper titles regardless of their official titles. The most common styling is to italicize the city name but not to capitalize or italicize the initial article.

> the *New York Times*
> the *Des Moines Register*
> the *Wall Street Journal*
> the *Washington Post*

81. Many publications, especially newspapers, do not use italics to style titles. They either simply capitalize the words of the title or capitalize the words and enclose them in quotation marks.

the Heard on the Street column in the Wall Street Journal
our review of "The Lives of a Cell" in last week's column

82. The first word following a colon in a title is capitalized.

John Crowe Ransom: An Annotated Bibliography

83. The titles of short poems, short stories, essays, lectures, dissertations, chapters of books, articles in periodicals, radio and television programs, and novellas that are published in a collection are capitalized and enclosed in quotation marks. The capitalization of articles, conjunctions, and prepositions is the same as it is for italicized titles, as explained in paragraph 78 above.

Robert Frost's "Dust of Snow"
Katherine Anne Porter's "That Tree"
John Barth's "The Literature of Exhaustion"
The talk, "Labor's Power: A View for the Eighties," will be given next week.
the third chapter of *Treasure Island,* entitled "The Black Spot"
Her article, "Computer Art on a Micro," was in last month's *Popular Computing*.
listening to "A Prairie Home Companion"
watching "The Tonight Show"
D. H. Lawrence's "The Woman Who Rode Away"

84. Common titles of sections of books (as a preface, introduction, or index) are capitalized but not enclosed in quotation marks when they refer to a section of the same book in which the reference is made. If they refer to another book, they are usually lowercased.

See the Appendix for further information.
In the introduction to her book, the author explains her goals.

85. Style varies regarding the capitalization of the word *chapter* when it is used with a cardinal number to identify a specific chapter in a book. In some publications the word is lowercased, but more commonly it is capitalized.

See Chapter 3 for more details.
is discussed further in Chapter Four
   but in the third chapter

86. The titles of long musical compositions such as operas and symphonies are capitalized and italicized; the titles of short compositions are capitalized and enclosed in quotation marks. The titles of musical compositions identified by the nature of the musical form in which they were written are capitalized only.

Verdi's *Don Carlos*
Ravel's "Bolero"
"America the Beautiful"
Serenade No. 12 in C Minor

Trademarks

87. Registered trademarks, service marks, collective marks, and brand names are capitalized.

Band-Aid	Diet Pepsi
College Board	Kleenex
Kellogg's All-Bran	Realtor
Jacuzzi	Lay's potato chips
Grammy	Planned Parenthood

Transportation

88. The names of individual ships, submarines, airplanes, satellites, and space vehicles are capitalized and italicized. The designations *U.S.S., S.S., M.V.,* and *H.M.S.* are not italicized.

Apollo 11	*Enola Gay*
Mariner 5	*Explorer 10*
Spirit of Saint Louis	M.V. *West Star*

Other Uses of Capitals

1. Full capitalization of a word is sometimes used for emphasis or to indicate that a speaker is talking very loudly. Both of these uses of capitals are usually avoided or at least used very sparingly in formal prose. Italicization of words for emphasis is more common. For examples of this use of italics, see paragraph 8 of the section on Other Uses of Italics in this chapter.

> Results are not the only criteria for judging performance. HOW we achieve results is important also.
>
> All applications must be submitted IN WRITING before January 31.
>
> The waiter rushed by yelling "HOT PLATE! HOT PLATE!"

2. A word is sometimes capitalized to indicate that it is being used as a philosophical concept or to indicate that it stands for an important concept in a discussion. Style manuals generally discourage this practice, but it is still in common use today even in formal writing.

> Many people seek Truth, but few find it.
>
> the three M's of advertising, Message, Media, and Management

3. Full capitals or a mixture of capitals and lowercase letters or sometimes even small capitals are used to reproduce the text of signs, labels, or inscriptions.

> a poster reading SPECIAL THRILLS COMING SOON
> a Do Not Disturb sign
> a barn with CHEW MAIL POUCH on the side
> a truck with WASH ME written in the dust

4. A letter used to indicate a shape is usually capitalized. If sans serif type is available, it is often used for such a letter, because it usually best approximates the shape that is being referred to.

> an A-frame house   V-shaped
> a J-bar

Other Uses of Italics

Italic type is used to indicate that there is something out of the ordinary about a word or phrase or about the way in which it is being used. For some of the uses listed below, quotation marks can be substituted. For more on this use of quotation marks, see the section on Quotation Marks, Double, in Chapter 1, "Punctuation," beginning on page 43. For each of the uses listed below, underlining is used in place of italicizing when the text is typewritten instead of typeset.

1. Foreign words and phrases that have not been fully adopted into the English language are italicized. The decision whether or not to italicize a word will vary according to the context of the writing and the audience for which the writing is intended. In general, however, any word that appears in the main A–Z vocabulary section of *Webster's Ninth New Collegiate Dictionary* does not need to be italicized.

> These accomplishments will serve as a monument, *aere perennius*, to the group's skill and dedication.
> They looked upon this area as a *cordon sanitaire* around the city.
> "The cooking here is *wunderbar*," he said.
> After the concert, the crowd headed en masse for the parking lot.
> The committee meets on an ad hoc basis.

NOTE: A complete sentence (such as a motto) can also be italicized. However, passages that comprise more than one sentence, or even a single sentence if it is particularly long, are usually treated as quotations; i.e., they are set in roman type and enclosed in quotation marks.

2. Unfamiliar words or words that have a specialized meaning are set in italics, especially when they are accompanied by a short definition. Once these words have been introduced and defined, they do not need to be italicized in subsequent references.

> *Vitiligo* is a condition in which skin pigment cells stop making pigment.

> Another method is the *direct-to-consumer* transaction in which the publisher markets directly to the individual by mail or door-to-door.

3. Style varies somewhat regarding the italicization of Latin abbreviations. During the first half of this century, these abbreviations were most commonly set in italic type. Some authors and publishers still italicize them, either by tradition or on the grounds that they should be treated like foreign words. However, most authors and publishers now set these abbreviations in roman type. (For an explanation of the use of *ibid., op. cit.,* and other Latin bibliographical abbreviations, see Chapter 7, "Notes and Bibliographies.")

> et al.   cf.   e.g.   i.e.   viz.

4. Italic type is used to indicate words referred to as words, letters referred to as letters, or numerals referred to as numerals. However, if the word referred to as a word was actually spoken, it is often enclosed in quotation marks. If the letter is being used to refer to its sound and not its printed form, virgules or brackets can be used instead of italics. And if there is no chance of confusion, numerals referred to as numerals are often not italicized. (For an explanation of the ways in which to form the plurals of words, letters, and numerals referred to as such, see the section on Plurals, beginning on page 82, in Chapter 3, "Plurals, Possessives, and Compounds."

> The panel could not decide whether *data* was a singular or plural noun.

> *Only* can be an adverb modifying a verb, as in the case of "I *only* tried to help."

> We heard his warning, but we weren't sure what "other repercussions" meant in that context.

> You should dot your *i*'s and cross your *t*'s.

> She couldn't pronounce her *s*'s.

> He was still having trouble with the /p/ sound.

> The first *2* and the last *1* are barely legible.

5. A letter used to indicate a shape is usually capitalized but not set in italics. For more on this use of capital letters, see the section on Other Uses of Capitals in this chapter.

6. Individual letters are sometimes set in italic type to provide additional typographical contrast. This use of italics is common when letters are used in run-in enumerations or when they are used to identify elements in an illustration.

> providing information about (*a*) typing, (*b*) transcribing, (*c*) formatting, and (*d*) graphics
> located at point *A* on the diagram

7. Italics are used to indicate a word created to suggest a sound.

> From the nest came a high-pitched *whee* from one of the young birds.
> We sat listening to the *chat-chat-chat* of the sonar.

8. Italics are used to emphasize or draw attention to a word or words in a sentence.

> Students must notify the dean's office *in writing* of all courses added or dropped from their original list.
> She had become *the* hero, the one everyone else looked up to.

NOTE: Italics serve to draw attention to words in large part because they are used so infrequently. Writers who overuse italics for giving emphasis may find that the italics lose their effectiveness.

Chapter 3

Plurals, Possessives, and Compounds

CONTENTS

This chapter describes the ways in which plurals, possessives, and compound words are most commonly formed. In doing so, it treats some of the simplest and some of the most problematic kinds of questions that are faced by writers and editors. For some of the questions raised in this chapter, various solutions have been developed over the years, but no single solution has come to be universally accepted. This chapter describes the range of solutions that are available; however, many of the questions raised in this chapter inevitably require arbitrary decisions and personal judgments. In cases like these, careful writers and editors usually make notes or keep a style sheet so that they can be consistent in the way that they form plurals, possessives, and compounds for certain specific words or categories of words. For more on keeping and using a style sheet, see pages 256–260 in Chapter 9, "Copyediting and Proofreading."

Writers and editors are frequently told that consulting a good dictionary will solve many of the problems that are discussed in this chapter. To some extent this is true, and this chapter does recommend consulting a dictionary at a number of points. In this regard, the best dictionary to consult is an unabridged dictionary, such as *Webster's Third New International Dictionary*. In the absence of such a comprehensive reference book, writers and editors should consult a good desk dictionary, such as *Webster's Ninth New Collegiate Dictionary*. Any dictionary that is much smaller than the *Ninth Collegiate* will often be more frustrating in what it fails to show than helpful in what it shows.

In giving examples of plurals, possessives, and compounds, this chapter uses both *or* and *also* to separate variant forms of the same word. The word *or* is used when both forms of the word are used with approximately equal frequency in standard prose; the form that precedes the *or* is probably slightly more common than the form that follows it. The word *also* is used when one form of the word is much more common than the other; the more common precedes the less common.

Plurals

The plurals of most English words are formed by adding -*s* to the singular. If the noun ends in -*s*, -*x*, -*z*, -*ch*, or -*sh*, so that an extra syllable must be added in order to pronounce the plural, -*es* is added to the singular. If the noun ends in a -*y* preceded by a consonant, the -*y* is changed to -*i*- and -*es* is added. Most proper nouns ending in -*y* (as *Mary* or *Germany*), however, simply add -*s* to the singular.

Many English nouns do not follow the general pattern for forming plurals. Most good dictionaries give thorough coverage to irregular and variant plurals, so they are often the best place to start to answer questions about the plural form of a specific word. The paragraphs that follow describe the ways in which plurals are formed for a number of categories of words whose plural forms are most apt to raise questions.

The symbol → is used throughout this section of the chapter. In each case, the element that follows the arrow is the plural form of the element that precedes the arrow.

Abbreviations

1. The plurals of abbreviations are commonly formed by adding -*s* or an apostrophe plus -*s* to the abbreviation; however, there are some significant exceptions to this pattern. For more on the formation of plurals of abbreviations, see the section on Plurals, Possessives, and Compounds, beginning on page 110, in Chapter 4, "Abbreviations."

COLA → COLA's	Ph.D. → Ph.D.'s
f.o.b. → f.o.b.'s	bldg. → bldgs.
CPU → CPUs	p. → pp.

Animals

2. The names of many fishes, birds, and mammals have both a plural formed with a suffix and one that is identical with the singular. Some have only the -*s* plural; others have only an uninflected plural.

flounder → flounder *or* flounders
quail → quail   *or*   quails
mink → mink   *or*   minks
buffalo → buffalo   *or*   buffalos

cow → cows	hen → hens
bison → bison	sheep → sheep
rat → rats	monkey → monkeys
shad → shad	moose → moose

3. Many of the animals that have both plural forms are ones that are hunted, fished, or trapped, and those who hunt, fish for, and trap them are most likely to use the uninflected form. The -s form is especially likely to be used to emphasize diversity of kinds.

> caught four trout
> *but*
> trouts of the Rocky Mountains
> a place where fish gather
> *but*
> the fishes of the Pacific Ocean

Compounds and Phrases

4. Most compounds composed of two nouns, whether styled as one word or two words or as hyphenated words, are pluralized by pluralizing the final element.

> matchbox → matchboxes
> judge advocate → judge advocates
> city-state → city-states
> face-lift → face-lifts
> spokeswoman → spokeswomen
> tree house → tree houses
> crow's-foot → crow's-feet
> battle-ax → battle-axes

5. The plural form of a compound consisting of an -er agent noun and an adverb is made by pluralizing the noun element.

> hanger-on → hangers-on
> looker-on → lookers-on
> onlooker → onlookers
> passerby → passersby

6. Nouns made up of words that are not nouns form their plurals on the terminal element.

> also-ran → also-rans
> put-down → put-downs
> changeover → changeovers
> ne'er-do-well → ne'er-do-wells
> set-to → set-tos
> blowup → blowups

7. Plurals of compounds that are phrases consisting of two nouns separated by a preposition are regularly formed by pluralizing the first noun.

> aide-de-camp → aides-de-camp
> auto-da-fe → autos-da-fe
> man-of-war → men-of-war
> attorney-at-law → attorneys-at-law
> lady-in-waiting → ladies-in-waiting
> power of attorney → powers of attorney
> base on balls → bases on balls
> mother-in-law → mothers-in-law
> coup d'état → coups d'état

8. Compounds that are phrases consisting of two nouns separated by a preposition and a modifier form their plurals in various ways.

> flash in the pan → flashes in the pan
> jack-in-the-box → jack-in-the-boxes *or* jacks-in-the-box
> jack-of-all-trades → jacks-of-all-trades
> son of a gun → sons of guns
> stick-in-the-mud → stick-in-the-muds

9. Compounds consisting of a noun followed by an adjective are regularly pluralized by adding a suffix to the noun.

> cousin-german → cousins-german
> heir apparent → heirs apparent
> knight-errant → knights-errant

NOTE: If the adjective in such a compound tends to be construed as a noun, the compound may have more than one plural form.

> attorney general → attorneys general *or* attorney generals
> sergeant major → sergeants major *or* sergeant majors
> poet laureate → poets laureate *or* poet laureates

Foreign Words and Phrases

10. Many nouns of foreign origin retain the foreign plural; most of them also have a regular English plural.

> alumnus → alumni
> beau → beaux *or* beaus
> crisis → crises
> emporium → emporiums *or* emporia
> index → indexes *or* indices
> larynx → larynges *or* larynxes
> phenomenon → phenomena *or* phenomenons
> schema → schemata *also* schemas
> seraph → seraphim *or* seraphs
> series → series
> tempo → tempi *or* tempos

NOTE: A foreign plural may not be used for all senses of a word or may be more commonly used for some senses than for others.

antenna (on an insect) → antennae
antenna (on a radio) → antennas

11. Phrases of foreign origin may have a foreign plural, an English plural, or both.

beau monde → beau mondes   *or*   beaux mondes
carte blanche → cartes blanches
charlotte russe → charlottes russe
felo-de-se → felones-de-se   *or*   felos-de-se
hors d'oeuvre → hors d'oeuvres

-ful Words

12. A plural -*fuls* can be used for any noun ending in -*ful,* but some of these nouns also have an alternative, usually less common plural with -*s*- preceding the suffix.

eyeful → eyefuls
barnful → barnfuls
mouthful → mouthfuls
worldful → worldfuls
barrelful → barrelfuls   *or*   barrelsful
bucketful → bucketfuls   *or*   bucketsful
cupful → cupfuls   *also*   cupsful
tablespoonful → tablespoonfuls   *also*   tablespoonsful

Irregular Plurals

13. A small group of English nouns form their plurals by changing one or more of their vowels.

foot → feet   mouse → mice
goose → geese   woman → women
louse → lice   tooth → teeth
man → men

14. A few nouns have -*en* or -*ren* plurals.

ox → oxen
child → children
brother → brethren

15. Some nouns ending in -*f,* -*fe,* and -*ff* have plurals that end in -*ves*. Some of these also have regularly formed plurals.

elf → elves
knife → knives
life → lives
loaf → loaves
beef → beefs   *or*   beeves
staff → staffs   *or*   staves
wharf → wharves   *also*   wharfs
dwarf → dwarfs   *or*   dwarves

Italic Elements

16. Italicized words, phrases, abbreviations, and letters in roman context are variously pluralized with either an italic or roman *s*. Most stylebooks urge use of a roman *s,* and our evidence indicates that that is the form used most commonly. If the plural is formed with an apostrophe and an *-s,* the *-s* is almost always roman.

> fifteen *Newsweek*s on the shelf
> answered with a series of *uh-huh*s
> a row of *x*'s

Letters

17. The plurals of letters are usually formed by the addition of an apostrophe and an *-s,* although uppercase letters are sometimes pluralized by the addition of an *-s* alone.

> p's and q's
> V's of geese flying overhead
> dot your *i*'s
> straight As

Numbers

18. Numerals are pluralized by adding an *-s,* or, less commonly, an apostrophe and an *-s.*

> two par 5s   1960's
> 1970s   the mid-$20,000s
> in the 80s   DC-10's

19. Spelled-out numbers are usually pluralized without an apostrophe.

> in twos and threes
> scored two sixes

-o Words

20. Most words ending in an *-o* are pluralized by adding an *-s;* however, some words ending in an *-o* preceded by a consonant have *-s* plurals, some have *-es* plurals, and some have both. When you are in doubt about such a word, consult a dictionary.

> alto → altos
> echo → echoes
> motto → mottoes   *also*   mottos
> tornado → tornadoes   *or*   tornados

Proper Nouns

21. The plurals of proper nouns are usually formed with *-s* or *-es.*

> Bruce → Bruces

Charles → Charleses
John Harris → John Harrises
Hastings → Hastingses
Velasquez → Velasquezes

22. Proper nouns ending in -*y* usually retain the -*y* and add -*s*.

Germany → Germanys
Mary → Marys
Mercury → Mercurys
  but
Ptolemy → Ptolemies
Sicily → The Two Sicilies
The Rockies

NOTE: Words that were originally proper nouns and that end in -*y* are usually pluralized by changing -*y* to -*i*- and adding -*es*, but a few retain the -*y*.

bobby → bobbies
Jerry → Jerries
johnny → johnnies
Tommy → Tommies
Bloody Mary → Bloody Marys
Typhoid Mary → Typhoid Marys

Quoted Elements

23. Style varies regarding the plural form of words in quotation marks. Some writers form the plural by adding an -*s* or an apostrophe plus -*s* within the quotation marks; others add an -*s* outside the quotation marks. Both arrangements look awkward, and writers generally try to avoid this construction.

too many "probably's" in the statement
didn't hear any "nays"
One "you" among millions of "you"s
a response characterized by its "yes, but"s

Symbols

24. Although symbols are not usually pluralized, when a symbol is being referred to as a character in itself without regard to meaning, the plural is formed by adding an -*s* or an apostrophe plus -*s*.

used &'s instead of *and*'s
his π's are hard to read
printed three *s

Words used as Words

25. Words used as words without regard to meaning usually form their plurals by adding an apostrophe and an -*s*.

five *and*'s in one sentence
all those *wherefore*'s and *howsoever*'s

NOTE: When a word used as a word has become part of a fixed phrase, the plural is usually formed by adding a roman -s without the apostrophe.

oohs and aahs
dos and don'ts

Possessives

The possessive case of most nouns is formed by adding an apostrophe or an apostrophe plus -s to the end of the word. For most other uses of the apostrophe, such as to form contractions, see the section on Apostrophe, beginning on page 5, in Chapter 1, "Punctuation." For the use of the apostrophe to form plurals, see the section on Plurals in this chapter.

Common Nouns

1. The possessive case of singular and plural common nouns that do not end in an *s* or *z* sound is formed by adding an apostrophe plus -s to the end of the word.

   the boy's mother   children's books
   men's clothing   the potato's skin
   at her wit's end   the symposia's themes

2. The possessive case of singular nouns ending in an *s* or *z* sound is usually formed by adding an apostrophe plus -s to the end of the word. Style varies somewhat on this point, as some writers prefer to add an apostrophe plus -s to the word only when the added -s is pronounced; if it isn't pronounced, they add just an apostrophe. According to our evidence, both approaches are common in contemporary prose, although always adding an apostrophe plus -s is the much more widely accepted approach.

   the press's books
   the boss's desk
   the index's arrangement
   the horse's saddle
   the audience's reaction   *also*   the audience' reaction
   the waitress's duties   *also*   the waitress' duties
   the conference's outcome *also*   the conference' outcome

NOTE: Even writers who follow the pattern of adding an apostrophe plus -s to all singular nouns will often make an exception for a multisyllabic word that ends in an *s* or *z* sound if it is followed by a word beginning with an *s* or *z* sound.

for convenience' sake
for conscience' sake
the illness' symptoms   *or*   the illness's symptoms
to the princess' surprise   *or*   to the princess's surprise

3. The possessive case of plural nouns ending in an *s* or *z* sound is formed by adding only an apostrophe to the end of the word. One exception to this rule is that the possessive case of one-syllable irregular plurals is usually formed by adding an apostrophe plus -*s*.

    horses' stalls
    consumers' confidence
    geese's calls
    mice's habits

Proper Names

4. The possessive forms of proper names are generally made in the same way as they are for common nouns. The possessive form of singular proper names not ending in an *s* or *z* sound is made by adding an apostrophe plus -*s* to the name. The possessive form of plural proper names is made by adding just an apostrophe.

    Mrs. Wilson's store   the Wattses' daughter
    Utah's capital   the Cohens' house
    Canada's rivers   Niagara Falls' location

5. As is the case for the possessive form of singular common nouns (see paragraph 2 above), the possessive form of singular proper names ending in an *s* or *z* sound may be formed either by adding an apostrophe plus -*s* or by adding just an apostrophe to the name. For the sake of consistency, most writers choose one pattern for forming the possessive of all singular names ending in an *s* or *z* sound, regardless of the pronunciation of individual names (for exceptions see paragraphs 6 and 7 below). According to our evidence, adding an apostrophe plus -*s* to all such names is more common than adding just the apostrophe.

    Jones's car   *also*   Jones' car
    Bliss's statue   *also*   Bliss' statue
    Dickens's novels   *also*   Dickens' novels

6. The possessive form of classical and biblical names of two or more syllables ending in -*s* or -*es* is usually made by adding an apostrophe without an -*s*. If the name has only one syllable, the possessive form is made by adding an apostrophe and an -*s*.

    Aristophanes' plays   Odysseus' journey

Judas' betrayal   Zeus's anger
Achilles' heel   Mars's help

7. The possessive forms of the names *Jesus* and *Moses* are always formed with just an apostrophe.

   Jesus' time
   Moses' law

8. The possessive forms of names ending in a silent *-s*, *-z*, or *-x* usually include the apostrophe and the *-s*.

   Arkansas's capital
   Delacroix's paintings
   Camus's *The Stranger*
   Josquin des Prez's work

9. For the sake of convenience and appearance, some writers will italicize the possessive ending when adding it to a name that is in italics; however, most frequently the possessive ending is in roman.

   the U.S.S. *Constitution*'s cannons
   Gone With the Wind's ending
   the *Mona Lisa*'s somber hues
   High Noon's plot

Pronouns

10. The possessive case of indefinite pronouns such as *anyone, everybody,* and *someone* is formed by adding an apostrophe and an *-s*.

    everyone's   anybody's
    everybody's   someone's
    anyone's   somebody's

    NOTE: Some indefinite pronouns usually require an *of* phrase rather than inflection to indicate possession.

    the rights of each
    the inclination of many
    the satisfaction of all

11. Possessive pronouns include no apostrophes.

    mine   his
    its   theirs
    yours   hers
    ours

Phrases

12. The possessive form of a phrase is made by adding an apostrophe or an apostrophe plus *-s* to the last word in the phrase.

    board of directors' meeting
    his brother-in-law's sidecar

from the student of politics' point of view
a moment or so's thought

NOTE: Constructions such as these can become awkward, and it is often better to rephrase the sentence to eliminate the need for the possessive ending. For instance, the last two examples above could be rephrased as follows:

from the point of view of the student of politics
thinking for a moment or so

Words in Quotation Marks

13. Style varies regarding the possessive form of words in quotation marks. Some writers place the apostrophe and -*s* inside the quotation marks; others place them outside the quotation marks. Either arrangement will look awkward, and writers usually try to avoid this construction.

the "Today Show' "s cohosts
the "Grande Dame's" escort
   but more commonly
the cohosts of the "Today Show"
escort to the "Grande Dame"

Abbreviations

14. Possessives of abbreviations are formed in the same way as those of nouns that are spelled out. The singular possessive is formed by adding an apostrophe plus -*s* to the abbreviation; the plural possessive, by adding an apostrophe only.

the AMA's executive committee
Itek Corp.'s Applied Technology Division
the Burns Bros.' stores
the MPs' decisions

Numerals

15. The possessive form of nouns composed of or including numerals is made in the same way as for nouns composed wholly of words. The possessive of singular nouns is formed by adding an apostrophe plus -*s*; the possessive form of plural nouns, by adding an apostrophe only.

1985's most popular model
Louis XIV's court
the 1980s' most colorful figure

Individual and Joint Possession

16. Individual possession is indicated when an apostrophe plus -*s* is added to each noun in a sequence. Joint possession is most commonly indicated by adding an apostrophe or an apostrophe plus -*s* to the last noun in the sequence. In some cases,

joint possession is also indicated by adding a possessive ending to each name.

> Kepler's and Clark's respective clients
> John's, Bill's, and Larry's boats
> Kepler and Clark's law firm
> Christine and James's vacation home
>   *or*   Christine's and James's vacation home

Compounds

A compound is a word or word group that consists of two or more parts working together as a unit to express a specific concept. Compounds can be formed by combining two or more words (as in *eye shadow, graphic equalizer, farmhouse, cost-effective, blue-pencil, around-the-clock,* or *son of a gun*), by combining word elements (as prefixes or suffixes) with words (as in *ex-president, shoeless, presorted, uninterruptedly,* or *meaningless*), or by combining two or more word elements (as in *supermicro* or *photomicrograph*). Compounds are written in one of three ways: solid (as *cottonmouth*), hyphenated (as *player-manager*), or open (as *field day*).

Some of the explanations in this section make reference to permanent and temporary compounds. Permanent compounds are those that are so commonly used that they have become established as permanent parts of the language; many of them can be found in dictionaries. Temporary compounds are those made up to fit the writer's need at the particular moment. Temporary compounds, of course, cannot be found in dictionaries and therefore present the writer with styling problems.

Presenting styling problems similar to those of temporary compounds are self-evident compounds. These are compounds (as *baseball game* or *economic policy*) that are readily understood from the meanings of the words that make them up. Self-evident compounds, like temporary compounds, are not to be found in dictionaries.

In other words, writers faced with having to use compounds such as *farm stand* (*farm-stand? farmstand?*), *wide body* (*wide-body? widebody?*), or *picture framing* (*picture-framing? pictureframing?*) cannot rely wholly on dictionaries to guide them in their styling of compounds. They need, in addition, to develop an approach for dealing with compounds that are not in the dictionary. A few of those approaches are explained below.

One approach is simply to leave open any compound that is not in the dictionary. Many writers do this, but there are drawbacks to this approach. A temporary compound may not be as easily recognized as a compound by the reader when it is left open. For instance if you need to use *wide body* as a term for a kind of jet airplane, a phrase like "the operation of wide bodies" may catch the reader unawares. And if you use the open style for a compound modifier, you may create momentary confusion (or even unintended amusement) with a phrase like "the operation of wide body jets."

Another possibility would be to hyphenate all compounds that aren't in the dictionary. Hyphenation would give your compound immediate recognition as a compound. But hyphenating all such compounds runs counter to some well-established American practice. Thus you would be calling too much attention to the compound and momentarily distracting the reader.

A third approach is to use analogy to pattern your temporary compound after some other similar compound. This approach is likely to be more complicated than simply picking an open or hyphenated form, and will not free you from the need to make your own decisions in most instances. But it does have the advantage of making your compound less distracting or confusing by making it look as much like other more familiar compounds as possible.

The rest of this section is aimed at helping you to use the analogical approach to styling compounds. You will find compounds listed according to the elements that make them up and the way that they function in a sentence.

This section deals first with compounds formed from whole English words, then compounds formed with word elements, and finally with a small collection of miscellaneous styling conventions relating to compounds. The symbol + in the following paragraphs can be interpreted as "followed immediately by."

Compound Nouns

Compound nouns are combinations of words that function in a sentence as nouns. They may consist of two or more nouns, a noun and a modifier, or two or more elements that are not nouns.

1. **noun + noun** Compounds composed of two nouns that are short, commonly used, and pronounced with falling stress—that is, with the most stress on the first noun and less or no stress on the second—are usually styled solid.

teapot	birdbath
catfish	handsaw
football	railroad
cottonmouth	handmaiden
sweatband	farmyard
handlebar	bandwagon

2. When a noun + noun compound is short and common but pronounced with equal stress on both nouns, the styling is more likely to be open.

bean sprouts	fire drill
fuel oil	head louse
fuel cell	pine tar
beach buggy	dart board
duffel bag	rose fever

3. Many short noun + noun compounds begin as temporary compounds styled open. As they become more familiar and better established, there is a tendency for them to become solid.

data base *is becoming* database
chain saw *is becoming* chainsaw
lawn mower *is becoming* lawnmower

4. Noun + noun compounds that consist of longer nouns, are self-evident, or are temporary are usually styled open.

wildlife sanctuary
football game
reunion committee
television camera

5. When the nouns in a noun + noun compound describe a double title or double function, the compound is hyphenated.

city-state	secretary-treasurer
decree-law	player-manager
dinner-dance	author-critic

6. Compounds formed from a noun or adjective followed by *man, woman, person,* or *people* and denoting an occupation are regularly solid.

salesman	salesperson
congresswoman	spokesperson
saleswoman	salespeople
handyman	policewoman

7. Compounds that are units of measurement are hyphenated.

foot-pound	column-inch
kilowatt-hour	light-year
man-hour	board-foot

8. **adjective + noun** Most temporary or self-evident adjective + noun compounds are styled open. Permanent compounds formed from relatively long adjectives or nouns are also open.

automatic weapons	minor seminary
religious freedom	modular arithmetic
pancreatic juice	graphic equalizer
modal auxiliary	white lightning
automatic pilot	

9. Adjective + noun compounds consisting of two short words may be styled solid when pronounced with falling stress. Just as often, however, short adjective + noun compounds are styled open; a few are hyphenated.

bigfoot	dry cleaner
blueprint	dry rot
drywall	dry run
highland	dry well
longboat	high gear
longhand	long haul
redline	red tape
shortcake	short run
shortcut	short story
shorthand	sick leave
sickbed	wet nurse
wetland	yellow jacket
yellowhammer	red-eye
big deal	red-hot

10. participle + noun Most participle + noun compounds are styled open, whether permanent, temporary, or self-evident.

frying pan	nagging backache
whipped cream	shredded wheat
furnished apartment	whipping boy

11. noun's + noun Compounds consisting of a possessive noun followed by another noun are usually styled hyphenated or open.

crow's-feet	cat's-eye
cat's cradle	fool's gold
stirred up a hornet's nest	cat's-paw
lion's share	

NOTE: Compounds of this type that have become solid have lost the apostrophe.

foolscap
menswear
sheepshead

12. noun + verb + -er; noun + verb + -ing Temporary compounds in which the first noun is the object of the verb to which the suffix has been added are most often styled open; however, many writers use a hyphen to make the relationships of the words immediately apparent. Permanent compounds like these are sometimes styled solid as well.

temporary		
	gene-splicing	career planning
	risk-taking	cost-cutting
	opinion maker	English-speakers

permanent	lifesaver	penny-pinching
	data processing	flyswatter
	lawn mower	fund-raising
	copyediting	bookkeeper
	bird-watcher	

13. **object + verb** Noun compounds consisting of a verb preceded by a noun that is its object are variously styled.

clambake	face-lift
car wash	turkey shoot

14. **verb + object** A few compounds are formed from a verb followed by a noun that is its object. These are mostly older words, and they are solid.

tosspot	carryall
cutthroat	pinchpenny
breakwater	pickpocket

15. **noun + adjective** Compounds composed of a noun followed by an adjective are styled open or hyphenated.

battle royal	mayor-elect
governor-designate	secretary-general
sum total	letters patent
consul general	president-elect
heir apparent	

16. **particle + noun** Compounds consisting of a particle (usually a preposition or adverb having prepositional, adverbial, or adjectival force in the compound) and a noun are usually styled solid, especially when they are short and pronounced with falling stress.

downpour	outpatient
output	aftershock
offshoot	crossbones
inpatient	input
throughput	overskirt
undershirt	upkeep

17. A few particle + noun compounds, especially when composed of longer elements or having equal stress on both elements, may be hyphenated or open.

off-season	off year
down payment	cross-fertilization

18. **verb + particle; verb + adverb** These compounds may be hyphenated or solid. Compounds with two-letter particles (*by, to, in, up, on*) are most frequently hyphenated, since the hyphen aids quick comprehension. Compounds with three-letter par-

ticles (*off, out*) are hyphenated or solid with about equal frequency. Those with longer particles or adverbs are more often but not always solid.

call-up	get-together	rollback
sign-on	giveaway	breakthrough
wrap-up	layout	takeover
brush-off	lead-in	letup
dropout	trade-in	sick-out
lay-up	flyby	tryout
sit-in	show-off	set-to
write-in	strikeout	warm-up
shoot-out	run-on	pileup
follow-through	turn-on	write-off
gadabout	breakdown	turnoff

19. **verb + -er + particle; verb + -ing + particle** Except for *passerby*, these compounds are hyphenated.

hanger-on	falling-out
summing-up	goings-on
diner-out	runner-up
talking-to	looker-on

20. **compounds of three or four elements** Compounds of three or four elements are styled either hyphenated or open. Those consisting of noun + prepositional phrase are generally open, although some are hyphenated. Those formed from other combinations are usually hyphenated.

base on balls	by-your-leave
lily of the valley	pick-me-up
good-for-nothing	lady of the house
love-in-a-mist	son of a gun
know-it-all	lady-in-waiting
justice of the peace	Johnny-jump-up
lord of misrule	stick-to-itiveness
jack-of-all-trades	

21. **letter + noun** Compounds formed from a single letter (or sometimes a combination of them) followed by a noun are either open or hyphenated.

A-frame	H-bomb
C ration	I beam
ABO system	Rh factor
B-girl	T-shirt
D day	T square
J-bar lift	H and L hinge

Compounds That Function as Adjectives
Compound adjectives are combinations of words that work together to modify a noun—that is, they work as unit modifiers. As

unit modifiers they should be distinguished from other strings of adjectives that may also precede a noun. For instance, in "a low, level tract of land" or "that long, lonesome road" the two adjectives each modify the noun separately. We are talking about a tract of land that is both low and level and about a road that is both long and lonesome. These are coordinate modifiers.

In "a low monthly fee" or "a wrinkled red necktie" the first adjective modifies the noun plus the second adjective. In other words, we mean a monthly fee that is low and a red necktie that is wrinkled. These are noncoordinate modifiers. But in "low-level radiation" we do not mean radiation that is low and level or level radiation that is low; we mean radiation that is at a low level. Both words work as a unit to modify the noun.

Unit modifiers are usually hyphenated. The hyphens not only make it easier for the reader to grasp the relationship of the words but also avoid confusion. The hyphen in "a call for more-specialized controls" removes any ambiguity as to which word *more* modifies. A phrase like "graphic arts exhibition" may seem clear to its author, but may have an unintended meaning for some readers.

22. **Before the Noun (attributive position)**   Most two-word permanent or temporary compound adjectives are hyphenated when placed before the noun.

> tree-lined streets
> an iron-clad guarantee
> class-conscious persons
> well-intended advice
> a profit-loss statement
> arrested on a trumped-up charge
> fast-acting medication
> a tough-minded negotiator
> Spanish-American relations
> the red-carpet treatment
> an input-output device
> a risk-free investment

23. Temporary compounds formed of an adverb (as *well, more, less, still*) followed by a participle (or sometimes an adjective) are usually hyphenated when placed before a noun.

> more-specialized controls
> a still-growing company
> these fast-moving times
> a just-completed survey
> a well-funded project
> a now-vulnerable politician

24. Temporary compounds formed from an adverb ending in *-ly* followed by a participle may sometimes be hyphenated but are

more commonly open, because adverb + adjective + noun is a normal word order.

> a widely-read feature
> internationally-known authors
> *but more often*
> generally recognized categories
> publicly supported universities
> a beautifully illustrated book
> our rapidly changing plans

25. The combination of *very* + adjective is not a unit modifier.

> a very satisfied smile

26. Many temporary compound adjectives are formed by using a compound noun—either permanent or temporary—to modify another noun. If the compound noun is an open compound, it is usually hyphenated so that the relationship of the words is more immediately apparent to the reader.

> the farm-bloc vote
> a short-run printing press
> a tax-law case
> a picture-framing shop
> a secret-compartment ring
> ocean-floor hydrophones

27. Some open compound nouns are considered so readily recognizable that they are frequently placed before a noun without a hyphen.

> a high school diploma   *or*   a high-school diploma
> a data processing course   *or*   a data-processing course
> a dry goods store   *or*   a dry-goods store

28. A proper name placed before a noun to modify it is not hyphenated.

> a Thames River marina
> a Korean War veteran
> a Huck Finn life
> a General Motors car

29. Compound adjectives of three or more words are hyphenated when they precede the noun. Many temporary compounds are formed by taking a phrase, hyphenating it, and placing it before a noun.

> spur-of-the-moment decisions
> higher-than-anticipated costs
> her soon-to-be-released movie

30. Compound adjectives composed of foreign words are not hyphenated when placed before a noun unless they are always hyphenated.

> the per capita cost
> a cordon bleu restaurant
> an a priori argument
> a ci-devant professor

31. Chemical names used as modifiers before a noun are not hyphenated.

> a sodium hypochlorite bleach
> a citric acid solution

32. Following the Noun (as a complement or predicate adjective) When the words that make up a compound adjective follow the noun they modify, they tend to fall in normal word order and are no longer unit modifiers. They are therefore no longer hyphenated.

> Controls have become more specialized.
> The company is still growing.
> a device for both input and output
> a statement of profit and loss
> arrested on charges that had been trumped up
> decisions made on the spur of the moment
> They were ill prepared for the journey.

33. Many permanent and temporary compounds keep their hyphens after the noun in a sentence if they continue to function as unit modifiers. Compounds consisting of adjective or noun + participle, adjective or noun + noun + -ed (which looks like a participle), or noun + adjective are most likely to remain hyphenated.

> Your ideas are high-minded but impractical.
> streets that are tree-lined
> You were just as nice-looking then.
> metals that are corrosion-resistant
> tends to be accident-prone

34. Permanent compound adjectives that are entered in dictionaries are usually styled in the way that they appear in the dictionary whether they precede or follow the noun they modify.

> The group was public-spirited.
> The problems are mind-boggling.
> is well-read in economics

35. Compound adjectives of three or more words are normally not hyphenated when they follow the noun they modify.

These remarks are off the record.

36. Permanent compounds of three or more words may be entered as hyphenated adjectives in dictionaries. In such cases the hyphens are retained as long as the phrase is being used as a unit modifier.

the plan is still pay-as-you-go
   but   a plan in which you pay as you go

37. It is possible that a permanent hyphenated adjective from the dictionary may appear alongside a temporary compound in a position where it would normally be open (as "one who is both ill-humored and ill prepared"). Editors usually try to resolve these inconsistencies, either by hyphenating both compounds or leaving both compounds open.

38. When an adverb modifies another adverb that is the first element of a compound modifier, the compound may lose its hyphen. If the first adverb modifies the whole compound, however, the hyphen should be retained.

a very well developed idea
a delightfully well-written book
a most ill-humored remark

39. Adjective compounds that are names of colors may be styled open or hyphenated. Color names in which each element can function as a noun (as *blue green* or *chrome yellow*) are almost always hyphenated when they precede a noun; they are sometimes open when they follow the noun. Color names in which the first element can only be an adjective are less consistently treated; they are often not hyphenated before a noun and are usually not hyphenated after.

blue-gray paint
paint that is blue-gray   *also*   paint that is blue gray
bluish gray paint   *or*   bluish-gray paint
paint that is bluish gray

40. Compound modifiers that include a number followed by a noun are hyphenated when they precede the noun they modify. When the modifier follows the noun, it is usually not hyphenated. For more on the styling of numbers, see Chapter 5, "The Treatment of Numbers."

five-card stud   ten-foot pole
an 18-inch rule   twelve-year-old girl
an essay that is one page   a child who is ten years old

41. An adjective that is composed of a number followed by a noun in the possessive is not hyphenated.

   a two weeks' wait
   a four blocks' walk

Compounds That Function as Adverbs

42. Adverb compounds consisting of preposition + noun are almost always written solid; however, there are a few well-known exceptions.

downtown	upstairs
downwind	upfield
onstage	offhand
overseas	underhand

   but

   in-house   off-line   on-line

43. Compound adverbs of more than two words are usually styled open, and they usually follow the words they modify.

every which way	hook, line, and sinker
little by little	off and on
high and dry	over and over

44. A few three-word adverbs are homographs of hyphenated adjectives and are therefore styled with hyphens. But many adverbs are styled open even if an adjective formed from the same phrase is hyphenated.

   back-to-back (adverb or adjective)
   face-to-face (adverb or adjective)
     but
   hand-to-hand combat
   off-the-cuff remarks
   fought hand to hand
   spoke off the cuff

Compound Verbs

45. Two-word verbs consisting of a verb followed by an adverb or a preposition are styled open.

get together	strike out
set to	run across
break through	put down
run around	print out
run wild	

46. A compound composed of a particle followed by a verb is styled solid.

upgrade	overcome
outflank	bypass

47. A verb derived from an open or hyphenated compound noun—permanent, temporary, or self-evident—is hyphenated.

blue-pencil   tap-dance
sweet-talk   poor-mouth
double-check   water-ski

48. A verb derived from a solid noun is styled solid.

bankroll   mainstream
roughhouse   steamroller

Compounds Formed with Word Elements

Many new and temporary compounds are formed by adding word elements to existing words or by combining word elements. There are three basic word elements: prefixes (as *anti-*, *re-*, *non-*, *super-*), suffixes (as *-er*, *-ly*, *-ness*, *-ism*), and what the dictionaries call combining forms (as *mini-*, *macro-*, *pseud-*, *ortho-*, *-ped*, *-graphy*, *-gamic*, *-plasty*). Prefixes and suffixes are usually attached to existing words; combining forms are usually combined to form new words.

49. prefix + word   Except as specified below, compounds formed from a prefix and a word are usually styled solid.

precondition   suborder
interagency   overfond
refurnish   postwar
misshapen   unhelpful

50. If the prefix ends with a vowel and the word it is attached to begins with the same vowel, the compound is usually hyphenated.

anti-inflation   de-emphasize
co-owner   multi-institutional

NOTE: Many exceptions to this styling (such as *cooperate* and *reentry*) can be found by checking a dictionary.

51. If the base word to which a prefix is added is capitalized, the compound is hyphenated.

anti-American   pro-Soviet
post-Victorian   inter-Caribbean

NOTE: The prefix is usually not capitalized in such compounds. But if the prefix and the base word together form a new proper name, the compound may be solid with the prefix capitalized (as *Postimpressionist*, *Precambrian*). Such exceptions can be found in a dictionary.

52. Compounds made with *self-* and *ex-* meaning "former" are hyphenated.

    self-pity
    ex-wife

53. If a prefix is added to a hyphenated compound, it may be either followed by a hyphen or closed up solid to the next element. Permanent compounds of this kind should be checked in a dictionary.

    unair-conditioned
    ultra-up-to-date
    non-self-governing
    unself-conscious

54. If a prefix is added to an open compound, the prefix is followed by a hyphen in typewritten material. In typeset material, this hyphen is often represented by an en dash. (For more on this use of the en dash, see paragraph 16 in the section on Dash, beginning on page 25, in Chapter 1, "Punctuation.")

    ex–Boy Scout
    post–coup d'état

55. A compound that would be identical with another word if styled solid is usually hyphenated to prevent misreading.

    a multi-ply fabric
    re-collect the money
    un-ionized particles

56. Some writers and editors like to hyphenate a compound that might otherwise be solid if they think the reader might be momentarily puzzled (as by consecutive vowels, doubled consonants, or simply an odd combination of letters.)

    coed   *or* co-ed
    coworker *or* co-worker
    overreact *or* over-react
    interrow *or* inter-row

57. Temporary compounds formed from *vice-* are usually hyphenated; however, some permanent compounds (as *vice president* and *vice admiral*) are open.

58. When prefixes are attached to numerals, the compounds are hyphenated.

    pre-1982 expenses
    post-1975 vintages
    non-20th-century ideas

59. Compounds formed from combining forms like *Anglo-*, *Judeo-*, or *Sino-* are hyphenated when the second element is an independent word and solid when it is a combining form.

Judeo-Christian   Francophone
Italophile   Sino-Soviet
Austro-Hungarian   Anglophobe

60. Prefixes that are repeated in the same compound are separated by a hyphen.

sub-subheading

61. Some prefixes and initial combining forms have related independent adjectives or adverbs that may be used where the prefix might be expected. A temporary compound with *quasi(-)* or *pseudo(-)* therefore may be written open as modifier + noun or hyphenated as combining form + noun. A writer or editor must thus decide which style to follow.

quasi intellectual   *or*   quasi-intellectual
pseudo liberal   *or*   pseudo-liberal

NOTE: in some cases (as *super, super-*), the independent modifier may not mean quite the same as the prefix.

62. Compounds consisting of different prefixes with the same base word and joined by *and* or *or* are sometimes shortened by pruning the first compound back to the prefix. The missing base word is indicated by a hyphen on the prefix.

pre- and postoperative care
anti- or pro-Revolutionary sympathies

63. word + suffix   Except as noted below, compounds formed by adding a suffix to a word are styled solid.

Darwinist   landscaper
fortyish   powerlessness

64. Permanent or temporary compounds formed with a suffix are hyphenated if the addition of the suffix would create a sequence of three like letters.

bell-like   a coffee-er coffee
will-less

65. Temporary compounds made with a suffix are often hyphenated if the base word is more than three syllables long, if the base word ends with the same letter the suffix begins with, or if the suffix creates a confusing sequence of letters.

tunnel-like   industry-wide
umbrella-like   jaw-wards
Mexican-ness   battle-worthy

66. Compounds made from a number + *odd* are hyphenated whether the number is spelled out or in numerals; a number + *-fold* is solid if the number is spelled out but hyphenated if it is in numerals.

> 20-odd   twenty-odd
> 12-fold   twelvefold

67. Most compounds formed from an open or hyphenated compound + a suffix do not separate the suffix by a hyphen. But such suffixes as *-like*, *-wide*, *-worthy*, and *-proof*, all of which are homographs of independent adjectives, are attached by a hyphen.

> good-humoredness   do-it-yourselfer
> dollar-a-yearism   a United Nations-like agency

NOTE: Open compounds often become hyphenated when a suffix is added unless they are proper nouns.

> middle age   *but*   middle-ager
> tough guy   *but*   tough-guyese
> New Englandism
> Wall Streeter

68. combining form + combining form   Many new terms in technical fields are created by adding combining form to combining form or combining form to a word or a word part. Such compounds are generally intended to be permanent, even though many never get into the dictionary. They are regularly styled solid.

Miscellaneous Styling Conventions

69. Compounds that would otherwise be styled solid according to the principles described above are written open or hyphenated to avoid ambiguity, to make sure of rapid comprehension, or to make the pronunciation more obvious.

> meat-ax   *or*   meat ax   umbrella-like
> re-utter   tri-city
> bi-level   un-iced

70. When typographical features such as capitals or italics make word relationships in a sentence clear, it is not necessary to hyphenate an open compound (as when it precedes a noun it modifies).

> a *Chicago Tribune* story
> I've been Super Bowled to death.
> a *noblesse oblige* attitude
> an "eyes only" memo

71. Publications (as technical journals) aimed at a specialized readership likely to recognize the elements of a compound and their relationship tend to use open and solid stylings more frequently than more general publications would.

> electrooculogram
> radiofrequency
> rapid eye movement

72. Words that are formed by reduplication and so consist of two similar-sounding elements (as *hush-hush, razzle-dazzle,* or *hugger-mugger*) present styling questions like those of compounds. Words like these are hyphenated if each of the elements is made up of more than one syllable. If each element has only one syllable, the words are variously styled solid or hyphenated. The solid styling is slightly more common overall; however, for very short words (as *no-no, go-go,* and *so-so*), for words in which both elements may have primary stress (as *tip-top* and *sci-fi*), and for words coined in the twentieth century (as *ack-ack* and *hush-hush*), the hyphenated styling is more common.

> | | |
> |---|---|
> | goody-goody | boo-boo |
> | palsy-walsy | tip-top |
> | teeter-totter | crisscross |
> | topsy-turvy | peewee |
> | agar-agar | knickknack |
> | ack-ack | singsong |

Chapter 4

Abbreviations

CONTENTS

Abbreviations are used for a variety of reasons. They serve to save space, to avoid repetition of long words and phrases that may distract the reader, and to reduce keystrokes for typists and thereby increase their output. In addition, abbreviations are used simply to conform to conventional usage.

The frequency of abbreviations in typewritten or printed material is directly related to the nature of the material itself. For example, technical literature (as in the military and in the fields of aerospace, engineering, data processing, and medicine) features many abbreviations, but formal literary writing has relatively few. By the same token, the number of abbreviations in a piece of business writing depends on the nature of the business, as do the particular abbreviations employed. A person working in a university English department will often see *ibid.*, *ll.*, and *TESOL*, while the employee of an electronics firm will instead see *CAD*, *CPU*, and *mm* from day to day.

Unfortunately, the contemporary styling of abbreviations is to a large extent inconsistent and arbitrary. No set of rules can hope to cover all the possible variations, exceptions, and peculiarities actually encountered in print. The styling of abbreviations—whether capitalized or lowercased, closed up or spaced, punctuated or unpunctuated—depends most often on the writer's preference or the organization's policy. For example, some companies style the abbreviation for *cash on delivery* as *COD*, while others prefer *C.O.D.*, and still others, *c.o.d.*

All is not confusion, however, and general patterns can be discerned. Some abbreviations (as *a.k.a.*, *e.g.*, *etc.*, *i.e.*, *No.*, and *viz.*) are governed by a strong tradition of punctuation, while others (as *NATO*, *NASA*, *NOW*, *OPEC*, and *SALT*) that are pronounced as words tend to be all-capitalized and unpunctuated. Styling problems can be dealt with by consulting a good general dictionary such as *Webster's Ninth New Collegiate Dictionary*, especially for capitalization guidance, and by following the guidelines of one's own organization or the dictates of one's own preference. An abbreviations dictionary such as *Webster's Guide to Abbreviations* may also be consulted.

Punctuation

The paragraphs that follow describe a few broad principles that apply to abbreviations in general; however, there are many specific situations in which these principles will not apply. For instance, U.S. Postal Service abbreviations for names of states are always unpunctuated, as are the abbreviations used within most branches of the armed forces for the names of ranks. The section on Specific Styling Conventions in this chapter contains more information on particular kinds of abbreviations.

1. A period follows most abbreviations that are formed by omitting all but the first few letters of a word.

   bull. for *bulletin*
   bro. for *brother*
   fig. for *figure*
   Fr. for *French*

2. A period follows most abbreviations that are formed by omitting letters from the middle of a word.

   secy. for *secretary*
   mfg. for *manufacturing*
   agcy. for *agency*
   Mr. for *Mister*

3. Punctuation is usually omitted from abbreviations that are made up of initial letters of words that constitute a phrase or compound word. However, for some of these abbreviations, especially ones that are not capitalized, the punctuation is retained.

   GNP for *gross national product*
   EFT for *electronic funds transfer*
   PC for *personal computer*
   f.o.b. for *free on board*

4. Terms in which a suffix is added to a numeral, such as *1st, 2nd, 3d, 8vo,* and *12mo,* are not abbreviations and do not require a period.

5. Isolated letters of the alphabet used to designate a shape or position in a sequence are not punctuated.

T square	I beam
A 1	V sign

6. Some abbreviations are punctuated with one or more virgules in place of periods.

c/o for *care of*
d/b/a for *doing business as*
w/o for *without*
w/w for *wall to wall*

Capitalization

1. Abbreviations are capitalized if the words they represent are proper nouns or adjectives.

F for *Fahrenheit*
NFL for *National Football League*
Nov. for *November*
Brit. for *British*

2. Abbreviations are usually capitalized when formed from the initial letters of the words or word elements that make up what is being abbreviated. There are, however, some very common abbreviations formed in this way that are not capitalized.

TM for *trademark*
ETA for *estimated time of arrival*
CATV for *community antenna television*
EEG for *electroencephalogram*
FY for *fiscal year*
a.k.a. for *also known as*
d/b/a for *doing business as*

3. Most abbreviations that are pronounced as words, rather than as a series of letters, are capitalized. If they have been assimilated into the language as words in their own right, however, they are most often lowercased.

OPEC	quasar
NATO	laser
MIRV	sonar
NOW account	scuba

Plurals, Possessives, and Compounds

1. Punctuated abbreviations of single words are pluralized by adding -*s* before the period.

bldgs.   figs.
bros.   mts.

2. Punctuated abbreviations that stand for phrases or compounds are pluralized by adding *-'s* after the last period.

   Ph.D.'s   J.P.'s
   f.o.b.'s   M.B.A.'s

3. Unpunctuated abbreviations that stand for phrases or compound words are usually pluralized by adding *-s* to the end of the abbreviation.

   COLAs   PCs
   CPUs   DOSs

   NOTE: Some writers pluralize such abbreviations by adding *-'s* to the abbreviation; however, this styling is far less common than the one described above.

4. The plural form of most lowercase single-letter abbreviations is made by repeating the letter. For the plural form of single-letter abbreviations that are abbreviations for units of measure, see paragraph 5 below.

   cc. for *copies*
   ll. for *lines*
   pp. for *pages*
   ff. for *and the following ones*
   nn. for *notes*
   vv. for *verses*

5. The plural form of abbreviations of units of measure is the same as the singular form.

   30 sec.   20 min.
   30 d.   50 m
   24 ml   200 bbl.
   24 h.   10 mi.

6. Possessives of abbreviations are formed in the same way as those of spelled-out nouns: the singular possessive is formed by the addition of *-'s*, the plural possessive simply by the addition of an apostrophe.

   the CPU's memory
   Brody Corp.'s earnings
   most CPUs' memories
   Bay Bros.' annual sale

7. Compounds that consist of an abbreviation added to another word are formed in the same way as compounds that consist of spelled-out nouns.

a Kalamazoo, Mich.-based company
an AMA-approved medical school

8. Compounds formed by adding a prefix or suffix to an abbreviation are usually styled with a hyphen.

an IBM-like organization
non-DNA molecules
pre-HEW years

Specific Styling Conventions

The following paragraphs describe styling practices commonly followed for specific kinds of situations involving abbreviations. The paragraphs are arranged under the following alphabetical headings.

A and An
A.D. and B.C.
Agencies, Associations, and
    Organizations
Beginning a Sentence
Books of the Bible
Company Names
Compass Points
Contractions
Dates
Degrees
Division of Abbreviations
Footnotes
Full Forms

Geographical and
    Topographical Names
Latin Words and Phrases
Latitude and Longitude
Laws and Bylaws
Military Ranks and Units
Number
Personal Names
Saint
Scientific Terms
Time
Titles
Units of Measure
Versus

A and An

1. The choice of the article *a* or *an* before abbreviations depends on the *sound* with which the abbreviation begins. If an abbreviation begins with a consonant sound, *a* is normally used. If an abbreviation begins with a vowel sound, *an* is used.

a B.A. degree   an FCC report
a YMCA club   an SAT score
a UN agency   an IRS agent

A.D. and B.C.

2. The abbreviations A.D. and B.C. are usually styled in typeset matter as punctuated, unspaced small capitals; in typed material they usually appear as punctuated, unspaced capitals.

in printed material	41 B.C.	A.D. 185
in typed material	41 B.C.	A.D. 185

3. The abbreviation A.D. usually precedes the date; the abbreviation B.C. usually follows the date. However, many writers and editors place A.D. after the date, thus making their placement of A.D. consistent with their placement of B.C. In references to whole centuries, the usual practice is to place A.D. after the century. The only alternative is not to use the abbreviation at all in such references.

> A.D. 185   *but also*   185 A.D.
> the fourth century A.D.

Agencies, Associations, and Organizations

4. The names of agencies, associations, and organizations are usually abbreviated after they have been spelled out on their first occurrence in a text. The abbreviations are usually all capitalized and unpunctuated.

EPA	NAACP	USO
SEC	NCAA	NOW

NOTE: In contexts where the abbreviation is expected to be instantly recognizable, it will generally be used without having its full form spelled out on its first occurrence.

Beginning a Sentence

5. Most writers and editors avoid beginning a sentence with an abbreviation that is ordinarily not capitalized. Abbreviations that are ordinarily capitalized, on the other hand, are commonly used to begin sentences.

> Page 22 contains . . .   *not*   P. 22 contains . . .
> Doctor Smith believes . . .   *or*   Dr. Smith believes . . .
> OSHA regulations require . . .
> PCB concentrations that were measured at . . .

Books of the Bible

6. Books of the Bible are generally spelled out in running text but abbreviated in references to chapter and verse.

> The minister based his sermon on Genesis.
> In the beginning God created the heavens and the earth.
> —Gen. 1:1

Capitalization—See section on Capitalization in this chapter.

Chemical Elements and Compounds—See **Scientific Terms** below.

Company Names

7. The styling of company names varies widely. Many published style manuals say that the name of a company should not be abbreviated unless the abbreviation is part of its official name; however, many publications routinely abbreviate words such as *Corporation, Company,* and *Incorporated* when they appear in company names. Words such as *Airlines, Associates, Fabricators, Manufacturing,* and *Railroad,* however, are spelled out.

> Ginn and Company   *or*   Ginn and Co.
> The Bailey Banks and Biddle Company
>   *or*   The Bailey Banks and Biddle Co.
> Gulf & Western Industries, Inc.
> Canon, U.S.A., Inc.

NOTE: An ampersand frequently replaces the word *and* in official company names. For more on this use of the ampersand, see paragraph 1 in the section on Ampersand, beginning on page 4, in Chapter 1, "Punctuation."

8. If a company is easily recognizable from its initials, its name is usually spelled out for the first mention and abbreviated in all subsequent references. Some companies have made their initials part of their official name, and in those cases the initials appear in all references.

> *first reference*   General Motors Corp. released figures
>   today . . .
> *subsequent reference* A GM spokesperson said . . .
> MCM Electronics, an Ohio-based electronics company . . .

Compass Points

9. Compass points are abbreviated when occurring after street names, though styling varies regarding whether these abbreviations are punctuated and whether they are preceded by a comma. When compass points form essential internal elements of street names, they are usually spelled out in full.

> 2122 Fourteenth Street, NW   *or*   2122 Fourteenth Street NW
>   *or*   2122 Fourteenth Street, N.W.
> 192 East 49th Street
> 1282 North Avenue

Compounds—See section on Plurals, Possessives, and Compounds above.

Computer Terms—See **Scientific Terms** below.

Contractions

10. Some abbreviations resemble contractions by including an apostrophe in place of omitted letters. These abbreviations are not punctuated with a period.

> sec'y for *secretary*   dep't for *department*
> ass'n for *association*

NOTE: This style of abbreviation is usually avoided in formal writing.

Courtesy Titles—See **Titles** below.

Dates

11. The names of days and months are usually not abbreviated in running text, although some publications do abbreviate names of months when they appear in dates that refer to a specific day or days. The names of months are not abbreviated in date lines of business letters, but they may be abbreviated in government or military correspondence.

> the December issue of *Scientific American*
> going to camp in August
> a report due on Tuesday
> a meeting held on August 1, 1985
>   *or* a meeting held on Aug. 1, 1985
>
> *general business date line*   November 1, 1985
> *military date line*   1 Nov 1985

NOTE: When dates are used in tables or in notes, the names of days and months are commonly abbreviated.

Degrees

12. Except for a few academic degrees with highly recognizable abbreviations (as *A.B.*, *M.S.*, and *Ph.D.*), the names of degrees and professional ratings are spelled out in full when first mentioned in running text. Often the name of the degree is followed by its abbreviation enclosed in parentheses, so that the abbreviation may be used alone later in running text. When a degree or professional rating follows a person's name it is usually abbreviated.

> Special attention will be devoted to the master of arts in teaching (M.A.T.) degree.
> Julia Ramirez, P.E.

13. Like other abbreviations, abbreviations of degrees and professional ratings are often unpunctuated. In general, punctuated abbreviations are more common for academic degrees, and unpunctuated abbreviations are slightly more common for professional ratings, especially if the latter comprise three or more capitalized letters.

R.Ph.	P.E.	CLA	CMET
Ph.D.	B.Sc.	M.B.A.	BGS

14. The initial letter of each element in abbreviations of all degrees and professional ratings is capitalized. Letters other than the initial letter are usually not capitalized.

D.Ch.E.   M.F.A.
Litt.D.   D.Th.

Division of Abbreviations

15. Division of abbreviations at the end of lines or between pages is usually avoided.

received an M.B.A.   *not*   received an M.B.-
degree   A. degree

Expansions—See **Full Forms** below.

Footnotes

16. Footnotes sometimes incorporate abbreviations.

ibid.   op. cit.   loc. cit.

NOTE: In current practice these abbreviations are usually not italicized.

Full Forms

17. When using an abbreviation that may be unfamiliar or confusing to the reader, many publications give the full form first, followed by the abbreviation in parentheses; in subsequent references just the abbreviation is used.

first reference   At the American Bar Association (ABA)
                     meeting in June . . .
subsequent reference   At that particular ABA meeting . . .

Geographical and Topographical Names

18. U.S. Postal Service abbreviations for states, possessions, and Canadian provinces are all-capitalized and unpunctuated, as are Postal Service abbreviations for streets and other geographical features when these abbreviations are used on envelopes addressed for automated mass handling.

addressed for automated handling   1234 SMITH BLVD
                                       SMITHVILLE, MN 56789
regular address styling   1234 Smith Blvd.
                             Smithville, MN 56789

19. Abbreviations of states are often used in running text to identify the location of a city or county. In this context they are set off with commas, and punctuated, upper- and lowercase state abbreviations are usually used. In other situations within running text, the names of states are usually not abbreviated.

John Smith of 15 Chestnut St., Sarasota, Fla., has won . . .

the Louisville, Ky., public library system

Boston, the largest city in Massachusetts, . . .

20. Terms such as *street* and *parkway* are variously abbreviated or unabbreviated in running text. When they are abbreviated, they are usually punctuated.

> our office at 1234 Smith Blvd. (*or* Boulevard)
> an accident on Windward Road (*or* Rd.)

21. Names of countries are typically abbreviated in tabular data, but they are usually spelled in full in running text. The most common exceptions to this pattern are the abbreviations *U.S.S.R.* and *U.S.* (see paragraph 23 below).

> *in a table*   Gt. Brit. *or* U.K. *or* UK
> *in text*   Great Britain and the U.S.S.R. announced the agreement.

22. Abbreviations for the names of most countries are punctuated. Abbreviations for countries whose names include more than one word are often not punctuated if the abbreviations are formed from only the initial letters of the individual words.

> Mex.   U.K. *or* UK
> U.S.S.R. *or* USSR   Scot.
> Can.   U.S. *or* US
> Gt. Brit.   U.A.E. *or* UAE

23. *United States* is often abbreviated when it is being used as an adjective, such as when it modifies the name of a federal agency, policy, or program. When *United States* is used as a noun in running text, it is usually spelled out, or it is spelled on its initial use and then abbreviated in subsequent references.

> U.S. Department of Justice
> U.S. foreign policy
> The United States has offered to . . .

24. *Saint* is usually abbreviated when it is part of the name of a geographical or topographical feature. *Mount, Point,* and *Fort* are variously spelled out or abbreviated according to individual preference. *Saint, Mount* and *Point* are routinely abbreviated when space is at a premium. (For more on the abbreviation of *Saint,* see paragraph 36 below.)

> St. Louis, Missouri   Fort Sumter
> Mount St. Helens   Mount McKinley
> St. Kitts   Point Pelee

Latin Words and Phrases—See also **Footnotes** above.

25. Words and phrases derived from Latin are commonly abbreviated in contexts where readers can reasonably be expected to recognize them. They are punctuated, not capitalized, and usually not italicized.

etc.	e.g.	et al.
i.e.	viz.	pro tem.

Latitude and Longitude

26. Latitude and longitude are abbreviated in tabular data but written out in running text.

> *in a table*   lat. 10°20′N   *or*   lat. 10-20N
>
> *in text*   from 10°20′ north latitude to 10°30′ south latitude

Laws and Bylaws

27. Laws and bylaws, when first mentioned, are spelled in full; however, subsequent references to them in a text may be abbreviated.

> *first reference*   Article I, Section 1
> *subsequent reference*   Art. I, Sec. 1

Military Ranks and Units

28. Military ranks are usually given in full when used with a surname only but are abbreviated when used with a full name.

> Colonel Howe
> Col. John P. Howe

29. In nonmilitary publications, abbreviations for military ranks are punctuated and set in capital and lowercase letters. Within the military (with the exception of the Marine Corps) these abbreviations are all-capitalized and unpunctuated. The Marine Corps follows the punctuated, capital and lowercase styling.

> *in the military*   BG John T. Dow, USA
>   LCDR Mary I. Lee, USN
>   Col. S. J. Smith, USMC
> *outside the military*   Brig. Gen. John T. Dow, USA
>   Lt. Comdr. Mary I. Lee, USN
>   Col. S. J. Smith, USMC

30. Abbreviations for military units are capitalized and unpunctuated.

> USA   SAC
> USAF   NORAD

Number

31. The word *number*, when used with figures such as *1* or *2* to indicate a rank or rating, is usually abbreviated. When it is, the *N* is capitalized, and the abbreviation is punctuated.

> The No. 1 priority is to promote profitability.

32. The word *number* is usually abbreviated when it is part of a set unit (as a contract number), when it is used in tabular data, or when it is used in bibliographic references.

> Contract No. N-1234-76-57
> Policy No. 123-5-X
> Publ. Nos. 12 and 13
> Index No. 7855

Period with Abbreviations—See section on Punctuation above.

Personal Names

33. First names are not usually abbreviated.

> George S. Patterson   *not*   Geo. S. Patterson

34. Unspaced initials of famous persons are sometimes used in place of their full names. The initials may or may not be punctuated.

> FDR   *or*   F.D.R.

35. Initials used with a surname are spaced and punctuated.

> F. D. Roosevelt

Plurals—See section on Plurals, Possessives, and Compounds above.

Possessives—See section on Plurals, Possessives, and Compounds above.

Saint

36. The word *Saint* is often abbreviated when used before the name of a saint or when it is the first element of the name of a city or institution named after a saint. However, when it forms part of a surname, it may or may not be abbreviated, and the styling should be the one used by the person or the institution.

> St. Peter   *or*   Saint Peter
> St. John's University
> Ruth St. Denis
> Augustus Saint-Gaudens
> St. Cloud, Minnesota
> Saint Joseph College

Scientific Terms—See also **Units of Measure** below.

37. In binomial nomenclature, a genus name may be abbreviated with its initial letter after the first reference to it is spelled out. The abbreviation is always punctuated.

> *first reference*   *Escherichia coli*
> *subsequent reference*   *E. coli*

38. Abbreviations for the names of chemical compounds or mechanical or electronic equipment or processes are usually not punctuated.

OCR   CPU
PCB   PBX

39. The symbols for chemical elements are not punctuated.

H   Pb
Cl   Na

Time—See also **A.D. and B.C.** and **Dates** above and **Units of Measure** below.

40. When time is expressed in figures, the abbreviations that follow are most often styled as punctuated lowercase letters; punctuated small capital letters are also common. For more on the use of *a.m.* and *p.m.*, see paragraph 44 in the section on Specific Styling Conventions, on page 145, in Chapter 5, "The Treatment of Numbers."

8:30 a.m.   8:30 A.M.
10:00 p.m.   10:00 P.M.

41. In transportation schedules *a.m.* and *p.m.* are generally styled in capitalized, unpunctuated, unspaced letters.

8:30 AM
10:00 PM

42. Time zone designations are usually styled in capitalized, unpunctuated, unspaced letters.

EST   PST   CDT

Titles—See also **Degrees** and **Military Ranks and Units** above.

43. The only courtesy titles that are invariably abbreviated in written references are *Mr., Ms., Mrs.,* and *Messrs.* Other titles, such as *Doctor, Representative,* or *Senator,* may be either written out or abbreviated.

Ms. Lee A. Downs
Messrs. Lake, Mason, and Nambeth
Doctor Howe   *or*   Dr. Howe
Senator Long   *or*   Sen. Long

44. Despite some traditional injunctions against the practice, the titles *Honorable* and *Reverend* are often abbreviated when used with *the.*

the Honorable Samuel I. O'Leary
  or   the Hon. Samuel I. O'Leary
the Reverend Samuel I. O'Leary   *or*   the Rev. Samuel I. O'Leary

NOTE: There is also a traditional injunction against using the titles *Honorable* and *Reverend* without *the* preceding them. However, in current practice, *Reverend* and *Rev.* are commonly used without *the*.

> Reverend Samuel I. O'Leary *or* Rev. Samuel I. O'Leary

45. The designations *Jr.* and *Sr.* may be used in conjunction with courtesy titles, with abbreviations for academic degrees, and with professional rating abbreviations. They may or may not be preceded by a comma according to the writer's preference. They are terminated with a period, and they are commonly only used with a full name.

> Mr. John K. Walker, Jr.
> Dr. John K. Walker, Jr.
> General John K. Walker Jr.
> The Honorable John K. Walker, Jr.
> John K. Walker Jr., M.D.

46. When an abbreviation for an academic degree, professional certification, or association membership follows a name, it is usually preceded by a comma. No courtesy title should precede the name.

> Dr. John Smith *or* John Smith, M.D.
>   *but not* Dr. John Smith, M.D.
> Katherine Derwinski, CLU
> Carol Manning, M.D., FACPS

47. The abbreviation *Esq.* for *Esquire* is used in the United States after the surname of professional persons such as attorneys, architects, consuls, clerks of the court, and justices of the peace. It is not used, however, if *the Honorable* precedes the first name. If a courtesy title such as *Dr., Hon., Miss, Mr., Mrs.,* or *Ms.* is used in correspondence, *Esq.* is omitted. *Esquire* or *Esq.* is frequently used in the United States after the surname of a woman lawyer, although the practice has not yet gained acceptance in all law offices or among all state bar associations.

> Carolyn B. West, Esq.

Units of Measure

48. Measures and weights may be abbreviated in figure plus unit combinations; however, if the numeral is written out, the unit should also be written out.

> 15 cu ft *or* 15 cu. ft. *but* fifteen cubic feet
> How many cubic feet does the refrigerator hold?

49. Abbreviations for metric units are usually not punctuated. In many scientific and technical publications, abbreviations for traditional nonmetric units are also unpunctuated. However, in most general-interest publications, abbreviations for traditional units are punctuated.

14 ml	22 mi.	4 sec.
12 km	8 ft.	20 min.

Versus

50. *Versus* is abbreviated as *v.* in legal contexts; it is either spelled out or abbreviated as lowercase roman letters *vs.* in general contexts. For more on the use of *v.* in legal contexts, see paragraph 35 in the section on Proper Nouns, Pronouns, and Adjectives, beginning on page 65, in Chapter 2, "Capitals, Italics, and Quotation Marks."

in a legal context	*Smith* v. *Vermont*
in a general context	honesty versus dishonesty
	or
	honesty vs. dishonesty

Chapter 5

The Treatment of Numbers

CONTENTS

The styling of numbers presents special difficulties to writers and editors because there are so many conventions to follow, some of which may conflict when applied to particular passages. The writer's major decision is whether to write out numbers in running text or to express them in figures. Usage varies considerably, in part because no single neat formula covers all the categories in which numbers are used. In general, the more formal the writing the more likely that numbers will be spelled out. In scientific, technical, or statistical contexts, however, numbers are likely to be expressed as figures. This chapter explains most of the conventions used in the styling of numbers. A discussion of general principles is followed by detailed information on specific situations involving numbers.

Numbers as Words or Figures

At one extreme of styling, all numbers, sometimes even including dates, are written out. This usage is uncommon and is usually limited to proclamations, legal documents, and some other types of very formal writing. This styling is space-consuming and time-consuming; it can also be ungainly or, worse, unclear. At the other extreme, some types of technical writing, such as statistical reports, contain no written-out numbers except at the beginning of a sentence.

In general, figures are easier to read than the spelled-out forms of numbers; however, the spelled-out forms are helpful in certain circumstances, such as in distinguishing different categories of numbers or in providing relief from an overwhelming cluster of numerals. Most writers follow one or the other of two common conventions combining numerals and written-out numbers. The conventions are described in this section, along with the situations that provide exceptions to the general rules.

Basic Conventions

1. The first system requires that a writer use figures for exact numbers that are greater than nine and words for numbers nine and below (a variation of this system sets the number ten as the dividing point). In this system, numbers that consist of a whole number between one and nine followed by *hundred, thousand, million,* etc. may be spelled out or expressed in figures.

   > She has performed in 22 plays on Broadway, seven of which won Pulitzer prizes.
   >
   > The new edition will consist of 25 volumes which will be issued at a rate of approximately four volumes per year.
   >
   > The cat show attracted an unexpected two thousand entries.
   >
   > They sold more than 2,000 units in the first year.

2. The second system requires that a writer use figures for all exact numbers 100 and above (or 101 and above) and words for numbers from one to ninety-nine (or one to one hundred) and for numbers that consist of a whole number between one and ninety-nine followed by *hundred, thousand, million,* etc.

   > The artist spent nearly twelve years completing these four volumes, which comprise 435 hand-colored engravings.
   >
   > The 145 participants in the seminar toured the area's eighteen period houses.
   >
   > In the course of four hours, the popular author signed twenty-five hundred copies of her new book.

Sentence Beginnings

3. Numbers that begin a sentence are written out, although some make an exception for the use of figures for dates that begin a sentence. Most writers, however, try to avoid spelled-out numbers that are lengthy and awkward by restructuring the sentence so that the number appears elsewhere than at the beginning and may then be styled as a figure.

   > Sixty-two species of Delphinidae inhabit the world's oceans.
   > *or*
   > The Delphinidae consist of 62 ocean-dwelling species.

Twelve fifteen was the year King John of England signed the Magna Carta.

or

1215 was the year King John of England signed the Magna Carta.

or

In 1215 King John of England signed the Magna Carta.

One hundred fifty-seven illustrations, including 86 color plates, are contained in the book.

or

The book contains 157 illustrations, including 86 color plates.

Adjacent Numbers and Numbers in Series

4. Generally, two separate sets of figures should not be written adjacent to one another in running text unless they form a series. So that the juxtaposition of unrelated figures will not confuse the reader, either the sentence is restructured or one of the figures is spelled out. Usually the figure with the written form that is shorter and more easily read is converted. When one of two adjacent numbers is an element of a compound modifier, the first of the two numbers is often expressed in words, the second in figures. But if the second number is the shorter, the styling is often reversed.

original	*change to*
16 ½-inch dowels	sixteen ½-inch dowels
25 11-inch platters	twenty-five 11-inch platters
20 100-point games	twenty 100-point games
78 20-point games	78 twenty-point games
By 1997, 300 more of the state's schools will have closed their doors.	By 1997, three hundred more of the state's schools will have closed their doors.

5. Numbers paired at the beginning of a sentence are usually styled alike. If the first word of the sentence is a spelled-out number, the second, related number is also spelled out. However, some writers and editors prefer that each number be styled independently, even if that results in an inconsistent pairing.

   Sixty to seventy-five acres were destroyed.
   Sixty to 75 acres were destroyed.

6. Numbers that form a pair or a series referring to comparable quantities within a sentence or a paragraph should be treated consistently. The style of the largest number usually determines the style of the other numbers. Thus, a series of numbers including some which would ordinarily be spelled out might all be styled as figures. Similarly, figures are used to ex-

press all the numbers in a series if one of those numbers is a mixed or simple fraction.

> Graduating from the obedience class were 3 corgis, 20 Doberman pinschers, 19 German shepherds, 9 golden retrievers, 10 Labrador retrievers, and 1 Rottweiler.
>
> The three jobs took 5, 12, and 4½ hours, respectively.

Round Numbers

7. Approximate or round numbers, particularly those that can be expressed in one or two words, are often written out in general writing; in technical and scientific writing they are more likely to be expressed as numerals.

> seven hundred people
> five thousand years
> four hundred thousand volumes
> seventeen thousand metric tons
> four hundred million dollars
> *but in technical writing*
> 50,000 people per year
> 20,000 species of fish

8. For easier reading, numbers of one million and above may be expressed as figures followed by the word *million, billion,* and so forth. The figure may include a decimal fraction, but the fraction is not usually carried past the first digit to the right of the decimal point, and it is never carried past the third digit. If a more exact number is required, the whole amount should be written in figures.

> about 4.6 billion years old
> 1.2 million metric tons of grain
> the last 600 million years
> $7.25 million
> $3,456,000,000
> *but* 200,000 years   *not*   200 thousand years

NOTE: In the United Kingdom, the word *billion* refers to an amount that in the United States is called *trillion*. In the American system each of the denominations above 1,000 millions (the American billion) is one thousand times the one preceding (thus, one trillion equals 1,000 billions; one quadrillion equals 1,000 trillions). In the British system the first denomination above 1,000 millions (the British milliard) is one thousand times the preceding one, but each of the denominations above 1,000 milliards (the British billion) is one million times the preceding one (thus, one trillion equals 1,000,000 billions; one quadrillion equals 1,000,000 trillions).

Ordinal Numbers

1. Ordinal numbers generally follow the styling rules for cardinal numbers that are listed above in the section on Numbers as Words or Figures: if a figure would be required for the cardinal form of a number, it should also be used for the ordinal form; if conventions call for a written-out form, it should be used for both cardinal and ordinal numbers. In technical writing, however, as well as in footnotes and tables, all ordinal numbers are written as figure-plus-suffix combinations. In addition, certain ordinal numbers—those specifying percentiles and latitudinal lines are common ones—are conventionally set as figures in both general and technical writing.

> the sixth Robert de Bruce
> the ninth grade
> the 9th and 14th chapters
> his twenty-third try
> the 20th century
> the 98th Congress
> the 12th percentile
> the 40th parallel

2. The forms *second* and *third* may be written with figures as *2d* or *2nd, 3d* or *3rd, 22d* or *22nd, 93d* or *93rd, 102d* or *102nd.* A period does not follow the suffix.

Roman Numerals

Roman numerals, which may be written either in capital or lower-case letters, are conventional in the specific situations described below. Roman numerals are formed by adding the numerical values of letters as they are arranged in descending order going from left to right. If a letter with a smaller numerical value is placed to the left of a letter with a greater numerical value, the value of the smaller is subtracted from the value of the larger. A bar placed over a numeral ($\bar{V}$) multiplies its value by one thousand. A list of Roman numerals and their Arabic equivalents is given in the table on page 128.

1. Roman numerals are traditionally used to differentiate rulers and popes that have identical names.

Elizabeth II	Innocent X
Henry VIII	Louis XIV

Arabic and Roman Numerals

Name	Arabic Numeral	Roman Numeral
zero	0	
one	1	I
two	2	II
three	3	III
four	4	IV
five	5	V
six	6	VI
seven	7	VII
eight	8	VIII
nine	9	IX
ten	10	X
eleven	11	XI
twelve	12	XII
thirteen	13	XIII
fourteen	14	XIV
fifteen	15	XV
sixteen	16	XVI
seventeen	17	XVII
eighteen	18	XVIII
nineteen	19	XIX
twenty	20	XX
twenty-one	21	XXI
twenty-two	22	XXII
twenty-three	23	XXIII
twenty-four	24	XXIV
twenty-five	25	XXV
twenty-six	26	XXVI
twenty-nine	29	XXIX
thirty	30	XXX
thirty-one	31	XXXI
thirty-two	32	XXXII
forty	40	XL
fifty	50	L
sixty	60	LX
seventy	70	LXX
eighty	80	LXXX
ninety	90	XC
one hundred	100	C
one hundred one *or* one hundred and one	101	CI
one hundred two *or* one hundred and two	102	CII
two hundred	200	CC
three hundred	300	CCC
four hundred	400	CD
five hundred	500	D
six hundred	600	DC
seven hundred	700	DCC
eight hundred	800	DCCC
nine hundred	900	CM
one thousand	1,000	M
two thousand	2,000	MM
five thousand	5,000	$\bar{\text{V}}$
ten thousand	10,000	$\bar{\text{X}}$
one hundred thousand	100,000	$\bar{\text{C}}$
one million	1,000,000	$\bar{\text{M}}$

2. Roman numerals are used to differentiate related males who have the same name. The numerals are used only with a person's full name and, unlike the similar forms *Junior* and *Senior,* they are placed after the surname with no intervening comma. Ordinals are sometimes used instead of Roman numerals.

James R. Watson II	James R. Watson 2nd *or* 2d
James R. Watson III	James R. Watson 3rd *or* 3d
James R. Watson IV	James R. Watson 4th

NOTE: Possessive patterns for these names are the following:

singular	James R. Watson III's (*or* 3rd's *or* 3d's) house
plural	the James R. Watson IIIs' (*or* 3rds' *or* 3ds') house

3. Roman numerals are used to differentiate certain vehicles and vessels, such as yachts, that have the same name. If the name is italicized, the numeral is italicized also. Names of American spacecraft formerly bore Roman numerals, but Arabic numerals are now used.

   Shamrock V

   The U.S. spacecraft *Rangers VII, VIII,* and *IX* took pictures of the moon.

   On July 20, 1969, *Apollo 11* landed on the moon.

4. Lowercase Roman numerals are often used to number book pages that precede the regular Arabic sequence, as in a foreword, preface, or introduction.

5. Roman numerals are often used in enumerations to list major headings. An example of an outline with Roman-numeral headings is shown on page 140.

6. Roman numerals are sometimes used to specify a particular act and scene of a play or a particular volume in a collection. In this system, capitalized Roman numerals are used for the number of the act, and lowercase Roman numerals for the number of the scene. Arabic numerals are increasingly used for these purposes, however.

Roman style	*Arabic style*
Richard II, Act II, scene i	Act 2, scene 1
Hamlet, I.i.63	Act 1, scene 1, line 63 *or* 1.1.63
II, iii, 13–20	2, 3, 13–20

7. Roman numerals are found as part of a few established technical terms such as blood-clotting factors, quadrant numbers, and designations of cranial nerves. Also, chords in the study of music harmony are designated by capital and lowercase Ro-

man numerals. For the most part, however, technical terms that include numbers express them in Arabic form.

blood-clotting factor VII
quadrant III
the cranial nerves II, IV, and IX
Population II stars
type I error
  but
adenosine 3′, 5′-monophosphate
cesium 137
PL/1 programming language

Punctuation, Spacing, and Inflection

This section explains general rules for the use of commas, hyphens, and spacing in compound and large numbers, as well as the plural forms of numbers. For the styling of specific categories of numbers, such as dates, money, and decimal fractions, see the section on Specific Styling Conventions in this chapter.

Commas and Spaces in Large Numbers

1. In general writing, with the exceptions explained in paragraph 3 below, figures of four digits may be styled with or without a comma; the punctuated form is more common. In scientific writing, these numerals are usually styled with a comma (but see paragraph 4 below). If the numerals form part of a tabulation, commas are necessary so that four-digit numerals can align with numerals of five or more digits.

   2,000 case histories   *or less commonly*   1253 people

2. Whole numbers of five digits or more (but not decimal fractions) use a comma or a space to separate three-digit groups, counting from the right. Commas are used in general writing; either spaces or commas are used in technical writing.

   a fee of $12,500
   15,000 units   *or*   15 000 units
   a population of 1,500,000   *or*   1 500 000

3. Certain types of numbers do not conform to these conventions. Decimal fractions and serial and multidigit numbers in set combinations, such as the numbers of policies, contracts, checks, streets, rooms, suites, telephones, pages, military hours, and years, do not contain commas. Numerals used in binary notation are also written without commas or spaces.

```
check 34567
page 209
Room 606
1650 hours
the year 1929
Policy No. 33442
10011
111010
```

NOTE: Year numbers of five or more digits (as geological or archeological dates) do contain a comma.

The Wisconsin glaciation lasted from approximately 70,000 to 10,000 years B.P.

4. In technical and scientific writing, lengthy figures are usually avoided by the use of special units of measure and by the use of multipliers and powers of ten. When long figures are written, however, each group of three digits may be separated by a space counting from the decimal point to the left and the right. If the digits are separated by a comma instead of a space, neither commas nor spaces are placed to the right of the decimal point. Whichever system is used should be applied consistently to all numbers with four or more digits.

```
27 483 241
23.000 003
27 483.241 755
27,483,241
23.000003
27,483.241755
```

Hyphens

5. Hyphens are used with written-out numbers between 21 and 99.

```
forty-one
forty-first
four hundred twenty-two
the twenty-fifth day
```

6. A hyphen is used between the numerator and the denominator of a fraction that is written out when that fraction is used as a modifier. A written-out fraction consisting of two words only (as *two thirds*) is usually styled open, although the hyphenated form is common also. Multiword numerators and denominators are usually hyphenated. If either the numerator or the denominator is hyphenated, no hyphen is used between them. For more on fractions, see pages 140–141.

```
a two-thirds majority of the staff
three fifths of her paycheck
```

> seven and four fifths
> forty-five hundredths
> four five-hundredths

7. Numbers that form the first part of a compound modifier expressing measurement are followed by a hyphen. An exception to this practice is that numbers are not followed by a hyphen when the second part of the modifier is the word *percent*.

> a 5-foot board
> a 28-mile trip
> a 10-pound weight
> an eight-pound baby
> a 680-acre ranch
> a 75 percent reduction

8. An adjective or adverb made from a numeral plus the suffix *-fold* contains a hyphen, while a similar term made from a written-out number is styled solid. (For more on the use of suffixes with numbers, see page 106 in Chapter 3, "Plurals, Possessives, and Compounds.")

> a fourfold increase
> increased 20-fold

9. Serial numbers, such as social security or engine numbers, often contain hyphens that make lengthy numerals more readable.

> 020-42-1691

10. Numbers are usually not divided at the end of a line. If division is unavoidable, the break occurs only after a comma. End-of-line breaks do not occur at decimal points, and a name with a numerical suffix (as *Elizabeth II*) is not divided between the name and the numeral.

Inclusive Numbers

11. Inclusive numbers—those which express a range—are separated either by the word *to* or by an en dash, which serves as an arbitrary equivalent of the phrase "(up) to and including" when used between dates and other inclusive numbers. (The en dash is explained further in the section on Dash, beginning on page 29, in Chapter 1, "Punctuation.") En dashes are used in tables, parenthetical references, and footnotes to save space. In running text, however, the word *to* is more often used.

> pages 40 to 98
> pages 40–98
> pp. 40–98

14–18 months
the years 1960–1965
spanning the years 1915 to 1941
the decade 1920–1930
the fiscal year 1984–1985

NOTE: Inclusive numbers separated by an en dash are not used in combination with the words *from* or *between,* as in "from 1955–60" or "between 1970–90." Instead, phrases like these are written as "from 1955 to 1960" or "between 1970 and 1990."

12. Units of measurement expressed in words or abbreviations are usually used only after the second element of an inclusive number. Symbols, however, are repeated.

an increase in dosage from 200 to 500 mg
running 50 to 75 miles every week
ten to fifteen dollars
30 to 35 degrees Celsius
  but
$50 to $60 million
45° to 48° F
45°–48°
3′–5′ long

13. Numbers that are part of an inclusive set or range are usually styled alike: figures with figures, spelled-out words with other spelled-out words. Similarly, approximate numbers are usually not paired with exact numbers.

from 8 to 108 absences
five to twenty guests
300,000 to 305,000   *not*   300 thousand to 305,000

14. Inclusive page numbers and dates that use the en dash may be written in full (1981–1982) or elided (1981–82). Both stylings are widely used. However, inclusive dates that appear in titles and other headings are almost never elided. Dates that appear with era designations are also not elided.

467–68   *or*   467–468
550–602
203–4   *or*   203–204
552–549 B.C.
1724–27   *or*   1724–1727
1463–1510
1800–1801

Plurals

15. The plurals of written-out numbers are formed by the addition of *-s* or *-es.*

Back in the thirties these roads were unpaved.

Christmas shoppers bought the popular toy in twos and threes.

16. The plurals of figures are formed by adding -*s*. Some writers and publications prefer to add an apostrophe before the -*s*. For more on the plurals of figures, see the section on Plurals, beginning on page 82, in Chapter 3, "Plurals, Possessives, and Compounds," and the section on Apostrophe, beginning on page 5, in Chapter 1, "Punctuation."

This ghost town was booming back in the 1840s.

The first two artificial hearts to be implanted in human patients were Jarvik-7s.

but also

linen manufacture in France in the 1700's

1's and *7*'s that looked alike

Specific Styling Conventions

The following paragraphs describe styling practices commonly followed for specific types of situations involving numbers. The paragraphs are arranged under the following alphabetical headings:

Addresses
Dates
Degrees of Temperature and Arc
Enumerations and Outlines
Fractions and Decimal Fractions
Money
Percentages
Proper Names
Ratios
Serial Numbers and Miscellaneous Numbers
Time of Day
Units of Measurement

Addresses

1. Arabic numerals are used for all building, house, apartment, room, and suite numbers except for *one*, which is written out.

6 Lincoln Road
1436 Fremont Street
Apt. 281, Regency Park Drive
Room 617, McClaskey Building
but
One Bayside Drive
One World Trade Center

NOTE: When the address of a building is used as its name, the number in the address is written out.

> Fifty Maple Street

2. Numbered streets have their numbers written as ordinals. There are two distinct conventions for the styling of numbered street names. The first, useful where space is limited, calls for Arabic numerals to denote all numbered streets above Twelfth; numbered street names from First through Twelfth are written out. A second, more formal, convention calls for the writing out of all numbered street names up to and including One Hundredth.

> 19 South 22nd Street
> 167 West Second Avenue
> One East Ninth Street
> 145 East 145th Street
> 122 East Forty-second Street
> 36 East Fiftieth
> in the Sixties (streets from 60th to 69th)
> in the 120s (streets from 120th to 129th)

NOTE: A disadvantage of the first convention is that the direct juxtaposition of the house or building number and the street number may occur when there is no intervening word such as a compass direction. In these cases, a spaced hyphen or en dash may be inserted to distinguish the two numbers, or the second convention may be used and the street number written out.

> 2018–14th Street
> 2018 Fourteenth Street

3. Arabic numerals are used to designate interstate, federal, and state highways and, in some states, county roads.

> U.S. Route 1   *or*   U.S. 1
> Interstate 91   *or*   I-91
> Massachusetts 57
> Indiana 60
> County 213

Dates

4. Year numbers are styled as figures. However, if a number representing a year begins a sentence, it may be written in full or the sentence rewritten to avoid beginning it with a figure. (For additional examples, see paragraph 3 in the section on Numbers as Words or Figures in this chapter.)

> in 323 B.C.
> before A.D. 40
> 1888–96

Fifteen eighty-eight marked the end to Spanish ambitions for the control of England.
or
Spanish ambitions for the control of England ended in 1588 with the destruction of their "Invincible Armada."

5. A year number may be abbreviated, or cut back to its last two digits, in informal writing or when an event is so well-known that it needs no century designation. In these cases an apostrophe precedes the numerals. For more on this use of the apostrophe, see the section on Apostrophe, beginning on page 5, in Chapter 1, "Punctuation."

   He always maintained that he'd graduated from Korea, Clash of '52.

   the blizzard of '88

6. Full dates (month, day, and year) may be styled in one of two distinct patterns. The traditional styling is the month-day-year sequence, with the year set off by commas that precede and follow it. An alternate styling is the inverted date, or day-month-year sequence, which does not require commas. This sequence is used in Great Britain, in U.S. government publications, and in the military.

   traditional style
   July 8, 1776, was a warm, sunny day in Philadelphia.
   the explosion on July 16, 1945, at Alamogordo
   military style
   the explosion on 16 July 1945 at Alamogordo
   Lee's surrender to Grant on 9 April 1865 at Appomattox

7. Ordinal numbers are not used in expressions of full dates. Even though the numbers may be pronounced as ordinals, they are written as cardinal numbers. Ordinals may be used, however, to express a date without an accompanying year, and they are always used when preceded in a date by the word *the*.

   December 4, 1829
   on December 4th   *or*   on December 4
   on the 4th of December
   on the 4th

8. Commas are usually omitted from dates that include the month and year but not the day. Alternatively, writers sometimes insert the word *of* between month and year.

   in November 1805
   back in January of 1981

9. Once a numerical date has been given, a reference to a related date may be written out.

> After the rioting of August 3 the town was quiet, and by the seventh most troops had been pulled out.

10. All-figure dating (as 6-8-85 or 6/8/85) is inappropriate except in the most informal writing. It also creates a problem of ambiguity, as it may mean either June 8, 1985, or August 6, 1985.

11. References to specific centuries are often written out, although they may be expressed in figures, especially when they form the first element of a compound modifier.

> the nineteenth century
> a sixteenth-century painting
> *but also*
> a 12th-century illuminated manuscript
> 20th-century revolutions

12. In general writing, the name of a specific decade often takes a short form. Although many writers place an apostrophe before the shortened word and a few capitalize it, both the apostrophe and the capitalization are often omitted when the context clearly indicates that a date is being referred to.

> in the turbulent seventies
> growing up in the thirties
> *but also*
> back in the 'forties
> in the early Fifties

13. The name of a specific decade is often expressed in numerals, usually in plural form. (For more on the formation of plural numbers, see paragraphs 15 and 16 in the section on Punctuation, Spacing, and Inflection in this chapter.) The figure may be shortened with an apostrophe to indicate the missing numerals, but any sequence of such numbers should be styled consistently. (For more on this use of the apostrophe, see the section on Apostrophe, beginning on page 5, in Chapter 1, "Punctuation.")

> during the 1920s   *or*   during the 1920's
> the 1950s and 1960s   *or*   the '50s and '60s
> *but not*
> the 1950s and '60s
> the 1930s and forties
> *and not*
> the '50's and '60's

14. Era designations precede or follow words that specify centuries or numerals that specify years. Era designations are unspaced and are nearly always abbreviated; they are usually printed as small capitals and typed as regular capitals, and they may or may not be punctuated with periods. Any date that is given without an era designation or context is understood to mean A.D. The two most commonly used abbreviations are B.C. (before Christ) and A.D. (*anno Domini,* "in the year of our Lord"). The abbreviation B.C. is placed after the date, while A.D. is usually placed before the date but after a century designation. (For more on the use of these abbreviations, see page 112 in Chapter 4, "Abbreviations.")

> 1792–1750 B.C.
> between 600 and 400 B.C.
> from the fifth or fourth millennium to c. 250 B.C.
> 35,000 B.C.
> between 7 B.C. and A.D. 22
> c. A.D. 1100
> the second century A.D.
> the seventeenth century

15. Less commonly used era designations include A.H. (*anno Hegirae,* "in the year of [Muhammad's] Hegira," or *anno Hebraico,* "in the Hebrew year"); B.C.E. (before the common era; a synonym for B.C.); C.E. (of the common era; a synonym for A.D.); and B.P. (before the present; often used by geologists and archeologists, with or without the word *year*). The abbreviation A.H. in both its meanings is usually placed before the year number, while B.C.E., CPE., and B.P. are placed after it.

> the tenth of Muharram, A.H. 61 (October 10, A.D. 680)
> the first century A.H.
> from the first century B.C.E. to the fourth century C.E.
> 63 B.C.E.
> the year 200 C.E.
> 5,000 years B.P.
> two million years B.P.

Degrees of Temperature and Arc

16. In technical writing, figures are generally used for quantities expressed in degrees. In addition, the degree symbol (°) rather than the word *degree* is used with the figure. With the Kelvin scale, however, neither the word *degree* nor the symbol is used with the figure.

> a 45° angle
> 6°40′10″N
> 32° F
> 0° C
> Absolute zero is zero kelvins or 0 K.

NOTE: In many technical and scientific publications, the figure, degree symbol, and the *F* or *C* that follows it are usually
written without any space between them or with a space before the degree symbol but not after it. Another style followed
in some scientific publications is to omit the degree symbol in
expressions of temperature.

100°F   *or*   100 °F   *or*   100F
39°C   *or*   39 °C   *or*   39C

17. In general writing, the quantity expressed in degrees may or
    may not be written out, depending upon the styling conven-
    tions being followed. A figure is followed by the degree sym-
    bol or the word *degree;* a written-out number is always
    followed by the word *degree*.

    latitude 43°19″ N
    latitude 43 degrees N
    a difference of 43 degrees latitude

    The temperature has risen thirty degrees since this morning.

Enumerations and Outlines

18. Both run-in and vertical enumerations are often numbered.
    In run-in enumerations, each item is preceded by a number
    (or an italicized letter) enclosed in parentheses. The items in
    the list are separated by commas if the items are brief and
    have little or no internal punctuation; if the items are com-
    plex, they are separated by semicolons. The entire run-in enu-
    meration is introduced by a colon if it is preceded by a full
    clause.

    We feel that she should (1) increase her administrative skills, (2)
    pursue additional professional education, and (3) increase her
    production.

    The oldest and most basic word-processing systems consist of the
    following: (1) a typewriter for keyboarding information, (2) a con-
    sole to house the storage medium, and (3) the medium itself.

    The vendor of your system should (1) instruct you in the care and
    maintenance of your system; (2) offer regularly scheduled mainte-
    nance to ensure that the system is clean, with lubrication and re-
    placement of parts as necessary; and (3) respond promptly to
    service calls.

19. In vertical enumerations, the numbers are usually not en-
    closed in parentheses but are followed by a period. Each item
    in the enumeration begins its own line, which is either flush
    left or indented. Runover lines are usually aligned with the
    first word that follows the number, and figures are aligned on
    the periods that follow them. Each item on the list is usually
    capitalized if the items on the list are syntactically indepen-

dent of the words that introduce them; however, style varies on this point, and use of a lowercase style for such items is fairly common. There is no terminal punctuation following the items unless at least one of the items is a complete sentence, in which case a period follows each item. Items that are syntactically dependent on the words that introduce them begin with a lowercase letter and carry the same punctuation marks that they would if they were a run-in series in a sentence.

Required skills include the following:
1. Shorthand
2. Typing
3. Transcription

To type a three-column table, follow this procedure:
1. Clear tab stops.
2. Remove margin stops.
3. Determine precise center of the page. Set a tab stop at center.

The vendor of your system should
1. instruct you in the care and maintenance of your system;
2. offer regularly scheduled maintenance to ensure that the system is clean, with lubrication and replacement parts as necessary; and
3. respond promptly to service calls.

20. Outlines make use of Roman numerals, Arabic numerals, and letters.

  I. Editorial tasks
    A. Manuscript editing
    B. Author contact
      1. Authors already under contract
      2. New authors
 II. Production responsibilities
    A. Scheduling
      1. Composition
      2. Printing and binding
    B. Cost estimates and bids
      1. Composition
      2. Printing and binding

Fractions and Decimal Fractions

21. In running text, fractions standing alone are usually written out. Common fractions used as nouns are usually styled as open compounds, but when they are used as modifiers they are usually hyphenated. For more on written-out fractions, see page 131.

two thirds of the paint
a two-thirds majority

three thirty-seconds
seventy-two hundredths
one one-hundredth

NOTE: Most writers try to find ways to avoid the necessity of writing out complicated fractions (as *forty-two seventy-fifths*).

22. Mixed fractions (fractions with a whole number, such as 3½) and fractions that form part of a unit modifier are expressed in figures in running text. A *-th* is not added to a figure fraction.

waiting 2½ hours
1¼ million population
a ⅞-mile course
a 2½-kilometer race

NOTE: When mixed fractions are typewritten, the typist leaves a space between the whole number and the fraction. The space is closed up when the number is set in print. Fractions that are not on the typewriter keyboard may be made up by typing the numerator, a virgule, and the denominator in succession without spacing.

23. Fractions used with units of measurement are expressed in figures.

⅒ km   ¼ mile

24. Decimal fractions are always set as figures. In technical writing, a zero is placed to the left of the decimal point when the fraction is less than a whole number. In general writing, the zero is usually omitted.

An example of a pure decimal fraction is 0.375, while 1.402 is classified as a mixed decimal fraction.
0.142857
0.2 gm
received 0.1 mg/kg diazepam i.v.
  but
a .40 gauge shotgun

25. A comma is never inserted in the numbers following a decimal point, although spaces may be inserted as described and illustrated in paragraph 4 in the section on Punctuation, Spacing, and Inflection in this chapter.

26. Fractions and decimal fractions are usually not mixed in a text.

5½ lb. 2⅕ oz.
5.5 lb. 2.2 oz.
  but not
5½ lb. 2.2 oz.

Money

27. Sums of money are expressed in words or figures, according to the conventions described in the first section of this chapter. If the sum can be expressed in one or two words, it is usually written out in running text. But if several sums are mentioned in the sentence or paragraph, all are usually expressed as figures. When the amount is written out, the unit of currency is also written out. If the sum is expressed in figures, the symbol of the currency unit is used, with no space between it and the numerals.

> We paid $175,000 for the house.
> My change came to 87¢.
> The shop charged $67.50 for hand-knit sweaters.
> The price of a nickel candy bar seems to have risen to more like forty cents.
> Fifty dollars was stolen from my wallet.
> forty thousand dollars
> fifty-two dollars

28. Monetary units of mixed dollars-and-cents amounts are expressed in figures.

> $16.75
> $307.02
> $1.95

29. Even-dollar amounts are often expressed in figures without a decimal point and zeros. But when even-dollar amounts are used in a series with or are near to amounts that include dollars and cents, the decimal point and zeros are usually added for consistency. The dollar sign is repeated before each amount in a series or inclusive range; the word *dollar* may or may not be repeated.

> The price of the book rose from $7.95 in 1970 to $8.00 in 1971 and then to $8.50 in 1972.
> The bids were eighty, ninety, and one hundred dollars.
>   *or*
> The bids were eighty dollars, one hundred dollars, and three hundred dollars.

30. Sums of money given in round units of millions or above are usually expressed in a combination of figures and words, either with a dollar sign or with the word *dollars*. For more on the handling of round numbers, see paragraphs 7 and 8 in the section on Numbers as Words or Figures in this chapter.

> 60 million dollars
> a $10 million building program
> $4.5 billion

31. In legal documents a sum of money is usually written out fully, with the corresponding figures in parentheses immediately following.

> twenty-five thousand dollars ($25,000)

Percentages

32. In technical writing and in tables and footnotes, specific percentages are styled as figure plus unspaced percent sign (%). In general writing, the percentage number may be expressed as a figure or spelled out, depending upon the conventions that apply to it. The word *percent* rather than the symbol is used in nonscientific texts.

> *technical*   *general*
> 15%   15 percent
> 13.5%   87.2 percent
>   Twenty-five percent of the
>   office staff was out with the flu.
>   a four percent increase

33. The word *percentage* or *percent,* used as a noun without an adjacent numeral, should never be replaced by a percent sign.

> Only a small percentage of the test animals exhibited a growth change.
>
> The clinic treated a greater percentage of outpatients this year.

34. In a series or unit combination the percent sign should be included with all numbers, even if one of the numbers is zero.

> a variation of 0% to 10%

Proper Names

35. Numbers in the names of religious organizations and of churches are usually written out in ordinal form. Names of specific ruling houses and governmental bodies may include ordinals, and these are written out if they are one hundred or below. A few ruling houses, however, are traditionally designated by Roman numerals that follow the name.

> First Church of Christ, Scientist
> Third Congregational Church
> Seventh-Day Adventists
> Fifth Republic
> Third Reich
> First Continental Congress
>   *but*
> Egyptian tombs from Dynasty XI

36. Names of electoral, judicial, and military units may include ordinal numbers that precede the noun. Numbers of one hundred or below may be either written out or styled as numerals.

> First Congressional District
> Twelfth Precinct
> Ninety-eighth Congress   *or*   98th Congress
> Circuit Court of Appeals for the Third Circuit
> United States Eighth Army   *or*   8th United States Army
> At H hour, the 32d would drive forward to seize the 77th Division's position southeast of Maeda.
> The assault was led by the 54th Massachusetts, the first black regiment recruited in a free state.

37. Specific branches of labor unions and fraternal organizations are conventionally identified by an Arabic numeral usually placed after the name.

> International Brotherhood of Electrical Workers Local 42
> Elks Lodge No. 61
> Local 98 Operating Engineers

Ratios

38. Ratios expressed in figures use a colon, a hyphen, a virgule, or the word *to* as a means of comparison. Ratios expressed in words use a hyphen, or the word *to*.

> a 3:1 chance
> odds of 100 to 1
> a 6-1 vote
> 22.4 mi/gal
> a ratio of ten to four
> a fifty-fifty chance

Serial Numbers and Miscellaneous Numerals

39. Figures are used to refer to things that are numbered serially, such as chapter and page numbers, addresses, years, policy and contract numbers, and so forth.

> Serial No. 5274
> vol. 5, p. 202
> Permit No. 63709
> column 2
> paragraphs 5–7
> Table 16
> pages 420–515

40. Figures are also used to express stock market quotations, mathematical calculations, scores, and tabulations.

> won by a score of 8 to 2
> the tally: 322 ayes, 80 nays
> $3\frac{1}{8}$ percent bonds
> $3 \times 15 = 45$

Time of Day

41. In running text the time of day is usually spelled out when expressed in even, half, or quarter hours.

> Quitting time is four-thirty.
> By half past eleven we were all getting hungry.
> We should arrive at a quarter past five.

42. The time of day is also usually spelled out when it is followed by the contraction *o'clock* or when *o'clock* is understood.

> I plan to leave here at eight o'clock.
> He should be here by four at the latest.
> My appointment is at eleven o'clock.
> *or*
> My appointment is at 11 o'clock.

43. Figures are used to delineate a precise time.

> The patient was discharged at 9:15 in the morning.
> Her plane is due in at 3:05 this afternoon.
> The program starts at 8:30 in the evening.

44. Figures are also written when the time of day is used in conjunction with the abbreviations *a.m. (ante meridiem)* and *p.m. (post meridiem)*. The punctuated lowercase styling for these abbreviations is most common, but punctuated small capital letters are also frequently used. These abbreviations should not be used in conjunction with the words *morning* or *evening;* and the word *o'clock* should not be combined with either *a.m.* or *p.m.*

> 8:30 a.m.   *or*   8:30 A.M.
> 10:30 p.m.   *or*   10:30 P.M.
> 8 a.m.   *or*   8 A.M.
> *but*
> 9:15 in the morning
> 11:00 in the evening
> nine o'clock

NOTE: When twelve o'clock is written, it is often helpful to add the designation *midnight* or *noon*, as *a.m.* and *p.m.* sometimes cause confusion.

> twelve o'clock (midnight)   *or*   12:00 midnight
> twelve o'clock (noon)   *or*   12:00 noon

45. For consistency, even-hour times should be expressed with a colon and two zeros, when used in a series or pairing with any odd-hour times.

> He came at 7:00 and left at 9:45.

46. The 24-hour clock system—also called military time—uses no punctuation and is expressed without the use of *a.m.*, *p.m.*, or *o'clock*.

> from 0930 to 1100
> at 1600 hours

Units of Measurement

47. In technical writing, numbers used with units of measurement—even numbers below ten—are expressed as numerals.

> 2 liters   12 miles
> 55 pounds   6 hectares
> 60 watts   15 cubic centimeters
> 20 kilometers   35 milligrams

48. General writing, on the other hand, usually treats these numbers according to the basic conventions explained in the first section of this chapter. However, in some cases writers achieve greater clarity by styling all numbers—even those below ten—that express quantities of physical measurement as numerals.

> The car was traveling in excess of 80 miles an hour.
> The old volume weighed three pounds and was difficult to hold in a reading position.
> *but also in some general texts*
> 3 hours, 25 minutes
> saw 18 eagles in 12 minutes
> a 6-pound hammer
> weighed 3 pounds, 5 ounces

49. When units of measurement are written as abbreviations or symbols, the adjacent numbers are always figures, in both general and technical texts.

> 6 cm   67.6 fl oz
> 1 mm   4'
> 10 cm^3 98.6°
> 3 kg $4.25

50. When two or more quantities are expressed, as in ranges or dimensions or series, an accompanying symbol is usually repeated with each figure.

> 2' x 4'
> 4" by 6" cards
> temperature on successive days of 30°, 55°, 43°, and 58°
> $400–$500

Chapter 6

Composition and Grammar

CONTENTS

No guide to effective communication can ignore the basic components of discourse: the word, the phrase, the clause, the sentence, and the paragraph. Each of these increasingly complex units contributes to the expression of a writer's ideas.

The simplest component of discourse is the word. The treatment of words in this chapter focuses on their grammatical function in a sentence. For a discussion of the ways in which plurals and possessives of words or compound words are formed, see Chapter 3, "Plurals, Possessives, and Compounds." General questions concerning the more complex language components of phrases, clauses, sentences, and paragraphs are also discussed in separate sections in this chapter.

Parts of Speech

Words have traditionally been classified into eight parts of speech: the adjective, adverb, conjunction, interjection, noun, preposition, pronoun, and verb. This classification system is based mainly on a word's inflectional features, its general grammatical functions, and its positioning within a sentence. On the following pages, these parts of speech are listed alphabetically and discussed briefly.

Adjective

An adjective is a word that typically describes or modifies the meaning of a noun. Adjectives serve to point out a quality of a thing named, to indicate its quantity or extent, or to specify a thing as distinct from something else.

Adjectives are often classified by the ways in which they modify or limit the meaning of a noun. The classifications commonly referred to are the following: descriptive adjectives, demonstrative adjectives, indefinite adjectives, interrogative adjectives, possessive adjectives, proper adjectives, relative adjectives, and articles.

A *descriptive adjective* describes something or indicates a quality, kind, or condition ("a *sick* person," "a *brave* soldier," "a *new* dress"). The *demonstrative adjectives,* such as *this* and *that,* point to what they modify in order to distinguish it from others. These two are the only adjectives with plural forms ("*this* child," "*these* children"; "*that* house," "*those* houses"). An *indefinite adjective* designates an unidentified or not immediately identifiable person or thing ("*some* books," "*other* hotels"). An *interrogative adjective* conveys the force of a question ("*Whose* office is this?" "*Which* book do you want?"). A *possessive adjective* is the possessive form of a personal pronoun ("*her* idea," "*his* job," "*my* car," "*our* savings plan," "*their* office," "*your* opinion"). A *proper adjective* is derived from a proper noun and takes its meaning from what characterizes the noun. It is usually capitalized ("*Victorian* furniture," "a *Puerto Rican* product," "*Keynesian* economics"). A *relative adjective* introduces an adjectival clause ("at the April conference, by *which* time the report should be finished") or a clause that functions as a noun ("the uncomfortable position of not knowing *which* course she should follow"). An *article* is one of a small group of words (as *a, an,* and *the*) that are used with nouns to limit or give definiteness to the application of a noun ("*a* condominium," "*an* honor," "*the* jetliner").

The following paragraphs describe some other types of adjectives. They also outline situations involving adjectives that are sometimes troublesome for writers.

1. **Absolute adjectives** Some adjectives (such as *prior, maximum, optimum, minimum,* and *first*) admit no comparison under ordinary circumstances (see paragraphs 4 and 5 below), because they represent ultimate conditions. These adjectives are called *absolute adjectives.* Some writers are careful to modify these adjectives with adverbs such as *almost, near,* or *nearly,* rather than *least, less, more, most,* or *very.*

> an almost fatal dose
> at near maximum capacity
> a more nearly perfect likeness

NOTE: Many writers do compare and qualify this type of adjective in order to show connotations and shades of meaning they consider less than absolute.

a more perfect union
a less complete account

When in doubt about the comparability of an absolute adjective, one should check the definitions and examples of usage given for the adjective in a dictionary.

2. **Adjective/noun agreement** Most American grammar books insist that demonstrative adjectives used with the words *kind,* *sort,* and *type* + *of* + noun should agree in number with both nouns.

   these kinds of typewriters   *not*   these kind of typewriters
   those sorts of jobs   *not*   those sort of jobs
   this type of person   *not*   these type of people

   This formulation generally accords with most formal American writing; however, in speech and in British English, usage patterns are more varied. In addition, the use of a plural demonstrative adjective with a singular *kind, sort,* or *type* is appearing more regularly in contemporary American writing, especially writing intended to have an informal or speechlike quality.

3. **Compared with adverbs** Both adjectives and adverbs describe or modify other words; however, adjectives can only modify nouns, while adverbs can modify verbs, adverbs, and adjectives. For more on the differences between adjectives and adverbs, see paragraph 14 below and paragraphs 4–6 under Adverb in this section.

4. **Comparison of adjectives** The main structural feature of an adjective is its ability to indicate degrees of comparison (positive, comparative, superlative) by addition of suffixal endings *-er/-est* to the base word, by addition of *more/most* or *less/least* before the base word, or by use of irregular forms.

positive	*comparative*	*superlative*
clean	cleaner	cleanest
meaningful	more meaningful	most meaningful
meaningful	less meaningful	least meaningful
bad	worse	worst

5. The comparative degree is used to show that the thing being modified has more (or less) of a particular quality than the one or ones to which it is being compared. The superlative degree is used to show that the thing being modified has the most (or least) of a quality out of all of the ones to which it is being compared. The superlative degree is most commonly used when there are more than two things being compared.

comparative
prices that were higher than those at other stores
a better report than our last one
the more expensive of the two methods

superlative
the highest prices in the area
the best report so far
the most expensive of the three methods

6. In general, the comparatives and superlatives of one-syllable adjectives are formed by adding *-er/-est* to the base word. The comparatives and superlatives of adjectives with more than two syllables are formed by adding *more* and *most* or *less* and *least* before the base word. The comparatives and superlatives of two-syllable adjectives are variously formed by adding *-er/-est* to the base word or using *more* and *most* or *less* and *least* before the base word. When in doubt about the inflection of a particular adjective, one should consult a dictionary.

positive	*comparative*	*superlative*
big	bigger	biggest
loose	looser	loosest
empty	emptier	emptiest
narrow	narrower	narrowest
complex	more complex	most complex
concise	less concise	least concise
important	more important	most important
troublesome	less troublesome	least troublesome

7. Some adjectives are ordinarily not compared, because they are felt to represent ultimate conditions. For more on these adjectives, see paragraph 1, above.

8. **Coordinate and noncoordinate adjectives** Adjectives that share equal relationships to the nouns they modify are called *coordinate adjectives* and are separated from each other by commas.

   a concise, coherent essay
   a hard, flickering light

9. When the first of two adjectives modifies the noun plus a second adjective, the result is a pair of *noncoordinate adjectives*. Noncoordinate adjectives are not separated by commas.

   a low monthly fee
   the first warm day

10. **Double comparisons** Double comparisons are considered nonstandard and should be avoided.

    an easier method   *not*   a more easier method
    the easiest solution   *not*   the most easiest solution

11. **Incomplete or understood comparisons** Some comparisons are left incomplete because the context clearly implies the comparison. These are commonly used especially in advertising. It should be understood, however, that the use of incomplete comparisons is often considered careless or illogical in formal writing.

> Get better buys here!
> We have lower prices.

12. **Nouns used as adjectives** Nouns are frequently used to describe other nouns, and in this way they act like adjectives. For more on the use of nouns as modifiers, see paragraph 6 under Noun in this section and the discussion under Compounds That Function as Adjectives, pages 97–102.

13. **Placement within a sentence** Adjectives may occur in the following positions within sentences: (1) preceding the nouns they modify, (2) following the nouns they modify, (3) following the verb *to be* and other linking verbs in the predicate-adjective position, and (4) following some transitive verbs used in the passive voice.

> (1) the black hat   a dark, shabby coat
> (2) an executive par excellence   painted the room blue
> (3) a hat that is black   food that tastes stale
>   while I felt sick
> (4) a room that was painted blue
>   passengers found dead at the crash site

14. **Predicate adjectives** A predicate adjective modifies the subject of a linking verb (as *be, become, feel, taste, smell, seem*) which it follows.

> She is happy.
> The milk tastes sour.
> The student seems puzzled.

NOTE: Because some linking verbs (as *feel, look, smell, taste*) can also function as active verbs, which can in turn be modified by adverbs, writers are sometimes confused over whether they should use the adverbial or adjectival form of a modifier after the verb. The answer is that an adjective is used if the subject of the sentence is being modified. If the verb is being modified, an adverb is used. (For more examples, see paragraph 5 under Adverb in this section.)

> Your report looks good. [adjective]
> The colors feel right. [adjective]
> The engine smells hot. [adjective]
> They looked quickly at each item. [adverb]
> He felt immediately for his wallet. [adverb]
> She felt the corners carefully for dampness. [adverb]

Adverb

An adverb is a word or combination of words typically serving as a modifier of a verb, an adjective, another adverb, a preposition, a phrase, a clause, or a sentence and expressing some relation of manner or quality, place, time, degree, number, cause, opposition, affirmation, or denial.

Most commonly, adverbs take the form of an adjective with an -ly ending added to it *(actually, congenially, madly, really)*. There are many exceptions to this pattern, however. For instance, adverbs based on adjectives ending in -ly *(costly, friendly, likely)* do not include an additional -ly ending but take the same form as the adjective. In addition, some adverbs do not end in -ly *(now, quite, too)*.

Adverbs answer such questions as the following: "when?" ("Please reply *at once*"); "how long?" ("This job is taking *forever*"); "where?" ("She works *there*"); "in what direction?" ("Move the lever *upward*"); "how?" ("The staff moved *expeditiously* on the project"); and "to what degree?" ("The book was *very* popular").

1. **Basic uses** Adverbs modify verbs, adjectives, and other adverbs.

    She *carefully* studied the balance sheet.
    She gave the balance sheet *very* careful study.
    She studied the balance sheet *very* carefully.

2. Conjunctive adverbs join clauses or link sentences. (For more on this use of adverbs, see paragraphs 13–15 under Conjunction in this section.)

    You are welcome to join our car pool; *however,* please be ready by 7:00 a.m.
    He thoroughly enjoyed the symposium. *Indeed,* he was fascinated by the presentations.

3. In addition, adverbs may be essential elements of two-word verbs commonly having separate entries in dictionaries.

    Our staff will work *up* the specifications.
    We can work them *up* later.

4. **Compared with adjectives** Adverbs but not adjectives modify action verbs.

    not
    He answered very *harsh.*
    instead
    He answered very *harshly.*

5. Complements referring to the subject of a sentence and occurring after linking verbs conventionally take adjectives but

not adverbs. (For more examples, see paragraph 14 under Adjective in this section.)

not
He looks *badly* these days.
The letter sounded *strongly*.

instead
He looks *bad* these days.
The letter sounded *strong*.

and also
He looks *good* these days.
He looks *well* these days.

NOTE: In the last two examples, either *good* or *well* is acceptable, because both words are here functioning as adjectives in the sense of "healthy."

6. Adverbs but not adjectives modify adjectives and other adverbs.

not
She looked *dreadful* tired.

instead
She looked *dreadfully* tired.

7. **Comparison of adverbs** Most adverbs have three different forms to indicate degrees of comparison (positive, comparative, superlative). The positive form is the same as the base word (*quickly, loudly, near*). The comparative form is usually shown by the addition of *more* or *less* before the base word (*more quickly, less quickly*); the superlative form is usually shown by the addition of *most* or *least* (*most quickly, least quickly*). However, a few adverbs (such as *fast, slow, loud, soft, early, late,* and *quick*) may be compared in two ways: by the method described above or by the addition of the suffixal endings *-er/-est* to the base word (*quick, quicker, quickest*). For an explanation of the uses of the comparative and superlative forms, see paragraph 5 under Adjective in this section.

8. As a general rule, one-syllable adverbs use the *-er/-est* endings to show comparison. Adverbs of three or more syllables use *more/most* and *less/least*. Two-syllable adverbs take either form.

fast	faster	fastest
late	later	latest
easy	easier	easiest
madly	more madly	most madly
happily	more happily	most happily

9. Some adverbs (such as *quite* and *very*) cannot be compared.

10. **Double negatives** A combination of two negative adverbs (such as *not, hardly, never,* and *scarcely*) used to express a single negative idea is avoided in all but the most speechlike or informal writing.

    not
    We *cannot* see *hardly* any reason why we should buy this product.

    instead
    We *cannot* see any reason why we should buy this product.

    We can see *hardly* any reason why we should buy this product.

    NOTE: Double negatives used as a means of understatement appear in all levels of writing, but their overuse can be annoying.

    We were *not unimpressed* by the progress he had made.

11. **Emphasis** Adverbs (such as *just* and *only*) are often used to emphasize other words. A writer should be aware of the various emphases that can result from the positioning of an adverb in a sentence.

    emphasis on the action itself
    He *just* nodded to me as he passed.

    emphasis on timing of the action
    He nodded to me *just* as he passed.

12. In some positions and contexts, these adverbs can be ambiguous.

    They will only tell it to you.

    It is not clear whether this writer means that they will only tell it, not put it in writing, or that they will tell no one else. If the latter interpretation is intended, a slight shift of position would remove the uncertainty.

    They will tell it only to you.

13. **Placement within a sentence** Adverbs are generally positioned as close as possible to the words they modify if such a position will not result in misinterpretation.

    unclear
    A project that the board would support *completely* occupied her thinking.

    It is unclear whether the writer means "would support completely" or "completely occupied her thinking." The adverb may be moved to another position, or the sentence may be recast, depending on intended meaning.

    clear
    A project that the board would completely support occupied her thinking.

or
Her thinking was *completely* occupied with a project that the board would support.

14. When an adverb separates *to* from the verbal element of an infinitive ("hope to really start"), the result is called a split infinitive. For a discussion of split infinitives, see paragraph 32 under Verb in this section.

15. In some cases, adverbs modify an entire sentence rather than a specific word or phrase within the sentence. Such adverbs are referred to as *sentence adverbs,* and their position can vary according to the emphasis one wishes to use.

   Fortunately they had already placed their order.
   They *fortunately* had already placed their order.
   They had already placed their order, *fortunately.*

16. **Relative adverbs** Relative adverbs (such as *when, where, why*) introduce subordinate clauses. (For more on subordinate clauses, see the section on Clauses, beginning on page 185.)

   They met at a time *when* prospects were good.
   I went into the room *where* they were sitting.
   Everyone knows the reason *why* she did it.

Conjunction

A conjunction is a word or phrase that joins together words, phrases, clauses, or sentences. Conjunctions may occur in many different positions in a sentence, although they ordinarily do not appear at the end of a sentence unless the sentence is elliptical. There are three main types of conjunctions: *coordinating, correlative,* and *subordinating.* In addition to these three types of conjunctions, the English language has transitional adverbs and adverbial phrases called *conjunctive adverbs.* These function as conjunctions even though they are customarily classified as adverbs. A definition and discussion of the three types of conjunctions and of conjunctive adverbs follows. (For information about punctuating sentences with conjunctions, see paragraphs 1–5, 23, and 26–28 under Comma, pages 13–15 and 19–20, and paragraphs 1–5 under Semicolon, pages 48–50.)

Coordinating conjunctions Coordinating conjunctions (such as *and, but, for, or, nor, so,* and *yet*) join together grammatical elements of equal weight. The elements may be words, phrases, subordinate clauses, main clauses, or complete sentences.

1. Coordinating conjunctions are used to join elements, to exclude or contrast, to offer alternatives, or to propose reasons, grounds, or a result.

joining elements
She ordered pencils, pens, *and* erasers.
Sales were slow, *and* they showed no sign of improvement.
excluding or contrasting
He is a brilliant *but* arrogant man.
They offered a promising plan, *but* it had not yet been tested.
alternative
She can wait here *or* go on ahead.
reason or grounds
The report is useless, *for* its information is no longer current.
result
His diction is excellent, *so* every word is clear.

2. A comma is used before a coordinating conjunction linking coordinate clauses, especially when these clauses are lengthy. For more on the use of Commas between clauses, see paragraphs 1–4 under Comma, pages 13–14.

   We encourage applications from all interested persons, *but* we do have high professional standards that the successful applicant must meet.

3. Coordinating conjunctions should link equal grammatical elements—for example, adjectives with other adjectives, nouns with other nouns, participles with other participles, clauses with other equal-ranking clauses, and so on. Combining unequal grammatical elements may result in unbalanced sentences.

   unbalanced (*and* links a participial phrase with an adverbial clause)
   Having become disgusted *and* because he was tired, he left the meeting.
   balanced (*and* links two adjectives)
   Because he was tired *and* disgusted, he left the meeting.
   Having become tired *and* disgusted, he left the meeting.

4. Coordinating conjunctions should not be used to string together excessively long series of elements, regardless of their grammatical equality.

   strung-out
   We have sustained enormous losses in this division, *and* we have realized practically no profits even though the sales figures indicate last-quarter gains, *and* we are therefore reorganizing the entire management structure as well as cutting back on personnel.
   tightened
   Because this division has sustained enormous losses and has realized only insignificant profits even with its last-quarter sales gains, we are totally reorganizing its management. We are also cutting back on personnel.

5. The choice of just the right coordinating conjunction for a particular verbal situation is important: the right word will pinpoint the writer's true meaning and intent and will emphasize the most relevant idea or point of the sentence. The following three sentences show increasingly stronger degrees of contrast through the use of different conjunctions:

> *neutral*
> He works hard *and* doesn't progress.
>
> *more contrast*
> He works hard *but* doesn't progress.
>
> *stronger contrast*
> He works hard, *yet* he doesn't progress.

6. The coordinating conjunction *and/or* linking two elements of a compound subject often poses a problem: should the verb that follows be singular or plural? A subject comprising singular nouns connected by *and/or* may be considered singular or plural, depending on the meaning of the sentence.

> *singular*
> All loss *and/or* damage is to be the responsibility of the sender. [one or the other and possibly both]
>
> *plural*
> John R. Westlake *and/or* Maria A. Artandi are hereby *appointed* as the executors of my estate. [both executors are to act, or either of them is to act if the other dies or is incapacitated]

Correlative conjunctions Correlative conjunctions are coordinating conjunctions that are regularly used in pairs, although they are not placed adjacent to one another.

7. Correlative conjunctions are used to link alternatives and equal elements.

> *alternatives*
> *Either* you go *or* you stay.
> He had *neither* looks *nor* wits.
>
> *equal elements*
> *Both* typist *and* writer should understand the rules of punctuation.
> *Not only* was there inflation, *but* there was *also* unemployment.

8. Because they link equal grammatical elements, correlative conjunctions should be placed as close as possible to the elements they join.

> *misplaced* (joining clause and verb phrase)
> *Either* I must send a telex *or* make a long-distance call.
>
> *repositioned* (joining two verb phrases)
> I must *either* send a telex *or* make a long-distance call.

9. The most common negative counterpart to *either . . . or* is *neither . . . nor,* although some people use *neither . . . or. Or* may also occur in combination with *no.*

>He received *neither* a promotion *nor* a raise.
>He received *neither* a promotion *or* a raise.
>He received *no* promotion *or* raise.

Subordinating conjunction Subordinating conjunctions join a subordinate or dependent clause to a main clause.

10. Subordinating conjunctions are used to express cause, condition or concession, manner, purpose or result, time, place or circumstance, and alternative conditions or possibilities.

>*cause*
>*Because* she learns quickly, she is doing well in her new job.
>*condition or concession*
>Don't call *unless* you have the information.
>*manner*
>He looks *as though* he is ill.
>We'll do it *however* you tell us to.
>*purpose or result*
>She routes the mail early *so that* they can read it.
>*time*
>She kept meetings to a minimum *when* she was president.
>*place or circumstance*
>I don't know *where* he has gone.
>He tries to help out *wherever* it is possible.
>*conditions or possibilities*
>It was hard to decide *whether* I should go or stay.

11. The subordinating conjunction *that* introduces several kinds of subordinate clauses, including those used as noun equivalents (such as a subject or an object of a verb or as a predicate nominative).

>Yesterday I learned *that* he has been sick for over a week.

12. In introducing subordinate clauses, subordinating conjunctions deemphasize less important ideas in favor of more important ideas. The writer must take care that the point he or she wishes to emphasize is in the main clause and that the points of less importance are subordinated. Notice how differently these two versions strike the reader.

>We were just coming out of the door *when* the building burst into flames.
>*As* we were just coming out of the door, the building burst into flames.

Conjunctive adverb Conjunctive adverbs are transitional adverbs and adverbial phrases that express relationships between two units of discourse (as two main clauses, two complete sentences, or two or more paragraphs). Conjunctive adverbs are classed as adverbs, but they function as conjunctions when they are used as connectives. Some common conjunctive adverbs are listed below.

accordingly	incidentally
also	in conclusion
anyhow	indeed
anyway	in fact
as a result	later
besides	likewise
consequently	moreover
e.g.	namely
finally	nevertheless
first	on the contrary
for example	otherwise
for instance	second
furthermore	still
further on	that is (to say)
hence	then
however	therefore
i.e.	to be sure
in addition	too

13. Conjunctive adverbs are used to express addition, to add emphasis, to express contrast or discrimination, to introduce illustrations or elaborations, to express or introduce conclusions or results, or to orient elements of discourse as to time or space.

addition
This employee deserves a substantial raise; *furthermore,* she should be promoted.

emphasis
He is brilliant; *indeed,* he is a genius.

contrast or discrimination
The major responsibility lies with the partners; *nevertheless,* associates should be competent in decision-making.

illustrations or elaborations
Losses were due to several negative factors; *namely,* inflation, foreign competition, and restrictive government regulation.

conclusions or results
Government overregulation in that country reached a prohibitive level in the last quarter. *Thus,* we are phasing out all of our operations there.

time or space
First, we can remind them that their account is long overdue; *second,* we can say that we must consider consulting our attorneys if they do not meet their obligation.

14. Conjunctive adverbs are usually placed at the beginning of a clause or sentence. When they are placed later in the clause or sentence, additional emphasis is placed on them.

> The overdue shipment arrived this morning; *however,* we must point out that it was incomplete.
> The overdue shipment arrived this morning; we must point out, *however,* that it was incomplete.

15. The misuse of conjunctive adverbs can lead to a problem known as *comma fault*. When a conjunctive adverb is used to connect two main clauses, a semicolon should be used; a comma will not suffice. (For more on comma fault and punctuation between main clauses, see paragraphs 1–4 under Comma, pages 13–14 and paragraph 5 under Semicolon, pages 49–50.)

> *comma fault*
> The company had flexible hours, *however* its employees were expected to abide by their selected arrival and departure times.
>
> *repunctuated*
> The company had flexible hours; *however,* its employees were expected to abide by their selected arrival and departure times.

Interjection

Interjections are exclamatory or interrupting words or phrases that express an emotion. Interjections are usually independent clauses that lack grammatical connection with the rest of the sentence. They often stand alone.

1. Interjections may be stressed or ejaculatory words, phrases, or even short sentences.

> Absurd!
> No, no!
> Get out!
> Not now!

2. Interjections may also be so-called "sound" words, such as those representing shouts, hisses, or cries:

> Shh! The meeting has begun.
> Pssst! Come over here.
> Ouch! That hurts.
> Ugh! What a horrible flavor.

3. Emphatic interjections expressing forceful emotions use exclamation points.

> Fire!
> What an awful time we had!

4. Mildly stressed words or sentences may be punctuated with commas and periods.

> *Ah,* that's my idea of a terrific deal.
> *Well, well,* so that's the solution.
> *Oh,* you're probably right.

5. Interjections should be sparingly used in discourse, and then only to signal genuine emotion or for strong emphasis.

Noun

A noun is a word that is the name of something (as a person, animal, place, object, quality, concept, or action). Nouns are used in a sentence as the subject or object of a verb, as the object of a preposition, as a predicate after a linking verb, as an appositive name, or as a name in an absolute construction.

Nouns exhibit these characteristic features: they are inflected for possession; they have number (that is, they are either singular or plural); they are often preceded by determiners (as *a, an, the; this, that, these, those; all, every,* and other such qualifiers; *one, two, three,* and other such numerical quantifiers; *his, her, their,* and other such pronominal adjectives); a few of them still show gender differences (as masculine *host, actor,* feminine *hostess, actress*); and many of them are formed by adding a suffix (such as *-ance, -ist, -ness,* and *-tion*).

1. Basic uses Nouns are used as subjects, direct objects, objects of prepositions, indirect objects, retained objects, predicate nominative, objective complements, and appositives and in direct address.

> *subject*
> The *office* was quiet.
> *direct object*
> He locked the *office.*
> *object of a preposition*
> The file is in the *office.*
> *indirect object*
> He gave his *client* the papers.
> *retained object*
> His client was given the *papers.*
> *predicate nominative*
> Mrs. Adams is the managing *partner.*
> *objective complement*
> They made Mrs. Adams managing *partner.*
> *appositive*
> Mrs. Adams, the managing *partner,* wrote that memorandum.
> *direct address*
> *Mrs. Adams,* may I present Mr. Bonkowski.

2. **Compound nouns** Because English is not a static and unchanging entity, many of its words undergo styling variations because of the changing preferences of its users. The styling of compound nouns (whether open, closed, or hyphenated) is especially subject to changing usage. No rigid set of rules can cover every possible variation or combination; however, some consistent patterns of usage can be discerned. For a description of these patterns, see the discussion under Compound Nouns, pages 93–97.

3. **Indefinite articles with nouns** Before a word or abbreviation beginning with a consonant *sound*, the article *a* is used. This is true even if the spelling of the word begins with a vowel.

a BA degree	a human
a hat	a U.S. Senator
a one	a door
a COD package	a union

4. Before *h-* in an unstressed or lightly stressed first syllable, the article *a* is more frequently used, although *an* is more usual in speech whether or not the *h-* is actually pronounced. Either is acceptable in speech or writing.

   a historian   *or*   an historian
   a heroic attempt   *or*   an heroic attempt
   a hilarious performance   *or*   an hilarious performance

5. Before a word or abbreviation beginning with a vowel *sound,* the article *an* is used. This is true even if the spelling (especially of an abbreviation) begins with a consonant.

an icicle	an MIT professor
an hour	an unknown
an FCC report	an nth degree
an orange	an Rh factor

6. **Nominals** Nominals are words or groups of words that function as nouns. Adjectives, gerunds, and infinitives act as nominals. An example of an adjective used as a noun is the word *good* in the phrase "the good die young." Examples of gerunds and infinitives used as nouns are *seeing* in the clause "seeing is believing" and *to see* in the clause "to see is to believe." Noun phrases and noun clauses are also considered to be nominals. For more information about gerunds and infinitives, see paragraphs 12–14 under Verb in this section. For information about noun phrases and noun clauses, see pages 184 and 185–186 respectively.

7. **Nouns used as adjectives** A frequent practice in English is to use a noun as an adjective by placing it before another noun

(in the attributive position), as in *school board* or *office manage-ment*. When nouns are frequently combined in this way, they become familiar compounds like *profit margin, systems analysis, money market, box lunch*. Such compounds provide useful verbal shortcuts (e.g., office management = the management of an office or offices). However, care should be taken not to pile up so many of these noun modifiers that the reader has difficulty sorting out their meanings.

> *shorter but unclear*
> Management review copies of the Division II sales department machine parts file should be indexed.

> *longer but clear*
> Copies of the machine parts file from the Division II sales depart-ment should be indexed before being sent to management for review.

NOTE: Both of these sentences could be made clearer by hy-phenating the compound nouns used as adjectives. For com-plete information about the treatment of this kind of compound, see the discussion under Compounds That Func-tion as Adjectives, pages 97–102.

> Management-review copies of the Division II sales-department machine-parts file should be indexed.

8. **Plurals** The plurals of nouns are usually indicated by addition of an *-s* or *-es* to the base word, although some nouns (such as those of foreign origin) have irregular plurals. For complete information about the formation of plurals, see the discussion under Plurals, pages 82–88.

9. **Possessives** The possessive case is the only noun case indicated by inflection. Typically, the possessives of nouns are formed by the addition of an apostrophe plus *-s* to singular nouns or just an apostrophe to plural words ending in *-s*. For complete information about the formation of possessives, see the discus-sion under Possessives, pages 88–92.

10. **Proper nouns** Proper nouns are nouns that name a particular person, place, or thing and distinguish it from other members of the same class. The most obvious feature of proper nouns is that they are almost always capitalized. For complete infor-mation about capitalizing proper nouns, see the discussion un-der Proper Nouns, Pronouns, and Adjectives, pages 56–77.

Preposition

A preposition is a word that combines with a noun, pronoun, or noun equivalent (as a phrase or clause) to form a phrase that usu-ally acts as an adverb, adjective, or noun.

Prepositions are not characterized by inflection, number, case, gender, or identifying suffixes. They can be identified chiefly by their position within sentences and by their grammatical functions. Prepositions may be simple, i.e., composed of only one element *(against, from, near, of, on, out,* or *without);* or they may be compound, i.e., composed of more than one element *(according to, by means of,* or *in spite of).*

1. **Basic uses** Prepositions are chiefly used to link nouns, pronouns, or noun equivalents to the rest of the sentence. A prepositional phrase is usually adverbial or adjectival in function.

   > She expected resistance *on* his part.
   > He sat down *beside* her.

2. **Conjunctions vs. prepositions** The words *after, before, but, for,* and *since* may function as either prepositions or conjunctions. Their position within the sentence identifies them as conjunctions or prepositions. Conjunctions link two words or sentence elements that have the same grammatical function. Prepositions precede a noun, pronoun, noun phrase, or noun equivalent.

   > *conjunction*
   > I was a bit concerned *but* not panicky. (*but* links two adjectives)
   > *preposition*
   > I was left with nothing *but* hope. (*but* precedes a noun)
   > *conjunction*
   > The device conserves fuel, *for* it is battery-powered. (*for* links two clauses)
   > *preposition*
   > The device conserves fuel *for* residual heating. (*for* precedes a noun phrase)

3. **Implied or unknown prepositions** If two words combine idiomatically with the same preposition, that preposition need not be used after both.

   > We were antagonistic [*to*] and opposed *to* the whole idea.
   >   *but*
   > We are interested *in* and anxious *for* raises.

4. **Position** Prepositions may occur in the following positions: before nouns or pronouns ("*below* the desk," "*beside* them"); after adjectives ("antagonistic *to*," "insufficient *in*," "symbolic *of*"); and after the verbal elements of idiomatically fixed verb + preposition combinations ("take *for*," "get *after*," "come *across*").

5. There is no reason why a preposition cannot terminate a sentence, especially when it is an integral element in an idiomatically fixed verb phrase.

> His lack of organization is only one of the things I put up *with*.
> What does all this add up to?

6. **Use of *between* and *among*** Despite an unfounded notion to the contrary, the preposition *between* can be used of more than two items. It is especially appropriate to denote a one-to-one relationship, regardless of the number of items. *Between* can be used when the number is unspecified, when more than two are enumerated, and even when only one item is mentioned (but repetition is implied).

> Treaties established economic cooperation *between* nations.
> This is *between* you and me and the lamppost.
> He paused *between* every sentence to clear his throat.

Among is more appropriate where the emphasis is on overall distribution rather than individual relationships.

> There was discontent *among* the peasants.

NOTE: When *among* is automatically chosen for more than two, the results can sound strained.

> The author alternates *among* quotes, clichés, and street slang.

Pronoun

A pronoun is a word that is used as a substitute for a noun or noun equivalent, takes noun constructions, and refers to persons or things named or understood in the context. The noun or noun equivalent for which it substitutes is called the *antecedent*.

Pronouns exhibit all or some of the following characteristic features: case (nominative, possessive, objective); number (singular, plural); person (first, second, third person); and gender (masculine, feminine, neuter). Pronouns are divided into seven major categories, each with its own function. Each pronoun category is listed and described alphabetically in this section.

Demonstrative pronouns The words *this, that, these,* and *those* are classified as pronouns when they function as nouns (they are classified as demonstrative adjectives when they modify nouns; see the discussion under Adjective in this section).

1. Demonstrative pronouns point out the person or thing referred to and distinguish it from others of the same type.

> *These* are the best cookies I've ever eaten.
> *Those* are strong words.

2. They also distinguish between a person or thing nearby and one further away.

    This is my desk; *that* is yours.

3. A potentially troublesome situation occurs when a demonstrative pronoun introduces a sentence referring back to something previously mentioned. The reference should be clear and not cloudy:

    cloudy
    The heir's hemophilia, the influence of an unprincipled faith healer on the royal family, devastating military setbacks, general strikes, mass outbreaks of typhus, and repeated crop failures contributed to the revolution. *This* influenced the course of history.

    clear
    None of the participants in the political scandal kept records of what they said or did. *That* is most unfortunate, and it should be a lesson for the future.

Indefinite pronouns   Indefinite pronouns designate an unidentified or not immediately identifiable person or thing. They are chiefly used as third-person references and do not distinguish gender. Examples of indefinite pronouns are the following: *all, another, any, anybody, anyone, anything, both, each, each one, either, everybody, everyone, everything, few, many, much, neither, nobody, none, no one, other, several, some, somebody, someone, something.*

4. Indefinite pronouns should agree in number with their verb. The following are singular and take singular verbs: *another, anything, each one, everything, much, nobody, no one, one, other, someone, something.*

    Much is being done.
    No one wants to go.

5. The following indefinite pronouns are plural and take plural verbs: *both, few, many, several.*

    Many were called; *few were* chosen.

6. Some indefinite pronouns (such as *all, any, none, some*) present problems because they may be either singular or plural, depending on whether they are used with mass nouns or count nouns (a *mass noun* identifies something not ordinarily thought of in terms of numbered elements; a *count noun* identifies things that can be counted).

    with mass noun
    All of the *property is* entailed.
    None of the *ink was* erasable.
    Not *any* of the *sky was* visible.

with count noun
All of our *bases are* covered.
None of the *clerks were* available.
Not *any* of the *stars were* visible.

7. The following are singular in form, and as such logically take singular verbs. However, because of their plural connotations, informal speech has established the use of plural pronoun references to them: *anybody, anyone, everybody, everyone, somebody.*

    I knew *everybody* by *their* first names.
    Don't tell *anyone; they* might spread the rumor.

8. Even in more formal contexts, expressions such as the following are used increasingly, especially as a result of attempts to avoid sexism in language:

    We called *everyone* by *their* first *names.*
    instead of
    We called *everyone* by *his* first *name.*

    For more about avoiding sexism in the use of personal pronouns, see paragraph 22 below.

9. In some constructions an apparently singular indefinite pronoun may take a plural verb if the context makes it seem plural. The following two sentences illustrate how a singular indefinite pronoun may take either a singular or plural verb, depending on how the writer interprets *either*:

    Either of these pronunciations *is* acceptable.
    Either of these pronunciations *are* acceptable.

    The conventional choice of verb would be *is,* because the subject of the sentence is the singular pronoun *either.* However, the proximity of the plural word *pronunciations,* together with the possibility of interpreting *either* to mean "one or both," lets the writer or speaker choose either a singular or a plural verb, depending on the interpretation of the subject.

10. The indefinite pronouns *any* and *anyone* are conventionally followed by *other(s)* or *else* when they form part of a comparison of two individuals in the same class.

    not
    Helen has more seniority than *anyone* in the firm.
    instead
    Helen has more seniority than *anyone else* in the firm.
    not
    Our house is older than *any* building on the block.
    instead
    Our house is older than *any other* building on the block.

The addition of *else* and *other* in the preceding sentences avoids the logical impossibility that Helen has more seniority than herself or that our house is older than itself. Likewise, it prevents the possible misreading that Helen is not a member of the firm or that our house is not on the block.

11. The antecedent of an indefinite pronoun should be clearly stated, not implied. A good check for a clear reference is to see if there is an antecedent in the sentence that could be substituted for the pronoun.

> *unclear*
> He's the author of a best-selling book on sailing, despite the fact that he's never set foot on *one*.
> *clear*
> He's the author of a best-selling book on sailing, despite the fact that he's never set foot on a sailboat.

12. Interrogative pronouns The interrogative pronouns *what, which, who, whom,* and *whose* as well as combinations of these words with the suffix *-ever* are used to introduce direct and indirect questions.

> *Who* is she?
> He asked me *who* she was.
> *Whom* did the article accuse?
> She asked *whom* the article accused.
> *Whoever* can that be?
> We wondered *whoever* that could be.

Personal pronouns Personal pronouns refer to beings and objects and reflect the person, number, and gender of those antecedents. Examples of personal pronouns are: *he, I, it, she, they, we, you.*

13. Most personal pronouns take different forms for the three cases.

	Nominative	Possessive	Objective
first person singular	I	my, mine	me
first person plural	we	our, ours	us
second person singular	you	your, yours	you
second person plural	you	your, yours	you
third person singular	he	his, his	him
	she	her, hers	her
	it	its, its	it
third person plural	they	their, theirs	them

14. A personal pronoun agrees in person, number, and gender with the word it refers to. However, the case of a pronoun is determined by its function within a sentence. The nominative case is used for a pronoun that acts as a subject of a sentence or as a predicate nominative (but see paragraph 15 below). The possessive case is used for pronouns that express possession or a similar relationship. The objective case is used for pronouns that are direct objects, indirect objects, retained objects, objects of prepositions, or objective complements.

> *You* and *I* thought the meeting was useful.
> My assistant and *I* attended the seminar.
> Our new candidate will be *you.*
> We all had *our* own offices.
> The vice president informed my assistant and *me* about the seminar.
> She gave *me* the papers.
> Just between *you* and *me,* the meeting was much too long.
> I was given *them* yesterday.
> That makes our new candidate *her.*

15. The nominative case after the verb *to be* (as in "It is I" and "This is she") is considered standard English and is preferred by strict grammarians, but the objective case (as in "It's me") also may be used without criticism, especially in spoken English.

> The only candidate left for that job may soon be she.
> *or*
> The only candidate left for that job may soon be her.

16. When a personal pronoun occurs in a construction introduced by *than,* the pronoun can be in the nominative or objective case. In formal writing, the use of the nominative case is the more frequent choice; in speech or informal writing, the objective case is often used.

> He received a bigger bonus than *she.*
> Kathy is ten years younger than *me.*

17. The suffixes *-self* and *-selves* combine only with the possessive case of the first- and second-person pronouns (*myself, ourselves, yourself, yourselves*) and with the objective case of the third-person pronouns (*himself, herself, itself, themselves*). Other combinations (as "hisself" and "theirselves") are considered nonstandard and should not be used.

18. Personal pronouns in the possessive case (such as *your, their, theirs, its*) do not contain apostrophes and should not be con-

fused with similar-sounding contractions (such as *you're,*
they're, there's, it's), which do contain apostrophes.

possessive personal pronoun	*contraction*
Put the camera in *its* case.	*It's* an expensive camera.
Whose camera is it?	*Who's* going to go?

19. When one uses the pronoun *I* or *me* with other pronouns or
    with other people's names, *I* or *me* should be last in the series:

    Mrs. Smith and *I* were trained together.

    He and *I* were attending the meeting.

    The memorandum was directed to Ms. Montgomery and *me.*

20. Some companies prefer that writers use *we* and not *I* when
    speaking for their companies in business correspondence. *I* is
    more often used when a writer is referring only to himself or
    herself. The following example illustrates use of both within
    one sentence:

    We [i.e., the writer speaks for the company] have reviewed the
    manuscript that you sent to *me* [i.e., the manuscript was sent only
    to the writer] on June 1, but *we* [a corporate or group decision]
    feel that it is too specialized a work to be marketable by *our*
    company.

21. While the personal pronouns *it, you,* and *they* are often used
    as indefinite pronouns in spoken English, they can be vague
    or even redundant in some contexts.

    vague
    They said at the seminar that the economy would experience a
    third-quarter upturn. (The question is: Who exactly is *they?*)
    explicit
    The economists on the panel at the seminar predicted a third-
    quarter economic upturn.
    redundant
    In the graph *it* says that production fell off by 50%.
    lean
    The graph indicates a 50% production drop.

22. Forms of the personal pronoun *he* and the indefinite pronoun
    one have been the standard substitutes for antecedents whose
    genders are mixed or irrelevant:

    Present the letter to the executive for *his* approval.

    Each employee should check *his* W-2 form.

    If *one* really wants to succeed, *one* can.

However, many writers today who are concerned about sexism in language recast such sentences, where possible, to avoid
generic use of the masculine pronoun:

Present the letter to the executive for approval.
All employees should check *their* W-2 forms.
Each employee should check *his or her* W-2 form.

The phrase *his or her* should be used sparingly, however, as it seems awkward and could certainly become tiresome if used frequently throughout a text. For more on avoiding the generic use of the masculine pronoun, see paragraph 8 above.

23. Reciprocal pronouns The reciprocal pronouns *each other* and *one another* are used in the object position to indicate a mutual action or cross relationship between the members comprised in a plural or compound subject.

They do not quarrel with *one another*.
Karen and Rachel spelled *each other* at driving on their trip.

24. Reciprocal pronouns may also be used in the possessive case:

The two secretaries borrowed *one another's* stationery.
The president and his vice president depend on *each other's* ideas.

25. Reflexive pronouns Reflexive pronouns express reflexive action or add extra emphasis to the subject of the sentence, clause, or verbal phrase in which they occur. Reflexive pronouns are formed by compounding the personal pronouns *him, her, it, my, our, them,* and *your* with *-self* or *-selves*. Reflexive pronouns are used when an object or subjective complement refers to the same thing as the foregoing noun or noun phrase.

She dressed *herself*.
The baby isn't *himself* this morning.
They asked *themselves* if they were being honest.
I *myself* am not afraid.
The cook told Jim to help *himself*.

Relative pronouns The relative pronouns are *that, what, which, who, whom,* and *whose,* as well as combinations of these with *-ever.* They introduce subordinate clauses acting as nouns or modifiers. While a relative pronoun itself does not exhibit number, gender, or person, it does determine the number, gender, and person of elements that follow it in the relative clause because of its implicit agreement with its antecedent. Consider, for instance, the following sentence:

People *who are* ready to start *their* jobs should arrive at 8:00 a.m.

In this sentence, the relative pronoun "who" refers to the plural subject "People," and it acts as the subject of the relative clause "who are ready to start their jobs." Because it refers to a plural word it acts like a plural word within its clause and therefore calls for the plural verb "are" and the plural pronoun "their."

26. The relative pronoun *who* typically refers to persons and some animals; *which*, to things and animals; and *that*, to both beings and things.

>   a man who sought success
>   a man whom we can trust
>   Seattle Slew, who won horse racing's Triple Crown
>   a book which sold well
>   a dog which barked loudly
>   a book that sold well
>   a dog that barked loudly
>   a man that we can trust

27. Relative pronouns can sometimes be omitted for the sake of brevity.

>   The man *whom* I was talking to is the president.
>   *or*
>   The man I was talking to is the president.

28. The relative pronoun *what* may be substituted for the longer and more awkward phrases "that which," "that of which," or "the thing which" in some sentences.

>   *stiff*
>   He was blamed for *that which* he could not have known.
>   *easier*
>   He was blamed for *what* he could not have known.

29. The problem of when to use *who* or *whom* has been blown out of proportion. The situation is very simple: formal written English makes a distinction between the nominative and objective cases of these pronouns when they are used as relatives or interrogatives.

>   *nominative case*
>   *Who* is she?
>   *Who* does she think she is, anyway?
>   She thinks she is the one *who* ought to be promoted.
>   Give me a list of the ones *who* you think should be promoted.
>   *objective case*
>   *Whom* are you referring to?
>   To *whom* are you referring?
>   He's a man *whom* everyone should know.
>   He's a man with *whom* everyone should be acquainted.

In speech and less formal writing, case distinctions and boundaries often become blurred, with *who* being freely used for *whom* except in set phrases such as *"To whom* it may concern."* In such contexts, then, *who* may be used not only as the subject of the clause it introduces but also as the object of a verb in a clause that it introduces or as an interrogative.

> See the manager, Mrs. Keats, *who* you should be able to find in her office.
> *Who* should we tell?

30. *Whom* is commonly used as the object of a preposition in a clause that it introduces; however, the form *who* is commonly used to introduce a question even when it is the object of a preposition:

> Presiding is a judge *about whom* I know nothing.
> He is a man *for whom* I would gladly work.
> *but*
> *Who* (rarely *whom*) are you going to listen to?
> *Who* (rarely *whom*) do you work for?

31. While the nominative form *who* can be used in the objective case in certain instances, substitution of the objective form *whom* in place of *who* is usually considered to be a hypercorrect, or overcompensating use. One should therefore avoid such usages as "*Whom* do you suppose is coming to the meeting?" which result from a mistaken notion that *whom* is somehow always more correct.

32. The relative pronouns *whoever* and *whomever* follow the same principles as *who* and *whom* in formal writing:

> *nominative*
> Tell *whoever* is going to research the case that . . . .
> He wants to help *whoever* needs it most.
>
> *objective*
> She makes friends with *whomever* she meets.

NOTE: In speech and less formal writing, however, as with *who* and *whom*, case distinctions become blurred, and *whoever* is used without criticism in most sentences:

> *Whoever* did she choose?

Verb

A verb is a word that is characteristically the grammatical center of a predicate and expresses an act, occurrence, or mode of being. Verbs are inflected for agreement with the subject and for mood, voice, or tense. Verbs typically have rather full descriptive meaning and characterizing quality, but they sometimes are almost completely devoid of these, especially when they are used as auxiliary or linking verbs.

Verbs exhibit the following characteristic features: inflection (*help, helps, helping, helped*), person (first, second, third person), number (singular, plural), tense (present, past, future), aspect (time relations other than the simple present, past, and future), voice (active, passive), mood (indicative, subjunctive, imperative), and suffixation (as by the typical suffixal markers *-ate, -en, -ify,* and *-ize*).

Inflection Regular verbs have four inflected forms signaled by the suffixes *-s* or *-es, -ed,* and *-ing.* The verb *help* as shown in the sentence above is regular. Most irregular verbs have four or five forms, as *see, sees, seeing, saw,* and *seen;* and one, the verb *be,* has eight: *be, is, am, are, being, was, were,* and *been.* When one is uncertain about a particular inflected form, one should consult a dictionary that indicates not only the inflections of irregular verbs but also those inflections resulting in changes in base-word spelling.

> blame; blamed; blaming
> spy; spied; spying
> picnic; picknicked; picnicking

A dictionary should also show variant inflected forms.

> bias; biased *or* biassed; biasing *or* biassing
> counsel; counseled *or* counselled; counseling *or* counselling
> diagram; diagramed *or* diagrammed; diagraming *or* diagramming
> travel; traveled *or* travelled; traveling *or* travelling

All of the foregoing forms may be found at their respective main entries in *Webster's Ninth New Collegiate Dictionary.* There are, however, a few rules that will aid one in ascertaining the proper spelling patterns of certain verb forms.

1. Verbs ending in a silent *-e* generally retain the *-e* before consonant suffixes (as *-s*) but drop the *-e* before vowel suffixes (as *-ed* and *-ing*).

   > arrange; arranges; arranged; arranging
   > hope; hopes; hoped; hoping
   > require; requires; required; requiring
   > shape; shapes; shaped; shaping

   NOTE: A few verbs ending in a silent *-e* retain the *-e* before vowel suffixes in order to avoid confusion with other words.

   > dye; dyes; dyed; dyeing (*vs.* dying)
   > singe; singes; singed; singeing (*vs.* singing)

2. Monosyllabic verbs ending in a single consonant preceded by a single vowel double the final consonant before vowel suffixes (as *-ed* and *-ing*).

brag; bragged; bragging
grip; gripped; gripping
pin; pinned; pinning

3. Polysyllabic verbs ending in a single consonant preceded by a single vowel and having an accented last syllable double the final consonant before vowel suffixes (as -*ed* and -*ing*).

commit; committed; committing
control; controlled; controlling
occur; occurred; occurring
omit; omitted; omitting

NOTE: The final consonant of such verbs is not doubled when two vowels occur before the final consonant or when two consonants form the ending of the verb.

daub; daubed; daubing
soil; soiled; soiling
help; helped; helping
lurk; lurked; lurking
peck; pecked; pecking

4. Verbs ending in -*y* preceded by a consonant regularly change the -*y* to -*i* before all suffixes except -*ing*.

carry; carried; carrying
marry; married; marrying
study; studied; studying

NOTE: If the final -*y* is preceded by a vowel, it remains unchanged in suffixation.

delay; delayed; delaying
enjoy; enjoyed; enjoying
obey; obeyed; obeying

5. Verbs ending in -*c* add a -*k* when a suffix beginning with -*e* or -*i* is added.

mimic; mimics; mimicked; mimicking
panic; panics; panicked; panicking
traffic; traffics; trafficked; trafficking

NOTE: Words derived from this type of verb also add a -*k* when such a suffix or the suffix -*y* is added to them.

panicky
trafficker

6. **Tense, aspect, voice, and mood** English verbs exhibit their simple present and simple past tenses by use of two single-word grammatical forms.

simple present = do
simple past = did

7. The future tense is expressed by *shall* or *will* followed by the base form of the verb or by use of the simple present or present progressive forms in a revealing context.

> I *shall do* it.
> He *will do* it.
> I *leave* shortly for New York.
> I *am leaving* shortly for New York.

8. Aspect is a property that allows verbs to indicate time relations other than the simple present, past, or future tenses. Aspect covers these relationships:

action occurring in the past and continuing to the present	has seen	*present perfect*
action completed at a past time or before the immediate past	had seen	*past perfect*
action that will have been completed by a future time	will have seen	*future perfect*
action occurring now	is seeing	*progressive*

In contexts that require it, the perfective and the progressive aspects can be combined to yield special verb forms, such as *had been seeing*.

9. Voice enables a verb to indicate whether the subject of a sentence is acting (he *loves* = active voice) or whether the subject is being acted upon (he *is loved* = passive voice).

10. Mood indicates manner of expression. The indicative mood states a fact or asks a question (He *is* here. *Is* he here?). The subjunctive mood expresses condition contrary to fact (I wish that he *were* here). The imperative mood expresses a command or request (*Come* here. Please *come* here).

11. **Transitive and intransitive verbs** Verbs may be used transitively or intransitively. A *transitive* verb acts upon a direct object.

> She *contributed* money.
> He *ran* the store.

An *intransitive* verb does not act upon a direct object.

> She *contributed* generously.
> He *ran* down the street.

NOTE: As in the examples above, many verbs are transitive in one sense and intransitive in another.

Verbals There is another group of words derived from verbs and called *verbals* that deserve added discussion. The members of this group—the gerund, the participle, and the infinitive—exhibit some but not all of the characteristic features of their parent verbs.

12. A gerund is an *-ing* verb form, but it functions mainly as a noun. It has both the active *(seeing)* and the passive *(being seen)* voices. In addition to voice, a gerund's verbal characteristics are as follows: it conveys the notion of a verb—i.e., action, occurrence, or being; it can take an object; and it can be modified by an adverb. In the following sentences, for instance, "Typing" and "driving" are gerunds, "data" and "cars" are their objects, and "daily" and "fast" are adverbs modifying the gerund.

> *Typing* tabular *data daily* is a boring task.
> He liked *driving cars fast.*

NOTE: Nouns and pronouns occurring before gerunds usually use the possessive case. However, writers often use objective pronouns or nouns not in the possessive case when they want to put emphasis on the noun or pronoun. In addition, plural nouns are often not expressed in the possessive before gerunds.

> She is trying to improve *her typing.*
> We objected to *their telling* the story all over town.
> We cannot imagine *him doing* anything less than is required.
> Talks began without the negotiating *parties having* any choice about the location.

13. Participles, on the other hand, function as adjectives and may occur alone ("a *broken* typewriter") or in phrases that modify other words ("*Having broken the typewriter,* she gave up for the day"). Participles have active and passive forms like gerunds.

> *active-voice participial phrase modifying "he"*
> *Having failed to pass the examination,* he was forced to repeat the course.
> *passive-voice participial phrase modifying "he"*
> *Having been failed* by his instructor, he was forced to repeat the course.

NOTE: Participles, unlike gerunds, are not preceded by possessive nouns or pronouns:

> We saw the *car waiting* outside the door.

14. Infinitives may exhibit active *(to do)* and passive *(to be done)* voices, and they may indicate aspect *(to be doing, to have done, to have been doing, to have been done)*. Infinitives may take complements and may be modified by adverbs. In addition, they can function as nouns, adjectives, and adverbs in sentences. Examples:

noun use
To be known is *to be castigated*. (subject and predicate nominative)
He tried everything except *to bypass his superior*. (object of preposition "except")

adjectival use
They had found a way *to increase profits greatly*. (modifies the noun "way")

adverbial use
He was too furious *to speak*. (modifies "furious")

NOTE: Although *to* is the characteristic marker of an infinitive, it is not always stated but may be understood:

He helped [to] complete the marketing report.

15. **Sequence of tenses** If the main verb in a sentence is in the present tense, any other tense or compound verb form may follow it in subsequent clauses, as:

I *realize* that you *are leaving*.
I *realize* that you *will be leaving*.
I *realize* that you *left*.
I *realize* that you *will leave*.
I *realize* that you *were leaving*.
I *realize* that you *will have been leaving*.
I *realize* that you *have been leaving*.
I *realize* that you *can be leaving*.
I *realize* that you *had left*.
I *realize* that you *may be leaving*.
I *realize* that you *had been leaving*.
I *realize* that you *must be leaving*.

16. If the main verb is in the past tense, that tense imposes time restrictions on any subsequent verbs in the sentence, thus excluding use of the present tense, as:

I *realized* that you *were leaving*.
I *realized* that you *would be leaving*.
I *realized* that you *left*.
I *realized* that you *could be leaving*.
I *realized* that you *had left*.
I *realized* that you *might be leaving*.
I *realized* that you *had been leaving*.
I *realized* that you *would leave*.

17. If the main verb is in the future tense, it imposes time restrictions on subsequent verbs in the sentence, thus excluding the possibility of using the simple past tense, as:

He *will see* you because he *is going* to the meeting too.
He *will see* you because he *will be going* to the meeting too.
He *will see* you because he *will go* to the meeting too.
He *will see* you because he *has been going* to the meetings too.
He *will see* you because he *will have been going* to the meetings too.

18. In general, most writers try to maintain an order of tenses throughout their sentences that is consistent with natural or real time, e.g., present tense = present-time matters, past tense = past matters, and future tense = matters that will take place in the future. However, there are two outstanding exceptions to these principles. First, if one is discussing the contents of printed or published material, one conventionally uses the present tense.

> In *Etiquette*, Emily Post *discusses* forms of address.
>
> This analysis *gives* market projections for the next two years.
>
> In his latest position paper on the Middle East, the Secretary of State *writes* that . . . .

Second, if one wishes to add the connotation of immediacy to a particular sentence, one may use the present tense instead of the future.

> I *leave* for Tel Aviv tonight.

19. The sequence of tenses in sentences which express contrary-to-fact conditions is a special problem frequently encountered in writing. The examples below show the sequence correctly maintained.

> If he *were* on time, we *would leave* now.
>
> If he *had been* (not *would have been*) on time, we *would have left* an hour ago.

20. At one time, *shall* was considered the only correct form to use with the first person in simple future tenses (*I shall, we shall*), while *will* was limited to the second and third persons (*you will, it will, they will*). Today, however, either of the following forms is considered correct for the first person:

> We *shall give* your request special attention.
>
> We *will give* your request special attention.

Subject-verb agreement   Verbs agree in number and in person with their grammatical subjects. At times, however, the grammatical subject may be singular in form, but the thought it carries—i.e., the notional subject—may have plural connotations. Here are some general guidelines. For discussion of verb agreement with indefinite-pronoun subjects, see paragraphs 4–9 under Pronoun in this section. For discussion of verb number as affected by a compound subject whose elements are joined by *and/or*, see paragraph 6 under Conjunction in this section.

21. Plural and compound subjects take plural verbs even if the subject is inverted.

Both dogs and cats *were* tested for the virus.
Grouped under the heading "fine arts" *are* music, theater, and painting.

22. **Compound subjects or plural subjects working as a unit take singular verbs in American English.**

Lord & Taylor *has* stores in the New York area.
Cauliflower and cheese *is* my favorite vegetable.
Five hundred dollars *is* a stiff price for a coat.
   but
Twenty-five milligrams of pentazocine *were* administered.

23. **Compound subjects expressing mathematical relationships may be either singular or plural.**

One plus one *makes* (or *make*) two.
Six from eight *leaves* (or *leave*) two.

24. **According to traditional guidelines, singular subjects joined by *or* or *nor* take singular verbs; plural subjects so joined take plural verbs. If one subject is singular and the other plural, the verb agrees with the number of the subject that is closer to it.**

A freshman or sophomore *is* eligible for the scholarship.
Neither freshmen nor sophomores *are* eligible for the scholarship.
Either the secretaries or the supervisor *has* to do the job.
Either the supervisor or the secretaries *have* to do the job.

NOTE: Some writers prefer using a plural verb with singular subjects joined by *nor* because they construe *neither . . . nor* as being the negative form of *both . . . and.*

Neither Michael nor his father *were* happy with the solution.

25. **Singular subjects introduced by *many a, such a, every, each,* or *no* take singular verbs, even when several such subjects are joined by *and.***

Many an executive *has* gone to the top in that division.
No supervisor and no assembler *is* excused from the time check.
Every chair, table, and desk *has* to be accounted for.

26. **The agreement of the verb with its grammatical subject ordinarily should not be skewed by an intervening phrase.**

One of my reasons for resigning *involves* purely personal considerations.
The president of the company, as well as members of his staff, *has* arrived.
He, not any of the proxy voters, *has* to be present.

27. The verb *to be* agrees with its grammatical subject and not with its complement.

> His mania *was* fast cars and beautiful women.
> Women in the work force *constitute* a new field of study.

NOTE: The verb *to be* introduced by the word *there* must agree in number with the subject following it.

> There *are* many complications here.
> There *is* no reason to worry about him.

28. Collective nouns—such as *orchestra, team, committee, family*—usually take singular verbs but can take plural verbs if the emphasis is on the individual members of the unit rather than on the unit itself.

> The committee *has agreed* to extend the deadline.
>   *but also*
> The committee *have been* at odds ever since the beginning.

29. The word *number* in the phrase *a number of* usually takes a plural verb, but in the phrase *the number of* it takes a singular verb.

> A number of errors *were* (also *was*) made.
> The number of errors *was* surprising.

30. A relative clause that follows the expression *one of those/these* + plural noun takes a plural or singular verb, depending on whether the singular notion of *one* or the plural notion of *those* or *these* is uppermost in the writer's mind.

> He is one of those executives who *worry* (or *worries*) a lot.
> This is one of those typewriters that *create* (or *creates*) perfect copies.

31. Linking and *sense* verbs Linking verbs (as the various forms of *to be*) and the so-called "sense" verbs (as *feel, look, taste, smell,* as well as particular senses of *appear, become, continue, grow, prove, remain, seem, stand,* and *turn*) connect subjects with predicate nouns or adjectives.

> He *is* a vice president.
> He *became* vice president.
> The temperature *continues* cold.
> The future *looks* prosperous.
> I *feel* bad.
> He *remains* healthy.

NOTE: Sense words often cause confusion, in that writers sometimes mistakenly use adverbs instead of adjectives following these words.

not
This perfume smells nicely.
instead
This perfume smells nice.
not
The meat tastes well.
instead
The meat tastes good.

32. **Split infinitives** A split infinitive is an infinitive that has a modifier between the *to* and the verbal (as in "to really care"). In the past, some grammarians disapproved of this construction, and many people still try to avoid it whenever they can. However, the split infinitive has been around a long time and has been used by a wide variety of distinguished English writers. It can be a useful device if a writer wants to stress the verbal element of an infinitive or express a thought that is most clearly shown with *to* + adverb + infinitive. In some cases where special emphasis on a word or a group of words is desirable, that emphasis cannot be achieved with an undivided infinitive construction. For example, in the phrase "to *thoroughly* complete the financial study" the position of the adverb as close as possible to the verbal element of the whole infinitive phrase strengthens the effect of the adverb on the verbal element. This situation is not necessarily true in the following reworded phrases:

> to complete *thoroughly* the financial study
> *thoroughly* to complete the financial study
> to complete the financial study *thoroughly*

In other instances, the position of the adverb may actually modify or change the entire meaning.

> *original*
> arrived at the office to *unexpectedly* find a new name on the door
> *recast with new meanings*
> arrived at the office *unexpectedly* to find a new name on the door
> arrived at the office to find a new name on the door *unexpectedly*

NOTE: Very long adverbial modifiers that interrupt an infinitive are clumsy and should be avoided or recast.

> *clumsy*
> He wanted to *completely and without mercy* defeat his competitor.
> *recast*
> He wanted to defeat his competitor *completely and without mercy*.

33. **Dangling participles** Dangling participles are participles occurring in a sentence without a normally expected syntactic rela-

tion to the rest of the sentence. They are best avoided, as they may create confusion for the reader or seem ludicrous.

dangling
Walking through the door, her coat was caught.

recast
While walking through the door, she caught her coat.
Walking through the door, she caught her coat.
She caught her coat while walking through the door.

dangling
Caught in the act, his excuses were unconvincing.

recast
Caught in the act, he could not make his excuses convincing.

dangling
Having been told that he was incompetent and dishonest, the executive fired the man.

recast
Having told the man that he was incompetent and dishonest, the executive fired him.
Having been told by his superior that he was incompetent and dishonest, the man was fired.

NOTE: Participles should not be confused with prepositions that end in *-ing*—like *concerning, considering, providing, regarding, respecting, touching,* etc.

prepositional usage
Concerning your complaint, we can tell you . . . .
Considering all the implications, you have made a dangerous decision.
Touching the matter at hand, we can say that . . . .

Phrases

A phrase is a brief expression that consists of two or more grammatically related words that may contain either a noun or a finite verb (that is, a verb that shows grammatical person and number) but not both, and that often functions as a particular part of speech with a clause or sentence.

Basic Types

There are seven basic types of phrases.

1. An *absolute phrase* consists of a noun followed by a modifier (such as a participle). Absolute phrases act independently within a sentence without modifying a particular element of the sentence. Absolute phrases are also referred to as *nominative absolutes*.

He stalked out, *his eyes staring straight ahead.*

2. A *gerund phrase* is a verbal phrase that includes a gerund and functions as a noun.

    Sitting on a patient's bed is bad hospital etiquette.

3. An *infinitive phrase* is a verbal phrase that includes an infinitive and that may function as a noun, adjective, or adverb.

    noun
    To do that would be stupid.

    adjective
    This was a performance *to remember.*

    adverb
    He struggled *to get free.*

4. A *noun phrase* consists of a noun and its modifiers.

    The concrete building is huge.

5. A *participial phrase* is a verbal phrase that includes a participle and that functions as an adjective.

    Listening all the time with great concentration, she began to line up her options.

6. A *prepositional phrase* consists of a preposition and its object. It may function as a noun, adjective, or adverb.

    noun
    Out of debt is where we'd like to be!

    adjective
    Here is the desk *with the extra file drawer.*

    adverb
    He now walked *without a limp.*

7. A *verb phrase* consists of a verb and any other terms that either modify it or that complete its meaning.

    She *will have arrived too late* for you to talk to her.

Usage Problems

1. Usage problems with phrases occur most often when a modifying phrase is not placed close enough to the word or words that it modifies. The phrase "On December 10" in the following sentence, for example, must be repositioned to clarify just what happened on that date.

    original
    We received your letter concerning the shipment of parts on December 10.

recast
On December 10 we received your letter concerning the shipment of parts.

or

We received your letter concerning the December 10 shipment of parts.

2. A very common usage problem with phrases involves dangling participial phrases. For a discussion of dangling participles, see paragraph 33 under Verb, pages 182–183.

Clauses

A clause is a group of words containing both a subject and a predicate. A clause functions as an element of a compound or a complex sentence. There are two general types of clauses: the *main* or *independent clause* and the *subordinate* or *dependent clause*. The main clause (such as "it is hot") is an independent grammatical unit and can stand alone. The subordinate clause (such as "because it is hot") cannot stand alone. A subordinate clause is either preceded or followed by a main clause.

Basic Types

Like phrases, clauses can perform as particular parts of speech within the total environment of the sentence. There are three basic types of clauses having part-of-speech functions.

1. The *adjective clause* modifies a noun or pronoun and typically follows the word it modifies.

> Her administrative assistant, *who was also a speech writer,* was overworked.
> I can't see the reason *why you're upset.*
> He is a man *who will succeed.*
> Anybody *who opts for a career like that* is crazy.

2. The *adverb clause* modifies a verb, an adjective, or another adverb and typically follows the word it modifies.

> They made a valiant effort, *although the risks were great.*
> *When it rains,* it pours.
> I'm certain *that he is guilty.*
> We accomplished less *than we did before.*

3. The *noun clause* fills a noun slot in a sentence and thus can be a subject, an object, or a complement.

subject
Whoever is qualified should apply.
object of a verb
I do not know *what his field is.*
object of a preposition
Route that journal to *whichever department you wish.*
complement
The trouble is *that she has no ambition.*

Elliptical Clauses

Some clause elements may be omitted if the context makes clear the understood elements:

I remember the first time [that] we met.
This typewriter is better than that [typewriter is].
When [she is] on the job, she is always competent and alert.

Placement of Clauses

A modifying clause should be placed as close as possible to the word or words it modifies. This placement will give maximum clarity, and it avoids the possibility that the reader will misinterpret written material. If intervening words muddy the overall meaning of a sentence, it should be rewritten or recast.

muddy
A memorandum is a piece of business writing, less formal than a letter, which serves as a means of interoffice communication.
recast
A memorandum, less formal than a letter, is a means of interoffice communication.

Restrictive and Nonrestrictive Clauses

Clauses that modify are also referred to as *restrictive* or *nonrestrictive.* Whether a clause is restrictive or nonrestrictive has a direct bearing on sentence punctuation. For information about punctuating restrictive and nonrestrictive clauses, see paragraph 10 under Comma, page 16.

1. Restrictive clauses are the so-called "bound" modifiers. They are absolutely essential to the meaning of the word or words they modify, they cannot be omitted without the meaning of the sentences being radically changed, and they are unpunctuated.

    Women who aren't competitive should not aspire to high corporate office.

    In this example, the restrictive clause "who aren't competitive" limits the classification of women, and thus is essential to the total meaning of the sentence. If, on the other hand, the restrictive clause is omitted as shown below, the classification of women is now not limited at all, and the sentence conveys an entirely different idea.

> Women should not aspire to high corporate office.

2. Nonrestrictive clauses are the so-called "free" modifiers. They are not inextricably bound to the word or words they modify but instead convey additional information about them. Nonrestrictive clauses may be omitted altogether without the meaning of the sentence being radically changed, and they are set off by commas; i.e., they are both preceded and followed by commas when they occur in mid-sentence.

> Our guide, who wore a green beret, was an experienced traveler.

In this example, the nonrestrictive clause "who wore a green beret" does not restrict the classification of the guide; i.e., it does not set him apart from all other guides but merely serves as a bit of incidental detail. Removal of the nonrestrictive clause does not affect the meaning of the sentence:

> Our guide was an experienced traveler.

Tacked-on *Which* Clauses

Many writers try to avoid tacking a *which* clause onto the end of a sentence when the clause actually refers to the total idea of the sentence. It can usually be avoided by recasting the sentence.

> *tacked-on*
> The company is retooling, which I personally think is a wise move.
>
> *recast*
> The company's decision to retool is a wise move in my opinion.
>   *or*
> I believe that the company's decision to retool is wise.

Sentences

A sentence is a grammatically self-contained unit that consists of a word or a group of syntactically related words and that (1) expresses a statement (declarative sentence); (2) asks a question (interrogative sentence); (3) expresses a request or command (imperative sentence); or (4) expresses an exclamation (exclamatory sentence). A sentence typically contains both a subject and a predicate, begins with a capital letter, and ends with a punctuation mark.

Basic Types

Sentences are classified into three main types on the basis of their clause structure.

1. The *simple sentence* is a complete grammatical unit having one subject and one predicate (either or both of which may be compound).

   Paper is costly.
   Bond and tissue are costly.
   Bond and tissue are costly and are sometimes scarce.

2. The *compound sentence* is made up of two or more main clauses.

   I could arrange to arrive late, or I could simply send a proxy.
   This commute takes at least forty minutes by car, but we can make it in twenty by train.
   A few of the executives had Ph.D.'s, even more of them had B.A.'s, but the majority of them had both B.A.'s and M.B.A.'s.

3. The *complex sentence* combines a main clause with one or more subordinate clauses (subordinate clauses are italicized in the examples).

   The committee meeting began *when the business manager and the secretarial staff supervisor walked in.*
   Although the city council made some reforms, the changes came so late *that they could not prevent these abuses.*

Construction

The construction of grammatically sound sentences can be achieved by following some general guidelines.

1. Sentence coordination should be maintained by the use of connectives linking phrases or clauses of equal rank. When a connective is used to link phrases or clauses that are not equal, the resulting sentence is ineffective at best, and can be confusing.

   faulty coordination with improper use of "and"
   I was sitting in on a meeting, and he stood up and started a long rambling discourse on a new pollution-control device.
   recast (one clause subordinated)
   I sat in on a meeting during which he stood up and rambled on about a new pollution-control device.
   recast (two sentences)
   I sat in on that meeting. He stood up and rambled on about a new pollution-control device.

faulty coordination with improper use of "and"
This company employs a full-time research staff and was founded in 1945.

recast (one clause subordinated)
This company, which employs a full-time research staff, was founded in 1945.

recast (one clause reworded into a phrase)
Established in 1945, this company employs a full-time research staff.

2. Parallel, balanced sentence elements are necessary in order to achieve good sentence structure. When clauses having unparallel subjects are linked together, the resulting sentence can be unclear.

   unparallel
   The report gives market statistics, but he does not list his sources for these figures.

   parallel
   The report gives market statistics, but it does not list the sources for these figures.

   unparallel
   We are glad to have you as our client, and please call on us whenever you need help.

   parallel
   We are glad to have you as our client and we hope that you will call on us whenever you need help.

   recast into two sentences
   We are glad to have you as our client. Please do call on us whenever you need help.

3. In order for a sentence to read effectively, its elements should be tightly linked together. When sentence elements are strung together by loose or excessive use of *and*, the sentence as a whole can be too lengthy and lacking in logical flow to be readily understood.

   faulty coordination/excessive use of "and"
   This company is a Class 1 motor freight common carrier of general commodities and it operates over 10,000 tractors, trailers, and city delivery trucks through 200 terminals, and serves 40 states and the District of Columbia.

   recast into three shorter, more effective sentences
   This company is a Class 1 motor freight common carrier of general commodities. It operates over 10,000 tractors, trailers, and city delivery trucks through 200 terminals. The company serves 40 states and the District of Columbia.

4. The correct choice of a conjunction to link clauses is important in writing an effective sentence. *And* is a general coordinating conjunction which functions to join sentence elements.

If a sentence is expressing more than simple linkage, as when one clause is being contrasted with another, or when a reason or result is being expressed, a more specific conjunction should be used. For more on the specific functions of coordinating and subordinating conjunctions, see paragraphs 1–6 and 10–12 under Conjunction, pages 155–157 and 158 respectively.

> *too general*
> The economy was soft *and* we lost a lot of business.
>
> *specific*
> We lost a lot of business *because* the economy was soft.
> The economy was soft, *so* we lost a lot of business.
>
> *specific*
> The soft economy has cost us a lot of business.

5. Unnecessary or unexpected grammatical shifts in a sentence interrupt the reader's train of thought and needlessly complicate the material. Some unnecessary grammatical shifts are shown below, along with their improvements:

> *unnecessary shifts in verb voice*
> Any information you *can give* us *will be* greatly *appreciated* and we *assure* you that discretion *will be exercised* in its use.
>
> *rephrased* (note the italicized all-active verb voice)
> We *will appreciate* any information that you *can give* us. We *assure* you that we *will use* it with discretion.
>
> *unnecessary shifts in person*
> *One* can use either erasers or correction fluid to remove typographical errors; however, *you* should make certain that *your* corrections are clean.
>
> *rephrased* (note that the italicized pronouns are consistent)
> *One* can use either erasers or correction fluid to eradicate errors; however, *one* should make certain that *one's* corrections are clean.
>   *or*
> *You* can use either erasers or correction fluid to eradicate errors; however, *you* should make certain that *your* corrections are clean.
>
> *unnecessary shift from phrase to clause*
> *Because of the current parts shortage* and *we are experiencing a strike,* we cannot fill any orders now.
>
> *rephrased*
> *Because of a parts shortage and a strike,* we cannot fill any orders now.
>   *or*
> *Because we are hampered by a parts shortage and we are experiencing a strike,* we cannot fill any orders now.

6. A rational, logical ordering of sentence elements is a writer's best guarantee that the material will be understood. Closely related elements, for example, should be placed as close together as possible for the sake of maximum clarity.

related elements separated
We would appreciate your sending us the instructions on copy-editing by mail or cable.

related elements joined
We would appreciate your sending us by mail or by cable the copy-editing instructions.

We would appreciate your mailing or cabling us the copy-editing instructions.

We would appreciate it if you would mail or cable us the copy-editing instructions.

7. Sentences should form complete, independent grammatical units containing both a subject and a predicate. Exceptions are dialogue or specialized copy where fragmentation may be used for particular reasons (as to reflect speech or to attract the reader's attention).

   incomplete grammatical units
   During the last three years, our calculator sales soared. While our conventional office machine sales fell off.

   complete grammatical units
   During the last three years, our calculator sales soared, but our conventional office machine sales fell off.

   While our conventional office machine sales fell off during the last three years, our calculator sales soared.

   sentences fragmented for special effects in advertising
   See it now. The car for the Nineties . . . A car you'll want to own.

Sentence Length

Sentence length is directly related to the writer's purpose: there is no magic number of words that guarantees a good sentence. For example, an executive covering broad and yet complex topics in a long memorandum may choose concise, succinct sentences for the sake of clarity, impact, fast dictation, and readability. On the other hand, a writer who wants the reader to reflect on what is being said may employ longer, more involved sentences. Still another writer may juxtapose long and short sentences to emphasize an important point. The longer sentences may build up to a climactic and forceful short sentence.

Sentence Strategy

1. **Coordination and subordination** Either coordination or subordination or a mixture of both can be used to create a variety of stylistic writing effects. Coordination links independent sentences and sentence elements by means of coordinating conjunctions, while subordination transforms elements into dependent structures by means of subordinating conjunctions. Coordination tends to promote rather loose sentence

structure, which can become a fault; subordination tends to tighten the structure and to emphasize a main clause.

coordination
During the balance of 1983, this Company expects to issue $100,000,000 of long-term debt and equity securities *and* may guarantee up to $200,000,000 of new corporate bonds.

subordination
While this Company expects to issue $100,000,000 of long-term debt and equity securities during the balance of 1983, it may also guarantee up to $200,000,000 of new corporate bonds.

2. **Interrupting elements** Interrupting the normal flow of discourse by inserting comments can be a useful device to call attention to an aside, to emphasize a word or phrase, to convey a particular tone (as forcefulness), or to make the prose a little more informal. Interrupting elements should be used with discretion; too many of them may distract the reader and disrupt his or her train of thought. The following are examples of effective interrupted sentences:

an aside
His evidence, if reliable, could send our client to prison.

emphasis
These companies—ours as well as theirs—must show more profits.

forcefulness
This, ladies and gentlemen, is the prime reason for your cost overruns. I trust it will not happen again?

3. **Parallelism and balance** While interruption breaks up the flow of discourse, parallelism and balance work together toward maintaining an even, rhythmic thought flow. Parallelism means a similarity in the grammatical construction of adjacent phrases and clauses that are equivalent, complementary, or antithetical in meaning.

These ecological problems are of crucial concern *to* scientists, *to* businessmen, *to* government officials, and *to* all citizens.

Our attorneys have argued *that* the trademark is ours, *that* our rights have been violated, and *that* appropriate compensation is required.

He was respected not only *for his intelligence* but also *for his integrity.*

Balance is the juxtaposition and equipoise of two or more syntactically parallel constructions (as phrases and clauses) that contain similar, contrasting, or opposing ideas:

To err is human; to forgive, divine.

—Alexander Pope

> Ask not what your country can do for you—ask what you can do for your country.
>
> —John F. Kennedy

And finally, a series can be an effective way to emphasize a thought and to establish a definite prose rhythm:

> The thing that interested me . . . about New York . . . was the . . . contrast it showed between the dull and the shrewd, the strong and the weak, the rich and the poor, the wise and the ignorant. . . .
>
> —Theodore Dreiser

4. Periodic and cumulative sentences Stylistically, there are two basic types of sentences—the periodic and the cumulative or loose. The periodic sentence is structured so that its main idea or its thrust is suspended until the very end, thereby drawing the reader's eye and mind along to an emphatic conclusion. In the example below, the main point follows the final comma.

> While the Commission would wish to give licensees every encouragement to experiment on their own initiative with new and different means of providing access to their stations for the discussion of important public issues, it cannot justify the imposition of a specific right of access by government fiat.
>
> —*Television/Radio Age*

The cumulative sentence, on the other hand, is structured so that its main point appears first, followed by other phrases or clauses expanding on or supporting it. In the following example, the main point precedes the first comma.

> The solution must be finely honed, lest strategists err too much on the side of sophistication only to find that U.S. military forces can be defeated by overwhelming mass.
>
> —William C. Moore

The final phrase or clause in a cumulative sentence theoretically could be deleted without skewing or destroying the essential meaning of the total sentence. A cumulative sentence is therefore more loosely structured than a periodic sentence.

5. Reversal A reversal of customary or expected sentence order is another effective stylistic strategy, when used sparingly, because it injects a dash of freshness, unexpectedness, and originality into the prose.

customary or expected order
I find that these realities are indisputable: the economy has taken a drastic downturn, costs on all fronts have soared, and jobs are at a premium.

reversal
That the economy has taken a drastic downturn; that costs on all fronts have soared; that jobs are at a premium—these are the realities that I find indisputable.

6. **Rhetorical questions** The rhetorical question is yet another device to focus the reader's attention on a problem or an issue. The rhetorical question requires no specific response from the reader but often merely sets up the introduction of the writer's own view. In some instances, a rhetorical question works as a topic sentence in a paragraph; in other instances, a whole series of rhetorical questions may spotlight pertinent issues for the reader's consideration.

What can be done to correct the problem? Two things, to begin with: never discuss cases out of the office, and never allow a visitor to see the papers on your desk.

7. **Variety** As a means of keeping the reader's attention, careful writers try to maintain a balance of different kinds of sentences. For example, they may use a combination of simple, compound, and complex sentences in a paragraph, together with a variey of short and long sentences. Writers also vary the beginnings of their sentences so that every sentence in a paragraph does not begin directly with the subject. Any kind of repetitious pattern creates monotony. Through judicious use of combinations of sentence patterns and the sentence strategies discussed in the preceding pragraphs, a writer can attain an interesting, diversified style.

Paragraphs

The underlying structure of any written communication—be it a memorandum, a letter, or a report—must be controlled by the writer if the material is to be clear, coherent, logical in progression, and effective. Since good paragraphing is a means to this end, it is essential that the writer become adept at using techniques of paragraph development and of transition between paragraphs. In order to do this, writers should be able to recognize various kinds of paragraphs and their functions as well as the potential problems that might arise in structuring a logical paragraph system. In this way, they should be able to spot possible discrepancies that might result in misinterpretation by the reader or that might detract from the total effect of the communication.

A paragraph is a subdivision in writing that consists of one or more sentences, that deals with one or more ideas, or that quotes a speaker or a source. The first line of a paragraph is indented in reports, studies, articles, theses, and books. However, the first line of a paragraph in business letters and memorandums may or may not be indented, depending on the style being followed.

Paragraphs should not be considered as isolated entities that are self-contained and mechanically lined up without transitions or interrelationship of ideas. Rather, paragraphs should be viewed as components of larger groups or blocks that are tightly interlinked and that interact in the sequential development of a major idea or cluster of ideas. The overall coherence of a communication depends on this interaction.

Individual paragraphs and paragraph blocks are flexible: their length, internal structure, and purpose vary according to the writer's intention and his own style. For example, one writer may be able to express his point in a succinct, one-sentence paragraph, while another may require several sentences to make his point. Writers' concepts of paragraphing also differ. For instance, some writers think of paragraphs as a means of dividing their material into logical segments with each unit developing one particular point in depth and in detail. Others view paragraphs as a means of emphasizing particular points or adding variety to long passages.

Development of Paragraphs

Depending on the writer's intentions, paragraph development may take any of the following directions:

1. The paragraph may move from the general to the specific.

2. The paragraph may move from the specific to the general.

3. The paragraph may exhibit an alternating order of comparison and contrast.

4. The paragraph may chronicle events in a set temporal order—e.g., from the beginning to the end, or from the end to the beginning.

5. The paragraph may describe something (as a group of objects) in a set spatial order—e.g., the items being described may be looked at from near-to-far, or vice versa.

6. The paragraph may follow a climactic sequence with the least important facts or examples described first followed by a buildup of tension leading to the most important facts or examples then followed by a gradual easing of tension. Other material can be so ordered for effectiveness; for example, facts or issues that are easy to comprehend or accept may be

set forth first and followed by those that are more difficult to comprehend or accept. In this way the easier material prepares the reader to comprehend or accept the more difficult points.

7. Anticlimactic order is also useful when the writer's intent is to persuade the reader. With this strategy, the writer sets forth the most persuasive arguments first so that the reader, having been influenced in a positive way by that persuasion, moves along with the rest of the argument with a growing feeling of assent.

Effective Paragraphing

The following material outlines some ways of building effective paragraphs within a text.

A topic sentence—a key sentence to which the other sentences in the paragraph are related—may be placed either at the beginning or at the end of a paragraph. A lead-in topic sentence should present the main idea in the paragraph and should set the initial tone of the material that follows. A terminal topic sentence should be an analysis, a conclusion, or a summation of what has gone before it.

A single-sentence paragraph can be used to achieve easy transition from a preceding to a subsequent paragraph (especially when the paragraphs are long and complex) if it repeats an important word or phrase from the preceding paragraph, if it contains a pronoun reference to a key individual mentioned in a preceding paragraph, or if it is introduced by an appropriate conjunction or conjunctive adverb that connects the paragraphs.

1. Since the very first paragraph sets initial tone, introduces the subject or topic under discussion, and leads into the main thrust of a communication, it should be worded so as to immediately attract the reader's attention and arouse interest. These openings can be effective:
   A. a succinct statement of purpose or point of view
   B. a concise definition (as of a problem)
   C. a lucid statement of a key issue or fact

2. These openings, by contrast, can blunt the point of the rest of the material:
   A. an apology for the material to be presented
   B. a querulous complaint or a defensive posture
   C. a detailed account of material presented earlier
   D. a presentation of self-evident facts
   E. a group of sentences rendered limp and meaningless because of clichés

3. The last paragraph ties together all of the ideas and points that have been set forth earlier and reemphasizes the main thrust of the communication. These can be effective endings:

   A. a setting forth of the most important conclusion or conclusions drawn from the preceding discussion
   B. a final analysis of the main problem or problems under discussion
   C. a lucid summary of the individual points brought up earlier
   D. a final, clear statement of opinion or position
   E. concrete suggestions or solutions if applicable
   F. specific questions asked of the reader if applicable

4. The following endings, by contrast, can reduce the effectiveness of a communication:

   A. apologies for a poor presentation
   B. qualifying remarks that blunt or negate incisive points made earlier
   C. insertion of minor details or afterthoughts
   D. a meaningless closing couched in clichés

5. The following are tests of good paragraphs:

   A. Does the paragraph have a clear purpose? Is its utility evident, or is it there just to fill up space?
   B. Does the paragraph clarify rather than cloud the writer's ideas?
   C. Is the paragraph adequately developed, or does it merely raise other questions that the writer does not attempt to answer? If a position is being taken, does the writer include supporting information and statistics that are essential to its defense?
   D. Are the length and wording of all the paragraphs sufficiently varied, or does the writer employ the same types of locutions again and again?
   E. Is the sentence structure coherent?
   F. Is each paragraph unified? Do all the sentences really *belong* there; or does the writer digress into areas that would have been better covered in another paragraph or that could have been omitted altogether?
   G. Are the paragraphs coherent so that one sentence leads clearly and logically to another? Is easy, clear transition between paragraphs effected by a wise selection of transitional words and phrases which indicate relationships between ideas and signal the direction in which the writer's presentation is moving?
   H. Does one paragraph simply restate in other terms what has been said before?

Chapter 7

Notes and Bibliographies

CONTENTS

Writers and editors often need to provide readers with documentation of the source of a quotation or a piece of information. Authors may also wish to provide additional information and commentary or cross-references. This type of information is usually included in a note, which may take the form of a footnote at the bottom of a page, an endnote at the end of a chapter or at the end of a work, or a note in parentheses.

Authors and editors use various methods to indicate the source of a given quotation or piece of information. In works related to the social and natural sciences, writers have relied on a system of parenthetical references within the text that refer readers to a list of sources at the end of the work or one of its divisions. In works related to the humanities, the footnote form has traditionally been preferred. In recent years, however, the footnote form has become slightly less popular, as some style books have urged writers in the humanities to adopt parenthetical references.

This chapter describes both the footnote or endnote system and the system of parenthetical references. For both of these systems, the examples in this chapter illustrate generally acceptable ways of styling references. However, writers and editors should be aware that many professions and academic disciplines have developed their own systems for documenting sources, and some of these systems differ from the stylings illustrated in this chapter.

Footnotes and Endnotes

A footnote or an endnote keys full bibliographical information about a source, including author, title, place of publication, publisher, date, and page number, to a specific text passage making use of that source. The text passage is marked with a number, and all such notes are set aside from the rest of the text. Notes that appear at the bottom of the page are called *footnotes*. Notes that appear at the end of the chapter or at the end of an entire work are called *endnotes*.

Some recently published style manuals have discouraged the use of footnotes and endnotes for providing readers with bibliographical information about sources. Among the obvious difficulties with footnotes is that they are troublesome for typists to type and expensive for typesetters to set. The problem is that it is necessary to reserve sufficient space at the bottom of each page to allow for the notes that go with the text on that page. While the last note on a page may go over to the next page, each note should begin on the same page on which its number appears in the text. If there are many notes on a page, the result can be an unattractive page with more space given to footnotes than to text. And in some cases, there may be no way to get each footnote to begin on the same page as its text reference without rewriting some portion of the main text or the footnote or both.

The disadvantage of endnotes is primarily one of inconvenience for the reader, who has to flip back and forth in the book from the main text to the notes. This can be especially frustrating when the note contains no more than a page reference to a work already cited.

The use of parenthetical references to document sources does not guarantee that writers and readers will be saved entirely from these disadvantages. However, it does usually result in fewer footnotes or endnotes, and it does allow authors to treat notes that provide strictly bibliographical information—the details of which readers are often willing to do without—differently from notes that provide commentary, cross-references, or additional information. For more on the styling of parenthetical references, see the section on Parenthetical References in this chapter.

Placement of the Elements

Footnotes and endnotes to a text are indicated by unpunctuated Arabic superior numbers (or reference symbols, discussed later in this section) placed immediately after the quotation or information with no intervening space. The number is usually placed at the end of a sentence or clause, or at some other natural break in the sentence when the reference material is not a quotation. The number follows all marks of punctuation except the dash. If a terminal quotation mark appears (as at the end of a short quotation that is included in the running text), the numeral is placed outside the final quotation mark with no space intervening (see the sample on page 200). The numbering may be consecutive throughout

According to Lesikar, if a "quoted passage is four lines or less in length, it is typed with the report text and is distinguished from the normal text by quotation marks."[17] However, a different procedure is used for longer quotations:

> But if a longer quotation (five lines or more) is used, the conventional practice is to set it in from both left and right margins (about five spaces) but without quotation marks. . . . The quoted passage is further distinguished from the report writer's work by single spacing. . . .[18]

A series of usually three periods called ellipsis is used to indicate omissions of material from a passage.[19]

Footnotes may be placed "at the bottom of the page . . . separated from the text by a horizontal line. If a line is used, it is typed a single space below the text and followed by one blank line."[20] Lesikar prefers the separation line to be one and one-half or two inches.[21] Generally, typewriting textbooks state that a two-inch line is adequate (20 pica strokes; 24 elite strokes). The line is constructed by striking the underscore key.

From a typing standpoint, reserve three lines of blank typing space per footnote at the bottom of the page.

---

17. Report Writing for Business (Homewood, Ill.: Richard D. Irwin, Inc., 1981), p. 187.

18. Ibid.

19. Ibid., p. 188.

20. Ruth I. Anderson et al., The Administrative Secretary: Resource (New York: McGraw-Hill Book Company, 1970), p. 391.

21. Lesikar, op. cit., p. 189.

Figure 7.1. A typewritten page with footnotes

the work or, as in the case of book-length works, it may begin again with each new chapter. Footnote numbers like 7a and 7b, which usually result from last-minute revisions in the manuscript, are to be avoided, even if it means renumbering all the notes in the copy.

The text of the note itself is introduced with the applicable Arabic numeral or reference symbol. The numeral may be a superior numeral, unpunctuated and separated from the first word of the footnote by one space, or it may be set on the line and followed by a period and one or two spaces. The latter styling has become more popular recently and is much easier to type.

traditional styling
⁷ Ibid., p. 223.

newer styling
7. Ibid., p. 223.

The indention of footnote and endnote text varies according to individual preference. Indenting the first line of the footnote to a paragraph indent with runover lines returning to flush left (as shown on pages 202 and 206) is probably the most common styling. However, the flush-left styling and the flush-and-hang styling, in which the first line is set flush left and succeeding lines are indented, are also common. The following examples reproduce the first three footnotes on page 202. In these examples, the reference number is set on the line in the flush-left styling and is raised in the flush-and-hang styling; however, either of the positions for reference numbers may be used with any of the indention styles.

flush left
1. Jennie Mason, *Introduction to Word Processing* (Indianapolis: Bobbs-Merrill, 1981), p. 55.
2. John E. Warriner and Francis Griffith, *English Grammar and Composition* (New York: Harcourt Brace Jovanovich, 1977), p. 208.
3. Ruth I. Anderson et al., *The Administrative Secretary: Resource* (New York: McGraw-Hill, 1970), p. 357.

flush and hang
¹ Jennie Mason, *Introduction to Word Processing* (Indianapolis: Bobbs-Merrill, 1981), p. 55.
² John E. Warriner and Francis Griffith, *English Grammar and Composition* (New York: Harcourt Brace Jovanovich, 1977), p. 208.
³ Ruth I. Anderson et al., *The Administrative Secretary: Resource* (New York: McGraw-Hill, 1970), p. 357.

In typewritten publications, the notes themselves are usually single-spaced, but double spacing is used between notes. When a

NOTES

1. Jennie Mason, *Introduction to Word Processing* (Indianapolis: Bobbs-Merrill, 1981), p. 55.

2. John E. Warriner and Francis Griffith, *English Grammar and Composition* (New York: Harcourt Brace Jovanovich, 1977), p. 208.

3. Ruth I. Anderson et al., *The Administrative Secretary: Resource* (New York: McGraw-Hill, 1970), p. 357.

4. Simone de Beauvoir, *The Second Sex,* trans. and ed. H. M. Parshley (New York: Alfred A. Knopf, 1953), p. 600.

5. Alfred H. Markwardt, *American English,* ed. J. L. Dillard (New York: Oxford University Press, 1980), p. 94.

6. Martha L. Manheimer, *Style Manual: A Guide for the Preparation of Reports and Dissertations,* Books in Library and Information Science, vol. 5 (New York: Marcel Dekker, 1973), p. 14.

7. Charles T. Brushaw, Gerald J. Alred, and Walter E. Oliu, *Handbook of Technical Writing,* 2d ed. (New York: St. Martins Press, 1982), pp. 182–184.

8. National Micrographics Association, *An Introduction to Micrographics,* rev. ed. (Silver Spring, Md.: National Micrographics Association, 1980), p. 42.

9. *The World Almanac and Book of Facts* (New York: Newspaper Enterprises Association, Inc., 1985), p. 310.

10. *Rules for Alphabetical Filing as Standardized by ARMA* (Prairie Village, Kans.: Association of Records Managers and Administrators, 1981), p. 14.

11. Peggy F. Bradbury, ed., *Transcriber's Guide to Medical Terminology* (New Hyde Park, N.Y.: Medical Examination Publishing Co., 1973), p. 446.

12. Kemp Malone, "The Phonemes of Current English," *Studies for William A. Read,* ed. Nathaniel M. Caffee and Thomas A. Kirby (Baton Rouge: Louisiana State University Press, 1940), p. 133–165.

13. Robert Chambers, *Cyclopaedia of English Literature,* 2 vols. (New York: World Publishing House, 1875), vol. 1, p. 45.

Figure 7.2. A page of endnotes illustrating footnote and endnote style for references to books

manuscript is being typed prior to typesetting, however, the notes should be double-spaced internally with triple spacing between the notes. In typeset material, footnotes and endnotes are usually set in type that is one or two points smaller than the text type. Extra space may or may not be placed between the notes according to individual preference.

When endnotes rather than footnotes are being used, all of the notes are gathered together in a single list (as shown on page 202) either at the end of a chapter or other section or at the end of an entire work. When a book uses a single note section at the end of the entire work, the section is usually divided with chapter headings to indicate where the notes of a particular chapter begin and end. An endnote may be styled in any of the ways that a footnote is styled.

Content and Styling for First References

Both footnotes and endnotes provide full bibliographical information for a source the first time it is cited; however, in subsequent references, this information is provided in an abbreviated manner. The following paragraphs describe the content and style used for first references. Subsequent references are discussed later in this section. Examples of the stylings described in this section are shown on pages 202 and 206. (The content and style for entries in bibliographies and lists of references are given in the section on Bibliographies and Lists of References later in this chapter.)

Books A footnote or endnote that refers to a book contains as many of the following elements as are relevant. Examples of each of the elements described below can be found in the references on page 202.

  1. *Author's name* In footnotes and endnotes, the author's first name comes first and the last name after. If there are more than three authors, the first author's name is followed by the phrase *et al.*, which is an abbreviation for the phrase *et alii* or *et aliae*, meaning "and others." (For examples of notes describing books with multiple authors, see notes 2, 3, and 7 on page 202.) If a publication is issued by a group or organization and no individual is mentioned on the title page, the name of the group or organization may be used in place of an author's name; in this case, the group or organization is thought of as being the corporate author. (For an example of a note describing a work with a corporate author, see note 8 on page 202.) In footnotes and endnotes, the author's name is followed by a comma.

2. *Title of the work* The title is underlined in typewritten manuscript and italicized in type. Each word of the title is capitalized except for articles and short prepositions other than the first word. In cases in which no author's name is used in the note, the title comes first. This is commonly the styling for well-known reference books and for publications that have corporate authors but are more likely to be known by their titles. (For examples of notes in which the title comes first, see notes 9 and 10 on page 202.)

3. *Portion of the book* If a reference is to one portion of a book (as an essay within a collection), the name of the portion should be included. The titles of chapters within nonfiction works by a single author are usually not part of a footnote reference. The titles of parts of books, such as short poems, short stories, and essays, are enclosed in quotation marks. (For an example of a reference to a work within a collection, see note 12 on page 202.)

4. *Editor, compiler, or translator* The name of an editor, compiler, or translator is preceded by the abbreviation *ed., comp.,* or *trans.* or some combination of them joined by *and.* The abbreviation is separated from the title that precedes it by a comma. (For examples of notes describing a book with a translator or editor, see notes 4, 5, and 12 on page 202.) If there is no author mentioned on the title page of the book, the name of the editor, compiler, or translator is placed first in the note, followed by the abbreviation *ed., comp.,* or *trans.* (For an example of a note in which the editor's name comes first, see note 11 on page 202.)

5. *Name of the series* If a book is part of a series, the name of the series should be included. If the book corresponds to a specific volume in that series, the volume number is also included. The volume number is separated from the title by a comma. The name of the series is separated from the title of the volume by a comma and is capitalized as a title, but it is not underlined or italicized. (For an example of a note describing a book that is part of a series, see note 6 on page 202.)

6. *Edition* If a work is other than the first edition, the number or the nature of the edition should be indicated. (For examples of notes describing books that are not first editions, see notes 7 and 8 on page 202.)

7. *Volume number* If a work has more than one volume, the total number of volumes is given after the title and edition data.

In addition, the number of the particular volume cited should precede the page number. In traditional footnote styling, a *vol.* or *vols.* precedes the volume number, but many authors now omit these abbreviations. (For an example of a note referring to a multivolume work, see note 13 on page 202.)

8. *Publishing data* The city of publication, the name of the publisher, and the year of publication should all be included. These items are usually placed within parentheses; a colon separates the city from the publisher's name. Names of states may be abbreviated, but not names of cities. A comma separates the publisher's name from the year of issue.

9. *Page number* The number of the page on which the quotation or piece of information can be found should be included. In traditional footnote styling a *p.* or *pp.* precedes the page number or numbers; however, many authors now omit those abbreviations.

Periodicals A footnote or endnote describing an article in a periodical should include all of the following information that is relevant. Examples of each of the elements described below can be found in the sample references on the next page.

1. *Author's name* The author's name is treated in the same way as described above for a reference to a book. The names of writers of letters to a periodical and contributors of signed book reviews are treated like names of authors. (For examples of references to a letter and to a signed review, see notes 6 and 7 in figure 7.3 on page 206.)

2. *Title of the article* The title of the article is enclosed in quotation marks. The words of the title are capitalized as in a book title. The title of the article is followed by a comma that is placed inside the quotation marks.

3. *Name of the periodical* The name of the periodical is treated in the way described above for the title of a book.

4. *Volume and number of the periodical* If a periodical uses both volume and number designations to identify an issue, both should be used. If a periodical uses some other system for identifying issues (as the month and year of issue), that system should be used. Note 1 on page 206 illustrates a reference to a periodical in which pages are numbered consecutively through a volume, and therefore only a volume number is required. Note 2 illustrates a reference to a periodical that uses a seasonal designation as well as volume and number designa-

---

NOTES

1. John Heil, "Seeing is Believing," *American Philosophical Quarterly* 19 (1982): 229–239.

2. Donald K. Ourecky, "Cane and Bush Fruits," *Plants & Gardens* 27, No. 3 (Autumn 1971): pp. 13–15.

3. Xan Smiley, "Misunderstanding Africa," *Atlantic* (Sept. 1982); pp. 70–79.

4. Shiva Naipaul, "A Trinidad Childhood," *New Yorker* (17 Sept. 1984): pp. 63–64.

5. Gail Pitts, "Money Funds Holding Own," *Morning Union* [Springfield, Mass.] (Aug. 23, 1982): p. 6.

6. Jeremy C. Rosenberg, "Letters," *Advertising Age* (7 June, 1982): p. M–1.

7. M. O. Vassell, rev. of *Applied Charged Particle Optics,* ed. A. Septier, *American Scientist* 70 (1982): 229.

8. Joyce A. Velasquez, "The Format of Formal Reports," report prepared for the Southern Engineering Company, Johnson City, Miss. (May 29, 1985).

9. Clive Johnson, letter to Elizabeth O'Hara, 9 Nov. 1916, Johnson Collection, item 5298, California State Historical Society, San Marino, Calif.

Figure 7.3. Sample notes showing footnote and endnote styling for references to periodicals and unpublished sources

tions for each issue, and which paginates each issue independently of the volume. Note 3 illustrates a reference to a monthly magazine. Most monthly magazines have a volume and number designation somewhere in them, but they are more commonly referred to by month and year.

5. *Issue date* Periodicals variously use months, days, and years to identify issues. The date is written in whatever form the periodical uses, but the names of the months may be abbreviated.

6. *Page number* The number of the page on which the quotation or piece of information can be found is included. The varying use and omission of the abbreviation *p.* or *pp.* as described above for books hold true for references to periodicals as well. One situation in which the abbreviation is almost always

dropped occurs when the reference is to a volume number and page number only. In that case, the volume number and page number are separated by a colon, and neither is identified with an abbreviation. Notes 1 and 7 on page 206 illustrate this styling.

NOTE: In making the decision of whether or not to include the abbreviation, writers and editors should keep in mind the needs of their readers. If most of the readers are well acquainted with footnote style, the abbreviation can be safely dropped. However, if a significant number of the readers of a text are unfamiliar with footnote styling, including the identifying abbreviation will help lessen the chances of confusion.

Unpublished materials A footnote referring to a work that is unpublished should include as many of the following elements as are known or are relevant. The elements described below are illustrated in notes 8 and 9 on page 206.

1. *Author's name* The author's name is treated in the same way as described above for a book.

2. *Title of the work* The title is enclosed in quotation marks and capitalized like a book title.

3. *The nature of the material* The reference should include a description of the document (as "letter" or "dissertation").

4. *Date* Include the date of the material if it is known.

5. *Folio number or other identification number* Include whatever kind of identification number is conventionally used with the material.

6. *Geographical location of the material* Include the name of the institution where the materials can be found and the city where the institution is located.

Style and Content for Subsequent References

There are two systems that are currently used to refer to a source that has already been cited. One makes use of a shortened footnote styling; the other uses Latin abbreviations. Both systems are described below.

Shortened footnotes When the same source is cited repeatedly with intervening footnotes, shortened footnotes may be used as space-saving devices. The following styling is generally acceptable for most publications.

1. If the author's name occurs in the running text, it need not be repeated in footnote references to the work after the first one.

   first reference

      1. Albert H. Marckwardt, *American English* (New York: Oxford University Press, 1980), p. 94.

   repeated reference

      2. *American English,* p. 95.

2. If the author's name does not appear in the running text prior to a repeated reference, either of the following stylings may be used. The styling of footnote 3 should be followed if more than one work by the same author is cited within the text.

   repeated reference

      3. Marckwardt, *American English,* p. 95.

      or

      4. Marckwardt, p. 95.

3. In repeated references to books by more than one author, the authors' names may be shortened. The styling of footnote 6 should be followed if more than one work by the same authors is cited within the text.

   first reference

      5. De Witt T. Starnes and Gertrude E. Noyes, *The English Dictionary from Cawdrey to Johnson 1604–1775* (Chapel Hill: University of North Carolina Press, 1946), p. 120.

   repeated reference

      6. Starnes and Noyes, *The English Dictionary from Cawdrey to Johnson 1604–1775,* p. 126.

      or

      7. Starnes and Noyes, p. 126.

4. A long title may be shortened if it has already been given in full in an earlier footnote.

      8. Starnes and Noyes, *The English Dictionary,* p. 126.

5. A shortened reference to an article in a periodical that has been cited earlier should include the author's last name; the title of the article, which can be shortened if it is a long one, and if no similar title by the same author is being cited; and the page number.

      9. Goldman, "Warren G. Harding," p. 45.

Latin abbreviations While the simplified and shortened footnote stylings described above have gained wide currency, some writers still prefer to use the traditional Latin abbreviations *ibid., loc. cit.,* and *op. cit.* as space-savers in repeated references to sources cited earlier. Current usage indicates that these abbreviations need no longer be typed with underscoring or italicized in type; however, some writers still prefer this traditional styling. When a page reference follows one of these abbreviations, it may or may not be set off with a comma.

>   10. Ibid. pp. 95–98.
>   *or*
>   11. Ibid., pp. 95–98.

These Latin abbreviations are capitalized when they appear at the beginning of a footnote or endnote, but not otherwise.

The abbreviation *ibid.* (for *ibidem,* "in the same place") is used when the writer is referring to the work cited in the immediately preceding footnote. The abbreviation may be used several times in succession.

> *first reference*
>   12. Simone de Beauvoir, *The Second Sex,* trans. and ed. H. M. Parshley (New York: Alfred A. Knopf, 1953), p. 600.

> *repeated reference* (immediately following note 12)
>   13. Ibid., p. 609.

> *repeated reference* (immediately following note 13)
>   14. Ibid.

When *ibid.* is used without a page number, it indicates that the same page of the same source is being cited as in the footnote immediately preceding. Thus, note 14 above cites page 609 of *The Second Sex.*

The abbreviations *loc. cit.* (for *loco citato,* "in the place cited") and *op. cit.* (for *opere citato,* "in the work cited") may be used only in conjunction with the author's name, which may occur in the running text or at the beginning of the first reference. When the writer cites a book or periodical, its complete title should be included the first time it is referred to in a footnote. In subsequent references, *loc. cit.* or *op. cit.* with or without page numbers may be substituted for the title, depending on the type of citation.

The difference between *loc. cit.* and *op. cit.* is that *loc. cit.* is used only when referring to the same page or pages of the same source cited earlier with footnotes intervening, while *op. cit.* is used to refer to a source cited earlier but not to the same page or pages of that source.

> *first reference*
>   15. De Witt T. Starnes and Gertrude E. Noyes, *The English Dictionary from Cawdrey to Johnson 1604–1775* (Chapel Hill: University of North Carolina Press, 1946), pp. 119–133.

repeated reference (with other footnotes intervening)
    18. Starnes and Noyes, loc. cit.
    21. Starnes and Noyes, loc. cit., p. 119.

The note without a page number indicates that pages 119–133 are being cited again.
    Examples of the use of *op. cit.* are as follows:

first reference
    22. Albert H. Marckwardt, *American English* (New York: Oxford University Press, 1980), p. 94.

repeated reference
    24. Marckwardt, op. cit., p. 98.

The title of the work rather than the Latin abbreviation should be used if the writer is using material from more than one work by the same author.

Nonbibliographical Footnotes and Endnotes

Nonbibliographical notes provide additional information, commentary, or cross-references that the author does not want to include in the main text. They are keyed to the text in the same way as bibliographical notes. In texts in which bibliographical notes are keyed with superior numerals, nonbibliographical notes are included in the same sequence, as in the examples below.

    1. Lyon Richardson, *A History of Early American Magazines* (New York: Thomas Nelson and Sons, 1931), p. 8.
    2. Total average circulation per issue of magazines reporting to the Bureau of Circulation rose from 96.8 million in 1939 to 147.8 million in 1945.
    3. For a particularly compelling account of this episode, see James P. Wood, *Magazines in the United States* (New York: The Ronald Press Company, 1949), pp. 92–108.
    4. Richardson, op. cit., p. 42.
    5. For more details, see Appendix.

Texts that rely on parenthetical references for bibliographical notes can still include footnotes or endnotes for other notes. When a nonbibliographical note mentions the name of a book or article that is not the source of a quotation or piece of information in the text, footnote styling is used to describe the reference.

In some publications, there are certain nonbibliographical notes that are not keyed to the text with any kind of symbol. These include notes that an editor places at the beginning of each part of a collection of works by different authors and that identify each author. They also include notes that an author uses to acknowledge those who gave assistance or contributed to the writing of the work. One reason that these notes are not keyed is that the only logical place to put the reference mark (described below) or number would be following the title of the work or the name of the author (both of which are often set in a larger distinctive type style), and some editors and designers are reluctant to use footnote symbols in this position. These unnumbered notes are conventionally placed in the footnote position on the first page.

Reference Marks

In texts that have only a limited number of footnotes or endnotes, writers sometimes substitute reference marks for reference numbers. The traditional footnote reference symbols are listed below in the order in which they are usually used.

- * asterisk
- † dagger
- ‡ double dagger
- § section mark
- ‖ parallels
- ¶ paragraph mark
- # number sign

The sequence of these symbols can begin anew with each page or with each chapter. If more than seven notes are needed in a sequence, the reference marks are doubled, as **, ††, etc.; however, if such a large number of footnotes is needed, reference numbers rather than reference symbols should probably be used. A common alternative to using the full set of symbols when only a few footnotes are needed is to use an asterisk for the first note, a double asterisk for the second, and so on without using the dagger or other marks. A variation on this that works for up to four footnotes in a sequence is to use the asterisk and dagger in the following order: *, **, †, ††.

Parenthetical References

Parenthetical references present very abbreviated bibliographical information (typically the name of the author followed by a page number, but sometimes just a page number) enclosed in parentheses. They are placed in the main body of the text, and they refer the reader to a list of references that is found at the end of the article, chapter, or book. A list of references is simply a bibliography, and details regarding its content and styling are presented in the section on Bibliographies and Lists of References, later in this chapter. For purposes of convenience, a sample list of references is included on page 213, and all parenthetical references in this section refer to it.

Parenthetical formats have the advantage of providing essential and useful information within the text, without providing so much information that reading the text is impeded. They can help the reader decide whether to turn to the list of references for further information.

The practice of using parenthetical references originated in the social and natural sciences; however, its adoption for writing in the humanities, and for all general writing that includes numerous bibliographical references, is being encouraged more and more. Most systems of parenthetical references are similar, but differences in details of styling do exist among the systems used by various academic disciplines and professional organizations. The examples in this section of the book are styled in accordance with the precepts of the *MLA Handbook for Writers of Research Papers,* second edition, to which readers of this book are referred for more details regarding parenthetical references. A discussion of a different parenthetical reference system used in the sciences follows at the end of this section.

Placement of the Reference

Parenthetical references are placed immediately after the quotation or piece of information whose source they refer to. The sample on page 214 reproduces the text of the sample on page 200 and shows how the same text would appear using parenthetical references instead of footnotes. Note especially that sentence punctuation (that is, punctuation not associated with a quotation) is placed after the reference. This means that periods and commas are placed outside of quotation marks and that run-in quoted sentences that end in an omission are styled with three spaced ellipsis points before the reference and a terminal period closed-up after the reference. If the final sentence of the extract quotation on page 214 had been set as a run-in quotation, it would appear as follows:

> Lesikar says, "The quoted passage is further distinguished from the report writer's work by single spacing . . ." (187).

Content and Style of Parenthetical References

The content and style are determined by two factors: (1) the style and content of the first element of the entry in the list of references to which it refers and (2) the bibliographical information that is included in the text around it.

These general principles are illustrated in the example on page 214. For instance, in the third paragraph, the parenthetical reference "(Anderson et al. 391)" is given because, in the list of

List of References

Anderson, Ruth I., et al. *The Administrative Secretary: Resource.* New York: McGraw-Hill, 1970.

"Aristotle." *Webster's New Biographical Dictionary.* Springfield, Mass.: Merriam-Webster Inc., 1983.

Brushaw, Charles T., Gerald J. Alred, and Walter E. Oliu. *Handbook of Technical Writing.* 2d ed. New York: St. Martin's Press, 1982.

Chambers, Robert. *Cyclopaedia of English Literature.* 2 vols. New York: World Publishing House, 1875.

Lesikar, Raymond V. *Report Writing for Business.* Homewood, Ill.: Richard D. Irwin, Inc., 1981.

National Micrographics Association. *An Introduction to Micrographics.* Rev. ed. Silver Spring, Md.: National Micrographics Association, 1980.

Rules for Alphabetical Filing as Standardized by ARMA. Prairie Village, Kans.: Association of Record Managers and Administrators, 1981.

Figure 7.4. A sample list of references

references, the full reference to this source begins "Anderson, Ruth I., et al."

The way that bibliographical information in the text determines the styling of the parenthetical reference is illustrated in the first sentence of the first paragraph. The parenthetical reference "(187)" is sufficient, because it is clear that Lesikar is the author of the source that is being quoted. In the second paragraph, the full parenthetical reference "(Lesikar 188)" is required because it is not clear from the sentence who is the source of the information being provided.

Sometimes a reference is supported by citations to two separate sources; the two citations are enclosed in the same parentheses but are separated by a semicolon, as "(Lesikar 189; Anderson et al. 390)." Lengthy parenthetical references should be avoided because they interrupt the flow of text. Authors can avoid unwieldy parenthetical references by incorporating as much of the bibliographical information within the text as can be smoothly absorbed.

According to Lesikar, if a "quoted passage is four lines or less in length, it is typed with the report text and is distinguished from the normal text by quotation marks" (187). However, a different procedure is used for longer quotations:

> But if a longer quotation (five lines or more) is used, the conventional practice is to set it in from both left and right margins (about five spaces) but without quotation marks. . . . The quoted passage is further distinguished from the report writer's work by single spacing. . . . (187)

A series of usually three periods called ellipsis is used to indicate omissions of material from a passage (Lesikar 188).

Footnotes may be placed "at the bottom of the page . . . separated from the text by a horizontal line. If a line is used, it is typed a single space below the text and followed by one blank line" (Anderson et al. 391). Lesikar prefers the separation line to be one and one-half or two inches (189). Generally, typewriting textbooks state that a two-inch line is adequate (20 pica strokes; 24 elite strokes). The line is constructed by striking the underscore key.

From a typing standpoint, reserve three lines of blank typing space per footnote at the bottom of the page.

The first line of a footnote is indented from one to six (but usually two or five) spaces from the left margin, depending on the writer's preference or the style manual being followed. The footnote may be introduced with the applicable superscript Arabic numeral, unpunctuated and separated from the first letter of the author's first name by one space; or it may be introduced by the

Figure 7.5. A typewritten page with parenthetical references

Matching the list of references The name in a parenthetical reference must correspond to a name that begins an entry in the list of references. In general, the last name of the author is usually sufficient within a parenthetical reference, as it was in the case of the references to Lesikar's book in the sample on page 214. However, if there had been another author with the last name Lesikar in the list of references, it would have been necessary to include both first and last name, as "(Lesikar, Raymond, 188)." Alternatively, if the list of references had included two different books both of which were by Raymond Lesikar, it would have been necessary to include both the author's name and the book's title (which may be shortened) in the parenthetical reference, as "(Lesikar, *Report Writing* 188)." The following paragraphs explain some other special cases.

1. *A work with two or three authors* The list of references on page 213 includes an entry for a book by Charles T. Brushaw, Gerald J. Alred, and Walter E. Oliu. A parenthetical reference to that work would take the following form:

   (Brushaw, Alred, and Oliu 182–184)

2. *A work with more than three authors* A work with more than three authors is listed in the list of references under the name of the first author, followed by the phrase *et al.* The reference to Anderson et al. in the third paragraph of the sample on page 214 illustrates this style.

3. *A work by a corporate author* The list of references on page 213 includes an entry in which National Micrographics Association is given as the author. A parenthetical reference to that work would also use National Micrographics Association as its author, although the name may be abbreviated.

   (National Micrographics 42)
   or
   (Natl. Micrographics 42)

4. *A work listed by its title* The list of references on page 213 includes an entry for a book *Rules for Alphabetical Filing as Standardized by ARMA.* A parenthetical reference to that work should also refer to it by its title, which may be shortened for convenience.

   (*Rules for Alphabetical Filing* 14)
   or
   (*Rules* 14)

Locators Usually the only locator that is required in a parenthetical reference is a page number. However, sometimes additional or alternate information is needed to help the reader find the original source. The following paragraphs describe some of these special situations. Note that in all cases no punctuation separates the author's name or the title from the locator and that no abbreviation is used to identify the nature of the locator unless confusion would result from its omission (but see the note following paragraph 1 below).

1. *A multivolume work* The list of references on page 213 includes a reference to Robert Chambers's two-volume *Cyclopaedia of English Literature*. A reference to that work would have to include a volume designation as well as a page number. The volume number and the page number are separated by an unspaced colon.

    (Chambers 1:45)

    NOTE: If an entire volume of a multivolume work is being referred to, the abbreviation *vol.* is used to make it clear that the number is a volume number and not a page number.

    (Chambers, vol. 1)

2. *A reference book* A reference to an entry in a reference book often begins with the name of the entry being cited, as in the entry for "Aristotle" on page 213. A parenthetic reference need only mention the name of the entry, as no page number is included in the list of references. The name of the reference book should be mentioned in the text preceding such a reference; otherwise, the reader must consult the list of references to know what source is being cited.

    ("Aristotle")

3. *Literary works* Parenthetical references to literary works often include references to stanzas, lines, verses, chapters, books, parts, and the like. This is often very useful to readers trying to find a particular passage, because they may be using an edition of the work whose pagination differs from that of the edition used by the author of the note. For more on giving references to literary works, see the section on Special Cases later in this chapter.

References to unpublished sources Parenthetical references are also used to cite unpublished sources that are not listed in a bibliography, such as letters to the author or telephone interviews. The following information should be included: the name of the person providing the information, the type of source, and the date, as "(Paul Roberts, letter to the author, Sept. 1984)." Any of these elements may be omitted from the parenthetical reference if in-cluded in the text.

Parenthetical Reference Styling in the Sciences

Another system of parenthetical citation that is used mostly in the social and natural sciences is the author-date system (also called the name-year system). In the author-date system the parentheti-cal reference contains the author's last name and the date of pub-lication with no intervening punctuation. A third element, a page number, is optional. If the author's name is mentioned in the in-troductory text, only the date and possibly the page number are needed within the parentheses. By referring to the list of refer-ences, the reader can find complete bibliographical information about the work. However, lists of references written in connection with the author-date system must also follow the scientific styling of placing the date after the author's name in each entry.

A book or article by two or more authors would be repre-sented by the following stylings:

(Martin and Zim 1951)
(Martin, Zim, and Nelson 1951)
(Martin et al. 1951)

A corporate author name or a title may be substituted when there are no individual authors. An editor's last name may also be sub-stituted, but the name is not followed by the abbreviation *ed.*

A page number or other number indicating a division of the work is often added to the date with a comma (a colon in some stylings) between date and page numbers. For citations to the short articles so prevalent in the scientific literature, page num-bers are unnecessary, but for books, page references are certainly helpful to the reader.

(Martin et al. 1951, 147–149) *or* (Martin et al. 1951:147–149)

Volumes are indicated by Arabic numerals. Thus, "(1.147–149)" denotes volume 1, pages 147–149.

More than one work by the same author can be readily shown with the listing of a second date that follows the first with a comma between them, as "(Martin et al. 1951, 1958)." Two or more separate citations can also be included within one parenthe-sis if they are separated by a semicolon.

More than one work published in the same year by the same author can be indicated by adding an *a, b,* or *c* to the date. The same letters should be added to the dates in the entries in the list of references.

(Martin and Zim 1952a)

Bibliographies and Lists of References

A bibliography differs from a list of references in that it lists all of the works that a writer has found relevant in writing the text. A list of references, on the other hand, includes only those works that are specifically mentioned in the text or from which a particular quotation or piece of information was taken. In all other respects, however, bibliographies and lists of references are quite similar. They both appear at the end of an article, chapter, or book, where they list sources of information that are relevant to the text. They differ from a section of bibliographical endnotes in that their entries are arranged alphabetically (as in the sample on page 213), and they use different patterns of indention, punctuation, and capitalization, as explained in the paragraphs that follow. Bibliographies and lists of references are punctuated and capitalized in the same way, and hereafter in this chapter, references to bibliographies should be understood to be inclusive of lists of references as well.

Additional detail regarding the styling of bibliographical entries is provided in the following paragraphs. For each of the kinds of entries that are described below, two examples are given. The first example is in a style used in the humanities, which is also the style used in most general writing and the style that is familiar to most writers. The second example is in a style that is representative of the social and natural sciences.

In general, bibliographical stylings used in the sciences differ from those used in general writing in that (1) the author's first and middle names are expressed with initials only, (2) the date, which is important in scientific writings, is often placed near the beginning instead of at the end of the entry, (3) less capitalization is used, (4) titles of articles are not enclosed in quotation marks, (5) book titles are not underlined or italicized, (6) dates are usually written as day-month-year, which results in less punctuation, and (7) more abbreviations are used. In content, however, the two stylings are much the same, and both rely on periods to separate each element of the bibliographical entry.

The examples used in this section by no means exhaust the possible variations on these two basic stylings. Different combinations of the styles illustrated here, as well as other alternatives, are found in print. Several of these variations are recommended by various professional organizations and academic disciplines within the social and natural sciences. The entries in this section that illustrate scientific style are based on the style described in the *CBE Style Manual,* fifth edition, published by the Council of Biology Editors. (NOTE: Some entries in this section may differ somewhat from preferred CBE style. Writers who need to style their bibliographies in strict accordance with CBE style should consult that manual.) Other style manuals that give details of bibliographical styling used in specialized fields within the social and natural sciences are published by professional organizations in those fields.

Books

Style and content of entries   A bibliographical entry that refers to a book includes as many of the following elements as are relevant. The order of elements listed here is the order in which they appear in entries written in the styling of the humanities. Each of these elements is illustrated in the examples that begin on page 221.

1. *Author's name*   The author's name or authors' names come first, whether the author is a single individual, or a group of individuals, or an organization. Names of coauthors are arranged in the order in which they are found on the title page. A work without an author but with an editor is styled with the editor's name first, followed by a comma and *ed.* (see paragraph 4 below). The name of the first author is inverted so that the surname comes first and can be alphabetized. In bibliographies that follow the style of the humanities, the author's name is written as it appears on the title page. In many stylings used in the social and natural sciences, the last name and first two initials are always used, regardless of how the author's name is printed on the title page. This is the style followed in this section for examples of bibliographical entries in the social and natural sciences; however, authors should remember that some confusion can result if more than one writer in the relevant subject area has the same initials and last name. The best way to avoid this difficulty is to include first names whenever there is a chance of confusion.

   In the humanities and in some stylings in the social and natural sciences, if there are more than three authors the first author's name is followed by *et al.*, which is an abbreviation for the Latin phrase *et alii* or *et aliae*, meaning "and others." In other stylings, the names of all the authors are included.

2. *Title of the work*   In the humanities, the title is underlined in typewritten manuscript and italicized in type. In the social and natural sciences, the title may follow this styling or it may be left without underlining or italicization. Capitalization is either headline-style (that is, all words are capitalized except for internal articles and prepositions) or sentence-style (that is, only the first word and proper nouns and adjectives are capital-

ized). In the humanities, headline-style capitalization is used; in the social and natural sciences, both styles of capitalization are used. The titles of references in the sciences that appear as examples in this chapter are unitalicized and use sentence-style capitalization. Another difference between the two stylings is that titles in the humanities include any subtitles, whereas subtitles are often omitted in bibliographies for the sciences. Subtitles are italicized and capitalized to match the styling of the titles that precede them.

3. *Portion of the book* Some bibliography entries cite only one portion of a book, as an essay within a collection or an article within a symposium. For these entries, the name of that portion is given first as a title. It is either italicized or enclosed in quotation marks, depending on its nature, or it is left alone as in stylings for the sciences. The title of the book is given next. The titles of chapters within nonfiction works by a single author are usually not included in the entry.

4. *Editor, compiler, or translator* In entries for books that have an author, the name of an editor, compiler, or translator comes after the title and is preceded or followed by the abbreviation *ed., comp.,* or *trans.* or some combination of these. If no author is listed, the name of the editor, compiler, or translator is placed first in the entry—styled like an author's name but followed by a comma and the lowercase abbreviation *ed., comp.,* or *trans.*

5. *Edition* If a book is other than the first edition, the number (as "2d ed." or "1986 ed.") or other description of the edition is written after the title. If the edition is identified by a word instead of a numeral, the first letter in that word is capitalized, as "Rev. ed."

6. *Volume number or number of volumes* In a bibliography entry that cites a multivolume work, the total number of volumes in that work is written before the publication information as, for example, "9 vols." There is no need to cite the volumes actually used, since this information will be in a note or in a parenthetical reference. On the other hand, if only one volume of a multivolume work was consulted, that volume alone is listed as an entry, so that the text references need cite only page numbers, not volume numbers as well.

7. *Name of the series* If the book is part of a series, the name of the series should be included, as well as the book or volume number if the book represents a specific numbered volume in that series. The series name is not italicized.

8. *Publication data* The city of publication (with the state abbreviation if the city is not well known), the name of the publisher, and the year of publication of the particular edition used— together these form the grouping called the publication data. A colon usually follows the city name, a comma follows the name of the publisher, and a period after the date ends the bibliographical entry if the styling is that used in the humanities. In stylings used in the sciences, the date often appears after the author's name.

All of this information comes from the title page and the copyright page. If the title page lists more than one city, only the first is mentioned in the bibliography. Some books are published under a special imprint name, which is usually printed on the title page above the publisher's name. In a bibliographical entry, the imprint name is joined to the publisher's name with a hyphen, as *Golden Press-Western Publishing Co.* Short forms of publisher's names are often used in bibliographies. This usage is acceptable if consistently applied. Also the word *and* and the ampersand are equally acceptable within a publisher's name if they are used consistently.

For a multivolume work that is published over a period of several years, inclusive numbers are given for those years. The phrase *in press* is substituted for the date in works that are about to be published.

9. *Locators* Page numbers are added to book entries in a bibliography only when the entry cites a portion of a book such as a story or essay in an anthology or an article in a collection. If that portion is in a volume of a multivolume work, both volume and page number are given.

Examples The following examples illustrate how each of the elements described above is styled in a number of different situations. In each case, the first example illustrates a typical style in the humanities and general publications; the second illustrates a representative style used in the social and natural sciences.

1. *Book with a single author*

   Chapman, R. F. *The Insects.* New York: American Elsevier, 1969.

   Chapman, R. F. 1969. The insects. New York: American Elsevier.

2. *Book with two or three authors*

   Starnes, De Witt T., and Gertrude E. Noyes. *The English Dictionary from Cawdrey to Johnson 1604–1775.* Chapel Hill: University of North Carolina Press, 1946.

   Starnes, D. T.; Noyes, G. E. 1946. The English dictionary from Cawdrey to Johnson 1604–1775. Chapel Hill: University of North Carolina Press.

3. *Book with more than three authors*

> Allee, W. C., et al. *Principles of Animal Ecology.* Philadelphia: W. B. Saunders Co., 1949.

> Allee, W. C.; Emerson, A. E.; Park, O.; Park, S.; Schmidt, K. D. 1949. Principles of animal ecology. Philadelphia: W. B. Saunders Co.

4. *Book with a corporate author*

> National Micrographics Association. *An Introduction to Micrographics.* Rev. ed. Silver Spring, Md.: National Micrographics Association, 1980.

> National Micrographics Association. 1980. An introduction to micrographics. Rev. ed. Silver Spring, Md.: National Micrographics Association.

5. *Book without an author listed*

> *The World Almanac & Book of Facts.* New York: Newspaper Enterprises Association, Inc., 1985.

> The world almanac & book of facts. 1985. New York: Newspaper Enterprises Association.

6. *Book with editor listed and no author*

> Bradbury, Peggy F., ed. *Transcriber's Guide to Medical Terminology.* New Hyde Park, N.Y.: Medical Examination Publishing Co., 1973.

> Bradbury, P. F., editor. 1973. Transcriber's guide to medical terminology. New Hyde Park, N.Y.: Medical Examination Publishing Co.

7. *Book with author and editor-translator*

> Beauvoir, Simone de. *The Second Sex.* Trans. and ed. H. M. Parshley. New York: Alfred A. Knopf, 1953.

> Beauvoir, S. 1953. The second sex. Parshley, H. M., translator and editor. New York: Alfred A. Knopf.

8. *Multivolume book*

> Farrand, John Jr., ed. *The Audubon Society Master Guide to Birding.* 3 vols. New York: Alfred A. Knopf, 1983.

> Farrand, J. Jr., editor. 1983. The Audubon Society master guide to birding. New York: Alfred A. Knopf, 3 vol.

9. *Multivolume book only one volume of which was consulted*

> Chambers, Robert. Vol. 1 of *Cyclopaedia of English Literature.* 2 vols. New York: World Publishing House, 1875.

> Chambers, R. 1875. Cyclopaedia of English literature. Vol. 1. New York: World Publishing House.

10. *Portion of a book*

> Malone, Kemp. "The Phonemes of Current English." *Studies for William A. Read.* Ed. Nathaniel M. Caffee and Thomas A. Kirby. Baton Rouge: Louisiana State University Press, 1940. pp. 133–165.
>
> Malone, K. 1940. The phonemes of current English. In: Caffee, N. M.; Kirby, T. A., eds. Studies for William A. Read. Baton Rouge: Louisiana State University Press: p. 133–165.

11. *Book in a series*

> Manheimer, Martha L. *Style Manual: A Guide for the Preparation of Reports and Dissertations.* Vol. 5 of Books in Library and Information Science. New York: Marcel Dekker, 1973.
>
> Manheimer, M. L. 1973. Style manual. New York: Marcel Dekker. (Books in library and information science; vol. 5.)

Articles in Journals or Other Periodicals

Style and Content of Entries A bibliography entry for an article in a journal or other periodical or in a newspaper includes as many of the following elements as are relevant. Examples of each of these elements can be found in the reference samples beginning on page 225. The elements are listed here in the order in which they appear in entries styled on the humanities pattern.

1. *Author's name* The author's name is written as it appears on the printed page and is styled in the way described above for an entry that refers to a book. Names of people who write letters to a periodical or who contribute signed reviews are treated like names of authors.

2. *Title of the article* The title of the article is written in full as it appears in the printed article. In most bibliography stylings used in the humanities, the title and subtitle are enclosed in quotation marks (with a period before the closing quotation mark) and capitalized headline-style. Titles of articles styled for use in the social and natural sciences tend to omit the quotation marks, use sentence-style capitalization, and omit subtitles.

3. *Name of the periodical* The name of the periodical is treated in the same way as described above for a book: underlined to indicate italics in bibliographies for the humanities but not italicized in bibliographies for the sciences. However, unlike book titles, periodical titles are fully capitalized in bibliographies in both the humanities and the sciences. In addition, there are special principles for the styling of periodical names in both categories. One is the omission of an initial article. Whereas

the initial article is included in a book title but ignored in alphabetizing, the initial article of a journal title is dropped completely. Another is the use of abbreviations for journal titles of more than one word. These abbreviations are widely used in technical writing. Each discipline has its own set of abbreviations for the journals that tend to be used in that discipline. For general writing, however, these titles are written in full for the reader's convenience, and the examples that follow show journal titles in unabbreviated form. Journal titles that begin with the words *Transactions, Proceedings,* and *Annals* are often reversed for the purpose of alphabetizing so that these words come last.

Names of newspapers are treated as they appear on the masthead, except that initial articles are omitted. Also, a place name is added in brackets after the newspaper's name if it is necessary to distinguish that particular paper.

4. *Volume and number of the periodical* This information comes after the name of the periodical and identifies the particular issue cited. An issue that is identified by both volume and number should be identified in that way in a bibliography entry, as "3(2):25–37" for volume 3, number 2, pages 25–37. If the issue is identified in some other manner, as by a full date, that method is used in the bibliography entry. Issue numbers are not commonly used, however, unless the issue is paginated independently of the volume as a whole and the number is needed to identify the issue. Examples 1 and 5 below illustrate entries for a periodical in which pages are numbered consecutively through a volume and which therefore needs only a volume number. If the volume number corresponds to a particular year, as in the examples, the year in parentheses follows the volume number—but not, of course, in the scientific stylings, where the year is placed after the author's name.

Example 2 on page 225 illustrates a reference to a periodical that uses a seasonal designation in addition to a volume and number designation; the pages in this issue are numbered independently of the volume as a whole. Example 3 illustrates a popular monthly magazine, issues of which are commonly referred to by date rather than by volume or issue number. Newspapers are always identified by date.

5. *Issue date* Periodicals issued daily, weekly, monthly, and bimonthly are usually designated by date of issue. The date follows the unpunctuated day-month-year order (27 May 1984) rather than the punctuated month-day-year order (May 27, 1984). Names of months that are spelled with more than four letters are usually abbreviated.

6. *Page numbers* Inclusive pages for the whole article are written
at the end of the entry. For newspaper entries, it may be necessary to add a section number or edition identification number as well, as "p. B6." Articles that are continued on later
pages are styled thus: "38–41, 159–160." The use of the abbreviations *p.* or *pp.* in bibliographies is the same as it is in
footnotes (see pages 206–207).

Examples The following examples illustrate how each of the elements described above is styled in a number of different situations. The first example of each group illustrates a style used in
the humanities and in general publications; the second illustrates
a style used in the social and natural sciences.

1. *Article in journal with continuous pagination of volume*

> Heil, John. "Seeing is Believing." *American Philosophical Quarterly*
> 19 (1982): 229–239.

> Heil, J. 1982. Seeing is believing. American Philosophical Quar-
> terly 19:229–239.

2. *Article in journal that paginates each issue separately*

> Ourecky, Donald K. "Cane and Bush Fruits." *Plants & Gardens* 27,
> No. 3 (Autumn 1971): pp. 13–15.

> Ourecky, D. K. 1971. Cane and bush fruits. Plants & Gardens
> 27(3):13–15.

3. *Articles in periodicals issued by date*

> Smiley, Xan. "Misunderstanding Africa." *Atlantic,* Sept. 1982, pp.
> 70–79.

> Smiley, X. 1982. Misunderstanding Africa. Atlantic, Sept.:70–79.

> Rosenberg, Jeremy C. "Letters." *Advertising Age,* 7 June 1982,
> p. M–1.

> Rosenberg, J. C. 1982. Letters. Advertising Age, 7 June: M–1.

4. *Article in newspaper*

> Pitts, Gail. "Money Funds Holding Own." *Morning Union* [Spring-
> field, Mass.], 23 Aug. 1982, p. 6.

> Pitts, G. 1982. Money funds holding own. Morning Union
> [Springfield, Mass.] 23 Aug.:6.

5. *Signed review*

> Vassell, M. O. Rev. of *Applied Charge Particle Optics,* ed. A. Septier.
> *American Scientist* 70 (1982): 229.

> Vassell, M. O. 1982. Rev. of A. Septier, ed., Applied charge parti-
> cle optics. American Scientist 70:229.

6. *Anonymous article*

   "Education at Home: A Showdown in Texas." *Newsweek,* 25 March 1985, p. 87.

   Anonymous. 1985. Education at home. Newsweek 25 March:87.

Unpublished Materials

Bibliography entries for unpublished materials include as many of the following elements as are known or are relevant.

1. *Author's name* The author's name is treated in the same way as described above for a book.

2. *Title of the work* If there is an official title, it is copied as it appears on the work. It is enclosed in quotation marks and capitalized like a book title in a bibliography using a styling from the humanities. If the work has no official title, a descriptive title is used, as in example 2 below, but it is not enclosed in quotation marks.

3. *The nature of the material* The entry should include a description of the document, such as "letter to the author" or "doctoral dissertation." For works without official author or title, this element is the first part of the entry.

4. *Date* The date must be included if it is known. If the date is known but is not written on the document, it is enclosed in brackets.

5. *Name of collection and identification number* Whatever information is necessary to completely identify the document is included.

6. *Geographical location* The name of the institution and the city where the materials can be located are often listed last in this kind of bibliographical entry.

Examples

1. *Unpublished report*

   Velasquez, Joyce A. "The Format of Formal Reports." Report prepared for the Southern Engineering Company. Johnson City, Miss., May 29, 1985.

   Velasquez, J. A. 1985. The format of formal reports. Report prepared for the Southern Engineering Company. 29 May. Johnson City, Miss.

2. *Letter in a collection*

   Johnson, Clive. Letter to Elizabeth O'Hara. 9 Nov. 1916. Johnson

Collection, item 5298. California State Historical Society, San Marino, Calif.

Johnson, C. 1916. Letter to Elizabeth O'Hara. 9 Nov. Located at California State Historical Society, San Marino, Calif.

Format of a Bibliography

Bibliographies are always typed beginning on a new page. Most are alphabetically arranged and indented flush-and-hang to set off the alphabetical sequence. Initial articles that are included in a title that begins an entry are ignored in determining the alphabetical order. All the entries are usually listed together in a single alphabetical arrangement, whether the first word is an author's surname or the title of an anonymous work. It is possible to divide a bibliography into categories by date of publication or by subject matter, but such divisions are not recommended unless the single-list form proves unmanageable.

More than one work by an author After the first listing of an entry by an author or group of coauthors who have more than one work listed in the bibliography, that person's name is replaced in succeeding, adjacent entries by a dash. In typewritten bibliographies, the dash is usually represented by three typed hyphens. The author is not usually expected to type this dash or its equivalent in hyphens; instead, the editor substitutes the dash for the author's names as needed on the copyedited page. The dash is followed by a period, just as a name would be, or by a comma and an abbreviation such as *ed.*

The dash substitutes for the author's full name (or the full names of the set of coauthors) but no more. Thus, the dash may be used only when the names are exactly the same in adjacent entries. For example, if an entry for a work by Kemp Malone is followed by an entry for a work coauthored by Malone and someone else, the second entry would be spelled out. But if Malone and his coauthor wrote more than one book together, the dash would be used to replace both names in the second reference. A work by a single author precedes a work by that author and another; and works edited by an author usually follow works written by the same person.

In the general bibliographical stylings, the various works by a single author or group of coauthors are arranged alphabetically by title. In bibliographies in the social and natural sciences, however, where the date appears after the author's name, these multiple entries are arranged by date of publication. Occasionally an author publishes more than one article during a year. In these cases, the work is identified by a letter (often italicized) that follows the year. Thus, an author's works may be listed as 1977, 1979a, 1979b, 1980, and so on.

Headings Depending on their scope as explained at the beginning of this section, bibliographies may be headed *Bibliography* or *List of References*. Writings in the sciences often list bibliographical entries under the heading *Literature Cited*. If this heading is used, then only "literature"—that is, published works—and only works actually cited can be included on the list. Unpublished works that are referred to in the text must carry information such as the author's name and the title and where the work can be located, as well as the word *unpublished,* within the text or within parentheses. To avoid having to refer to an unwieldy number of unpublished works in the text, the author or editor may head the reference list *References Cited,* which allows the inclusion of unpublished works. Works in press are usually listed under *Literature Cited* heads even though they are not yet published. In lieu of the date, the entry contains the phrase *in press.*

Annotated bibliographies Annotated bibliographies are those in which the entries are written as for a regular bibliography but are then followed by a sentence or paragraph of description. Annotated bibliographies are designed to lead the reader to the most useful works for further study. Comments may be added to all or just some of the entries. The descriptive part may be run in with the bibliographical entry, or it may be set off typographically by lines of space, indention, italics, or smaller type.

Special Cases

Lists of references frequently contain items that do not fit neatly into any of the categories described in the previous sections of this chapter. Some are printed items like government publications, others are nonprint items. These special references are styled, as far as possible, in formats similar to those used for the published and unpublished works described and illustrated in the previous sections. They are arranged and punctuated in a way that corresponds to whatever styling has been chosen for the publication's notes, parenthetical references, and bibliography entries.

In the following paragraphs there are several references to the styling of titles in quotation marks or italics. These statements refer only to the documentation styles used in the humanities and in general-purpose writing. As was pointed out in the preceding section, titles have no special styling in the documentation formats used in the social and natural sciences. Also the date of publication, which occurs near the end of the references discussed here, is set after the author's name in the bibliographical stylings used in the sciences.

Nonprint Sources

Many sources in the following categories are often not cited in bibliographies and lists of references. When they are not, however, full documentation should be supplied within the text or in a note.

Personal communications The name of the person who supplied information in a personal communication is listed first in this kind of reference; the name is styled like an author's name. A descriptive word or phrase (like *personal communication* or *telephone interview*) follows, unitalicized and without quotation marks. The place, if applicable, and date of the communication are also given. This type of source is rarely included in a list of references. In scientific publications a form like the following is often found as a parenthetical reference: "(J. Scott, pers. comm. 1985)."

Speeches Lectures and other addresses are listed with the speaker's name first, then the title of the speech in quotation marks (or a descriptive term if the speech has no title), the name of the meeting or sponsoring organization or the occasion, then the place and date.

Radio and television programs The title of the program is usually listed first and is underlined or italicized. However, if the program is an episode of a multipart series, the episode title is placed in quotation marks and the name of the series follows without underlining or italics. If the reference in the text is to a particular performer, composer, or other person, that person's name may be listed before the title. Following the title are the names of the network, the local station and city (in a bibliography entry these two are separated by a comma not a period), and the date of the broadcast. Depending on its relevance, additional information may be given after the title, such as the names of the performers, the composer, or the director.

Sound recordings, films, and videotapes Sound recordings, films and filmscripts, and videotapes are usually documented according to their titles. If the name of a particular writer, composer, or performer is stressed in the text, and especially if the source is a recording, that person's name may be listed first. The italicized title is usually followed by whatever names are needed to identify the work, such as writers, performers, and others. Some programs may need to be further identified by a descriptive term like *filmstrip*, *slide program*, or *videocassette*. The director's name follows, preceded by the abbreviation *dir*. Finally, the name of the distributor, the year, the catalog number, and other information is added as needed to complete the identification of the work. The following example illustrates a bibliography entry for a recording.

> Brahms, Johannes. *A German Requiem (Ein deutsches Requiem)*, Op. 45. Cond. Erich Leinsdorf. Boston Symphony Orchestra. RCA, LSC-7054, 1969.

Works of art   References to works of art include the artist's name, which is styled like an author's name, an italicized title, the name of the proprietary institution, and the city.

Computer software   References to computer software contain the following elements: the name of the program's writer, if known; the title of the program, which is italicized; the descriptive term *computer software;* the name and location of the distributor; and the year of publication. Additional information, such as the machines or the operating systems the software is designed for, may be added at the end of the note or bibliographical entry.

Microforms   Materials in microform are documented in whatever styling is appropriate for their contents—as periodical articles, unpublished reports, etc.—except that to the end of the note or the bibliography entry is added a term that describes the form (as *microfiche*) and also the name and location of the commercial service that supplied the form. However, regular published material that has been microfilmed and preserved in a library is cited as if the actual works had been handled, and there is no mention of the microform process.

Material from an information service   Sources from an information service are documented like books, articles, reports, and other printed materials, but at the end of the note or bibliography entry is added the name of the service, its location, and any identification numbers for the material.

Government Publications

If a publication by a government agency has a named author, that name may go first in a note or bibliography entry. Most government publications, however, are authored by an agency. The name of the government (as United States, Montana, or Chicago) often comes first, then the name of the department if applicable, then the name of the specific agency responsible for the publication. These names are not abbreviated when they precede the title of the work.

Next is the title, italicized like a book title and further identified as needed by series or publication numbers or by whatever format the agency uses to identify the work. As with other kinds of documentation, publication data is also included. Most U.S.

government publications are published by the Government Printing Office, which is usually referred to in notes and bibliographies as *GPO*. References to congressional documents usually omit the GPO publication data, because it is understood. Standardized abbreviations are often used in these references, but names may also be spelled out, especially in writings for the general public.

> United States. Department of Labor. Employment and Training Administration. *Dictionary of Occupational Titles*. 4th ed. Washington: GPO, 1977.

Congressional documents are often attributed first to the "U.S. Congress" in notes and bibliography entries but not in parenthetical references. The name of the appropriate house follows (the short forms *House* and *Senate* are used), and then the name of the committee, if applicable. The document title is listed next in the reference, followed by the number and session of Congress. The year is listed next, then the number or other description of the document. The *Congressional Record* needs to be identified only by date and page number, as in the following bibliography entry:

> *Congressional Record*. 96th Cong., 2d sess., 1976. Vol. 5, pt. 7, pp. 13–27.

Bills in Congress are identified in a special way. *H.R.* is the conventional abbreviation for the House of Representatives in this case, and *S.* for the Senate. Thus, bills are referred to as "H.R. 93" or "S. 120." In citations to congressional reports, however, the House is abbreviated *H.* (as in "H. Rept. 1303"), while a Senate report would be styled "S. Rept. 671." In each case, the number and session of the congress follow the document title.

Laws and constitutions References to laws and constitutions are documented in notes and bibliography entries unless full information is provided in the text. These citations are not italicized. In legal writing, a large number of standard abbreviations is used, but in most writing for a general audience the abbreviations are limited to those which can be readily understood by the public. Roman numerals are traditionally used to denote certain sections of constitutions, as shown in the first two examples below.

> U.S. Constitution, Amendment XIII.
>
> Indiana Constitution, Art. III, sec. 2, cl. 4.
>
> Trade Agreements Act, Public Law 96–39, sec. 32, 96th Cong., 1st sess., July 26, 1979.
>
> 90 Stat. 1113 (1976).

The fourth reference in the list above is an example of the abbreviated form that is typical of legal citations. It is also typical in that the volume number comes *before* the name of a multivolume work.

The reference points to a statute that is found in volume 90 of the *U.S. Statutes at Large* beginning on page 1113. Inclusive numbers are not used in legal references. The examples below illustrate a reference to a federal statute that has been codified in the *U.S. Code* and that can be found in volume 28, section 17 of that work, together with its supplement.

> 28 U.S.C. sec. 17. (1964).
> 28 U.S.C. sec. 17 (1964), as amended (Supp. II, 1966).

Regulations of the federal government also conform to official citation form. Like codified statutes, regulations codified in the *Code of Federal Regulations* or the *Federal Register* are identified first by volume number, then by section or page number and date.

> 33 C.F.R. sec. 403.2 (1980).
> 43 Fed. Reg. 54221 (1978).

Court Cases

Titles of court cases are italicized within the text, whether they involve two opposing parties (as *Surner* v. *Kellogg*) or whether they have titles like *In re Watson* or *In the matter of John Watson*. When these cases are listed in a bibliography, however, they are not italicized. The *v.* (for versus) within a case title is usually set roman in printed matter, but on a typewritten page the underscore is usually extended throughout the case title. A citation to a court case gives the name of the case, the number, title, and page of the volume in which it is recorded, and the date.

> *A Minor* v. *State*, 85 Nev. 323, 454 P. 2d 895 (1969).

The example above refers the reader to two sources in one reference: volume 85 of *Nevada Reports* on page 323, and also volume 454 of the second series of the *Pacific Reporter,* on page 895. Frequently the name of the court that decided the case is listed before the date.

Literary Works

Since literary works are printed in so many different editions, each of which is paginated differently, documentation of such works as poems, stories, plays, and novels does not always involve page numbers. Instead, reference is frequently made to the divisions of the work, such as chapter, book, part, act, scene, or line. Page numbers are referred to, however, in prose works if the edition used is clearly identified in a list of references or in a note; but in poetry and verse plays, where each line has a number, documentation refers to lines rather than to pages.

In cases where the author wishes to lead the reader to a particular chapter or part of a work of prose, the page number may be given in a reference, followed by a semicolon and the appropriate location, as "22; ch. 2" or "433; pt. 7."

Numerals alone, without accompanying terms like *chapter, verse, act, scene,* or *line,* are used in footnotes and endnotes and especially in parenthetical references, where they take up little space. Numerals are used wherever they can be easily understood without accompanying words or abbreviations. Frequently two numerals are used together, one that indicates a large division of the work and another that indicates a smaller division, as "4.122" for book 4, line 122. The two numerals are separated by a period or sometimes by a comma. Some stylings use capital and lowercase Roman numerals to denote the act and scene of a play, as "*Hamlet* III.ii" for act 3, scene 2; but the Arabic form 3.2 is also found, as in "*Hamlet* 3.2."

A single numeral is generally not used in a reference without an identifying word or abbreviation because it could be confusing. Thus, parenthetical references such as the following should include an identifying term: (*Hamlet,* Act 3) and ("The Waste Land," part 4). The abbreviations for line and lines (*l.* and *ll.*) should be used with great care, since they are easily confused with the numbers 1 and 11.

The Bible

Biblical references are not usually listed in a bibliography unless a particular version or edition is specified in the text. A text reference includes the name of the book, which is not italicized and which is often abbreviated, followed by Arabic numerals representing chapter and verse. Chapter and verse numerals are traditionally separated by a colon, but a period is a common alternative. A book with two or more parts is styled with an Arabic numeral before the name of the book, as "2 Chron. 2:18." Page numbers are never used to refer to biblical material.

Chapter 8

The Treatment of Quotations

CONTENTS

Authors rely on two common conventions to indicate that a passage of prose or poetry is being quoted from another source. Short quotations are most commonly run in with the rest of the text and set off with quotation marks. Longer passages are most commonly indented as separate paragraphs without enclosing quotation marks. These paragraphs are usually referred to as *extracts, excerpts,* or *block quotations.* This chapter tells how authors decide which format to use. It also explains the conventions that apply to the treatment of long quotations set as extracts and specifies the conditions under which authors are allowed to alter the original source.

Most of the information needed to punctuate short run-in passages can be found in Chapter 1, "Punctuation," especially in the section on Quotation Marks, Double, beginning on page 43, but also in the sections on Brackets, Colon, Comma, Ellipsis Points, and Virgule. Information about the capitalization of run-in quotations can be found in the section on Beginnings, starting on page 53, in Chapter 2, "Capitals, Italics, and Quotation Marks."

Choosing between Run-in and Block Quotations

The length of a quotation usually determines whether it is run into the text or set as a block quotation. For prose quotations, length can be assessed in terms of the number of words, the number of typewritten or typeset lines, or the number of sentences in the passage. Authors who consider the number of words in making this decision usually run in quotations of less than 100 words and set off quotations of more than 100 words. Authors who base their decisions on the number of lines in the passage use cutoff points ranging from four to ten lines. When the number of sentences is the criterion, passages of one sentence in length are run in; passages of two or more sentences are set off as extracts, although some authors add the condition that the quotation must also run to at least four lines.

Each of these approaches relies on an arbitrary cutoff, and no matter which approach is used, the writer will want to make exceptions for certain sentences. For instance, writers who want to make a passage read more smoothly may prefer to run in the longer quotations, even if the system they are using would dictate that the quotations be set as extracts. Alternatively, writers who want to emphasize quoted passages to make them easier for the reader to locate will set even short quotations as extracts.

For quotations of poetry, different criteria are used. Full lines of poetry are usually set as extracts, although it is also common to run one or two lines into the text.

Styling Block Quotations

Block quotations are set off from the text that precedes and follows them by a number of devices, including (1) the addition of extra space between the quotation and the text; (2) indenting each line of the quoted matter—on the left only or on both right and left margins; (3) setting the quotation in smaller type; and (4) leaving less space between the lines of quoted material than there is between lines of the main text. Most often some combination of these devices is used, as in the examples below.

typeset passage with extra space between text and quotation, smaller type for the quotation, and each line indented

He took the title for his biography of Henry David Thoreau from a passage in *Walden*, one of Thoreau's most well-known books:

> I long ago lost a hound, a bay horse, and a turtle-dove, and am still on their trail. . . . I have met one or two who had heard the hound, and the tramp of the horse, and even seen the dove disappear behind a cloud, and they seemed as anxious to recover them as if they had lost them themselves.

However, the title *A Hound, a Bay Horse, and a Turtle-dove* probably puzzled some readers.

typewritten passage with less space between lines of the quotation and each line indented

```
He took the title for his biography of Henry David

Thoreau from a passage in Walden, one of Thoreau's most

well-known books:

    I long ago lost a hound, a bay horse, and a
    turtle-dove, and am still on their trail. . . . I
    have met one or two who had heard the hound, and the
    tramp of the horse, and even seen the dove disappear
    behind a cloud, and they seemed as anxious to recover
    them as if they had lost them themselves.

However, the title A Hound, a Bay Horse, and a

Turtle-dove probably puzzled some readers.
```

Introductory Punctuation, Capitalization, and Indention

Typically, block quotations are preceded by a full sentence ending with a colon, and they begin with a full sentence whose first word is capitalized. However, if the opening words of the quoted passage can be made to flow with the syntax of an incomplete sentence that precedes the quotation, then no punctuation is required to introduce the extract, and the quotation can begin with a lowercase letter. (For an explanation of the conditions under which authors can alter the original capitalization of a quoted passage, see the section on Alterations, Omissions, and Interpolations in this chapter.)

> The chapter begins with a general description of interoffice memorandums:
>
> > The interoffice memorandum or memo is a means of informal communication within a firm or organization. Its special arrangement replaces the salutation, complimentary close, and written signature of the letter with identifying headings.
>
> They describe the interoffice memorandum as
>
> > a means of informal communication within a firm or organization. Its special arrangement replaces the salutation, complimentary close, and written signature of the letter with identifying headings.

If the sentence that precedes the quotation does not introduce it or refer directly to it, the sentence ends in a period.

> As of the end of April she believed that the product had been introduced well and that it stood a good chance of success.
>
> > Unit sales are strong, revenues are better than forecast, shipments are being made on schedule, and inventory levels are stable.

A block quotation is sometimes introduced by a sentence that includes words or sentence fragments quoted from the same source as the quotation that follows.

The report spoke of a "sense of direction" and "newfound optimism" in the community.

> This community is building for its future. New institutions are being created, and existing ones are being strengthened. Civic, cultural, and social events are once again well attended.

When the beginning of a block quotation is also the beginning of a paragraph in the original, the first line of the quotation begins with extra indention.

> The first chapter includes a statement that should be encouraging to secretaries:
>
> > In the past, many secretaries have been placed in positions of responsibility without being delegated enough authority to carry out the responsibility. The current pressures affecting managers have caused them to rethink the secretarial function and to delegate more responsibility and authority to their secretaries.

Quotations that include two or more consecutive paragraphs follow the paragraphing form of the original; each new paragraph is indented.

Quotations within an Extract

If a block quotation itself contains quoted material, that material is enclosed in double quotation marks.

> The authors of the book recommend the following procedures for handling reports:
>
> > The presiding officer will call for the appropriate report from an officer, a board member, a standing committee, or a special committee by saying, "Will the chairperson of the Ways and Means Committee please present the committee's report?" After the report is presented, a motion is heard to accept the report.

Dialogue in a block quotation is enclosed in quotation marks. The beginning of each speech is also marked by extra indention. If a speech runs to more than one paragraph, open quotation marks appear at the beginning of each paragraph of the extract; closing quotation marks appear only at the end of the final paragraph.

> Marion makes her invitation at the end of the first chapter, but Richard's reply is at least somewhat tentative.
>
> > "Would you like to come visiting again on your next vacation?" she asked.
> > "Yes, I would," I replied, "but I don't know when that will be. It's becoming harder and harder for me to find the time to get away.
> > "By the way," I went on, "I want to thank you for introducing me to those people last night."
> > "It was my pleasure," she said.
> > "I really appreciate it."
> > "I do hope you will come again."
> > "I'd like to."

Alterations, Omissions, and Interpolations

Although absolute accuracy is always of first importance when quoting from another source, there are certain kinds of alterations, omissions, and additions that authors and editors are traditionally allowed to make. Most of these alterations occur at the beginning or end of the quotation. The following paragraphs explain the kinds of changes that authors and editors may make and how these changes are indicated. All of the conventions described in this section are illustrated with block quotations; however, the conventions are equally applicable to run-in quotations. Examples of alterations, omissions, and interpolations occurring in run-in quotations can be found in the section on Brackets, beginning on page 6, and in the section on Ellipsis Points, beginning on page 30, in Chapter 1, "Punctuation."

Changing Capital or Lowercase Letters

If the opening words of a quotation act as a sentence within the quotation, the first word is capitalized, even if that word did not begin a sentence in the original version. (In the following example, the full version of the passage being quoted appears in the example on page 237.)

> The authors make exactly this point in the first chapter:
>
>> Many secretaries have been placed in positions of responsibility without being delegated enough authority to carry out the responsibility. The current pressures affecting managers have caused them to rethink the secretarial function and to delegate more responsibility and authority to their secretaries.

In situations in which meticulous handling of original source material is required, the capital *M* would be placed in square brackets to indicate that it was not capitalized in the source.

> The authors make exactly this point in the first chapter:
>
>> [M]any secretaries have been placed in positions of responsibility without being delegated enough authority to carry out the responsibility.

When the opening words of a quoted passage are joined syntactically to the sentence that precedes the quotation, the first word is generally not capitalized, even if it was capitalized in the original version. A few writers, however, retain the capital letter of the original in these circumstances. (Once again, the full version of the passage quoted below appears on page 237.)

> The author of this chapter knows full well that
>
>> in the past, many secretaries have been placed in positions of responsibility without being delegated enough authority to carry out the respon-

sibility. The current pressures affecting managers have caused them to rethink the secretarial function and to delegate more responsibility to their secretaries.

Omissions at the Beginning or End of a Quotation

If an omission is made from the beginning of a quotation, no ellipsis points are required. However, style varies somewhat on this point, and some writers will use ellipsis points for this kind of omission, although usually only in very formal contexts.

> They describe an interoffice memorandum as
>
> ... a means of informal communication within a firm or organization. Its special arrangement replaces the salutation, complimentary close, and written signature of the letter with identifying headings.

> *but more commonly*

> They describe an interoffice memorandum as
>
> a means of informal communication within a firm or organization. Its special arrangement replaces the salutation, complimentary close, and written signature of the letter with identifying headings.

A quoted passage that is cut off before a period in the original may be concluded with a period and a set of three ellipsis points to show that the last part of the original sentence was omitted. Any original punctuation at the end of the quotation—with the exception of question marks and exclamation points, which are discussed in the next paragraph—may then be dropped. In the example given below, the quoted passage ended with a comma in the original version. In the extract, the first of the four periods at the end of the passage marks the end of the sentence; the periods that follow are ellipsis points that indicate the omission of material.

> The book offers this advice about overseas calls:
>
> Give the Overseas Operator the same information that you would give to the regular Long-distance Operator. There may be a delay, but it is possible to call practically every telephone in the world by this method. Direct dialing is also available to many countries. ...

If the final sentence in the original version ends in an exclamation point or a question mark, that mark of punctuation is retained and is preceded by three ellipsis points. In the example given below, words that immediately precede the question mark in the original version are omitted.

> The authors recommend that secretaries take the following steps to improve their working environment:
>
> You could think of ways to improve the flow of paperwork: Where do backlogs occur, for example, and where and why do most errors occur? Can you design a new rubber stamp or sticker to help speed the flow of paper? Are there ways to reduce interruptions to your work ... ?

Omissions within Quotations

Omission of a full paragraph   If a full paragraph or more is omitted from a block quotation, the omission is indicated by ellipsis points at the end of the paragraph that comes before the omission. In the example that follows, the quoted passage includes text from two different paragraphs in the original version and omits entirely an intervening paragraph.

> The chapter offers the following advice regarding preconference preparations:
>
>> After the cutoff date for preregistration, and usually one week before the meeting, the rooming list of conference participants should be sent to the conference manager. . . .
>>
>> Whenever possible, the conference name tags or badges should be prepared ahead of time and arranged in a system that will facilitate easy distribution. These items are often included in the conference packets. All convention- or conference-related materials should be assembled in packets for the participants. These items include the convention program, appropriate brochures, relevant reports, minutes, and other materials.

Omission at the beginning of a paragraph   If text is omitted from the beginning of any paragraph other than the first paragraph of the extract, the omission is marked by three ellipsis points at the beginning of the paragraph from which the omission has been made. Regular paragraph indention precedes the ellipsis points. The example that follows shows how the preceding example would look if the writer doing the quoting decided to omit the first two sentences of the final paragraph.

> The chapter offers the following advice regarding preconference preparations:
>
>> After the cutoff date for preregistration, and usually one week before the meeting, the rooming list of conference participants should be sent to the conference manager. . . .
>>
>> . . . All convention- or conference-related materials should be assembled in packets for the participants. These items include the convention program, appropriate brochures, relevant reports, minutes, and other materials.

Omission within a sentence   Omissions from quoted material that fall within a sentence are indicated by three ellipsis points.

> The chapter offers the following advice regarding preconference preparations:
>
>> Whenever possible, the conference name tags should be . . . arranged in a system that will facilitate easy distribution.

Punctuation used in the original that falls on either side of the ellipsis points is often omitted; however, it may be retained, especially if such retention helps clarify the meaning or structure of the sentence.

> The chapter offers the following advice regarding preconference preparations:

> > After the cutoff date for preregistration . . . the rooming list of conference participants should be sent to the conference manager. . . .
> >   Whenever possible, . . . badges should be prepared ahead of time and arranged in a system that will facilitate easy distribution.

> > *or*

> > After the cutoff date . . . , the rooming list of conference participants should be sent to the conference manager. . . .

Omission of a full sentence   If an omission comprises an entire sentence or the beginning or end of a sentence within a paragraph, the end punctuation preceding or following the omission is retained and followed by three periods.

> The chapter offers the following advice regarding preconference preparations:

> > Whenever possible, conference name tags or badges should be prepared ahead of time and arranged in a system that will facilitate easy distribution. . . . All convention- or conference-related materials should be assembled in packets. . . . These items include the convention program, appropriate brochures, relevant reports, minutes, and other materials.

> On pages 234–235 we presented the following description of how authors choose between block and run-in formats for prose quotations:

> > The length of a quotation usually determines whether it is run into the text or set as a block quotation. . . . Length can be assessed in terms of the number of words, the number of typewritten or typeset pages, or the number of sentences in the passage.

The capitalization of the word *Length* in the second example is generally acceptable, although in some situations in which meticulous handling of original source material is required, the capital *L* would be placed in square brackets. For an example of this use of square brackets, see the second example on page 238.

Other Minor Alterations

Archaic spelling and punctuation   Archaic spellings and styles of punctuation should be preserved in direct quotations if they do not interfere with a reader's comprehension. If they occur frequently in a quotation, the author may wish to modernize them. An explanation to this effect should be placed in the text, in a note, or in a general statement within the preface if such modernizing has been done throughout the work. On the other hand, obvious typographical errors in modern works may be corrected without explanation.

Insertions   Sometimes an author wishes to insert into a quotation a brief explanation, clarification, summary of omitted material, or correction. These insertions (also called *interpolations*) are enclosed in square brackets. This use of brackets is explained and illustrated in the section on Brackets, beginning on page 6, in Chapter 1, "Punctuation."

Italics added   Words that were not italicized in the original version of a text may be italicized in the quoted passage in order to give emphasis to a particular word or phrase if the author informs the reader of the change. Any of several notations may be used. The notation may appear in the quoted passage, following the italicized portion, or at the end of the passage.

In works that include footnotes or other kinds of source notes, the notation may be set as a footnote or added to a source note. Common examples of notations are "italics mine," "emphasis added," and "italics added."

> The first chapter includes a statement that should be encouraging to secretaries:
>
>> In the past, many secretaries have been placed in positions of responsibility *without being delegated enough authority to carry out the responsibility*. The current pressures affecting managers have caused them to rethink the secretarial function and to delegate more responsibility and authority to their secretaries. [Italics mine.]
>
> The chapter offers the following advice regarding preconference preparations:
>
>> Whenever possible, conference name tags or badges should be prepared ahead of time and arranged in a system for early distribution. These items are often included in the conference packets. *All convention- or conference-related materials should be assembled in packets for the participants.* [Emphasis added.] These items include the convention program, appropriate brochures, relevant reports, minutes, and other materials.

If the note is placed at the end of the passage, parentheses may be used in place of brackets.

Footnote or endnote reference symbols or numbers are usually omitted from short quotations. In their place, authors often insert their own references.

Quoting Verse

The major difference between quotations of prose and poetry is that lines of poetry keep their identity as separate lines when set as extracts and also when run in with the text. When more than one line is run in, the poetic lines are separated by a virgule.

When poetic lines are set as extracts, the lines are divided exactly as in the original.

> When Gerard Manley Hopkins wrote that "Nothing is so beautiful as spring— / When weeds, in wheels, shoot long and lovely and lush," he probably had my yard in mind.

> The experience was one that reminded them of the wisdom of Pope's observation:

> > A little learning is a dang'rous thing;
> > Drink deep, or taste not the Pierian spring:
> > There shallow draughts intoxicate the brain,
> > And drinking largely sobers us again.

Style varies regarding spacing around the virgule. Some authors and publishers put no space on either side; others prefer a word space on each side. The virgule is sometimes omitted when each line of the original begins with a capital letter and the quotation contains no other capitals. Up to three or four lines of poetry are sometimes run in if they are closely integrated with the text. However, quotations of as few as two lines of poetry are commonly set off from the text as extracts.

> It was a fatalistic view of life that seemed to say, as James Payn did, "I never had a piece of toast / Particularly long and wide; / But fell upon the sanded floor, / And always on the buttered side."

> Some lines from Wordsworth seemed to express their attitude:

> > Bliss was it in that dawn to be alive,
> > But to be young was very heaven!

Horizontal Spacing

In typeset material, poetry quoted as an extract is usually arranged so that the longest line is centered on the page and the first word of all other flush-left lines align above or below the first word of the longest line. If the poem includes varied line lengths and indention, the alignment in the original version should be preserved. In typewritten material, authors will frequently choose a uniform indention for all lines that are flush left in the original version rather than center each poetry extract separately. Authors using this approach still indent lines that are not flush left in such a way as to preserve the alignment in the original.

> Consider these excerpts from Edgar Allen Poe, the first from "Annabel Lee," the second from "The Bells."

> > She was a child and I was a child,
> >   In this Kingdom by the sea,
> > But we loved with a love that was more than love—
> >   I and my Annabel Lee—
> > With a love that the wingèd seraphs of Heaven
> >   Coveted her and me.

> Hear the sledges with the bells—
> 　Silver bells!
> What a world of merriment their melody foretells!
> 　How they tinkle, tinkle, tinkle,
> 　　In the icy air of night!
> 　While the Stars that oversprinkle
> All the heavens seem to twinkle
> 　With a crystalline delight;
> 　Keeping time, time, time,
> 　In a sort of Runic rhyme
> To the tintinnabulation that so musically wells
> 　From the bells, bells, bells, bells,
> 　　Bells, bells, bells—
> From the jingling and the tinkling of the bells.

If the quotation does not start at the beginning of the line, the alignment in the quotation should still follow the original.

He praised her with words taken from Shelley:

> 　　　Wit and sense,
> Virtue and human knowledge, all that might
> Make this dull world a business of delight,

For an explanation of how to style poetry quotations that do not end in a period, see page 245.)

Sometimes the lines of a poem are too long to center. In these cases, the quotation may be set using a standard indention; run-over lines are indented further.

They were asked to comment on the following lines by Walt Whitman:

> You flagg'd walks of the cities! you strong curbs at the edges!
> You ferries! you planks and posts of wharves! you
> 　timber-lined sides! you distant ships!
> You rows of houses! you window-pierc'd façades! you roofs!
> You porches and entrances! you copings and iron guards!
> You windows whose transparent shells might expose so much!
> You doors and ascending steps! you arches!
> You gray stones of interminable pavements! You trodden crossings!
> From all that had touch'd you I believe you have imparted to yourselves
> 　and now impart the same secretly to me,
> From the living and the dead you have peopled your impassive sur-
> 　faces, and the spirits thereof would be evident and amicable with
> 　me

Quotation Marks in Poetry

If a quotation mark occurs at the beginning of a line of poetry, it should be aligned with the first letter of other lines. In a speech that extends over several lines, quotation marks are placed at the beginning of the speech and at the beginning of each stanza within the speech as well as at its conclusion.

They based their comments on the following lines from Matthew Arnold's "Stanzas from the Grande Chartreuse":

O children, what do ye reply? —
"Action and pleasure, will ye roam
Through these secluded dells to cry
And call us? — but too late ye come!
Too late for us your call ye blow,
Whose bent was taken long ago.

"Long since we pace this shadowed nave,
We watch those yellow tapers shine,
Emblems of hope over the grave,
In the high altar's depth divine;
The organ carries to our ear
Its accents of another sphere.

"Fenced early in this cloistral round
Of reverie, of shade, of prayer,
How should we grow in other ground?
How can we flower in foreign air?
—Pass, banners, pass, and bugles, cease;
And leave our desert to its peace!"

Omissions from Poetry

When a full line or several consecutive lines of poetry are omitted
from a quotation, the omission is indicated by a line of spaced
points. The lines of points extend the length of the preceding line
or of the missing line.

Whitman's attitude on the subject is revealed in these lines from
"When I Heard the Learned Astronomer":

When I heard the learned astronomer,
. . . .
How soon unaccountable I became tired and sick,
Til rising and gliding out I wandered off by myself,
In the mystical moist night-air, and from time to time,
Looked up in perfect silence at the stars.

Style varies regarding the treatment of poetry quotations that
do not end in a period. Sometimes authors indicate an omission
with ellipsis points, sometimes they prefer not to use ellipsis points
but rather to reproduce the text exactly as it appeared in the original version.

Whitman's attitude on the subject is revealed in these lines from
"When I Heard the Learned Astronomer":

When I heard the learned astronomer,
. . . .
How soon unaccountable I became tired and sick, . . .

or

Whitman's attitude on the subject is revealed in these lines from
"When I Heard the Learned Astronomer":

When I heard the learned astronomer,
. . . .
How soon unaccountable I became tired and sick,

Attribution of Sources

The ways in which authors acknowledge the sources of quotations vary with the kind of publication they are writing for and the kind of system that they are using to document sources of information throughout the work. In some cases, simply including the author's name is sufficient; in other cases, full bibliographical information is required, including publisher's name, date of publication, and page number of the passage quoted. The following paragraphs describe some of the alternative methods that are available to authors. For more on the details of styling such documentation, see Chapter 7, "Notes and Bibliographies."

In Works without Notes or a Bibliography

In works that do not include footnotes, endnotes, or a bibliography, authors often include all necessary information in the body of the text preceding the quotation.

> Levin summarizes these points in an article entitled "The Office in the Electronic Age" on page 46 of the March, 1982, issue of *The Office*:
>
> > The quality of work in general, whether involving electronic equipment or not, is based on the manager's knowing the responsibilities of each worker, careful assignment of tasks, effective written and oral communication, and periodic evaluation and modification of procedures.

An alternative method used in books that do not include notes or a bibliography is to run in all bibliographical information in a parenthetical note that follows the quotation. If the quotation is a run-in quotation the note comes between the closing quotation mark and the terminal punctuation of the sentence. If the quotation is set as an extract, the note follows the terminal punctuation.

> Levin makes the same points when she says, "The quality of work in general, whether involving electronic office equipment or not, is based on the manager's knowing the responsibilities of each worker, careful assignment of tasks, effective written and oral communication, and periodic evaluation and modification of procedures" ("The Office in the Electronic Age," *The Office,* March 1982, 46).

> Levin has summarized these points as follows:
>
> > The quality of work in general, whether involving electronic office equipment or not, is based on the manager's knowing the responsibilities of each worker, careful assignment of tasks, effective written and oral communication, and periodic evaluation and modification of procedures. ("The Office in the Electronic Age," *The Office,* March 1982, 46)

In each of these examples, it is assumed that the author's full name has already been given in the text and therefore does not need to be repeated.

In Works with Footnotes or Endnotes

In works that include footnotes or endnotes, the source of a quotation can be indicated by a raised reference number or reference mark that is placed at the end of the quoted passage after any terminal punctuation. For a full description of how to style footnotes and endnotes, see the section on Footnotes and Endnotes, beginning on page 198, in Chapter 7, "Notes and Bibliographies."

> Levin makes the same point when she says, "The quality of work in general, whether involving electronic office equipment or not, is based on the manager's knowing the responsibilities of each worker, careful assignment of tasks, effective written and oral communication, and periodic evaluation and modification of procedures."[17]

> Levin has summarized these points as follows:

> The quality of work in general, whether involving electronic office equipment or not, is based on the manager's knowing the responsibilities of each worker, careful assignment of tasks, effective written and oral communication, and periodic evaluation and modification of procedures.[17]

If a work with footnotes and endnotes includes more than one quotation from the same source, reference to full bibliographical information is required only at the first quotation. The usual practice is to include an explanation with the footnote to the first quotation that all subsequent references to that work in the text are from the same source. Having done that, one needs only to mention the page number at subsequent references.

> Levin makes the same point when she says, "The quality of work in general, whether involving electronic office equipment or not, is based on the manager's knowing the responsibilities of each worker, careful assignment of tasks, effective written and oral communication, and periodic evaluation and modification of procedures" (p. 46).

> Levin has summarized these points as follows:

> The quality of work in general, whether involving electronic office equipment or not, is based on the manager's knowing the responsibilities of each worker, careful assignment of tasks, effective written and oral communication, and periodic evaluation and modification of procedures. (p. 46)

In a Work with Parenthetical References

In a work utilizing parenthetical references to provide bibliographical information, the parenthetical reference is either included in the sentence that precedes the quotation or placed after the quotation, as were the page references in the preceding examples. Note that these references are placed before the terminal punctuation of a run-in quotation, but after the terminal punctuation of an extract. For more on the placement of parenthetical references, see the section on Parenthetical References, beginning on page 211, in Chapter 7, "Notes and Bibliographies."

In Other Contexts

In a context in which only the author's name or the author's name and the title of the work quoted are required, the attribution can be placed on its own line following the quotation. The attribution is usually set flush right and either enclosed in parentheses or preceded by an em dash. In a variation on this arrangement, the attribution may be run in with the quotation and either enclosed in parentheses or preceded by a dash.

> I went to the woods because I wished to live deliberately, to front only the essential fact of life, and see if I could not learn what it had to teach, and not, when I came to die, discover that I had not lived.
> —Henry David Thoreau, *Walden*

> That things always collapse into the *status quo ante* three weeks after a drive is over, everybody knows and apparently expects. . . . And yet many managements fail to draw the obvious conclusion. . . .
> (Peter F. Drucker)

> Winter lies too long in country towns; hangs on until it is stale and shabby, old and sullen. —Willa Cather, *My Ántonia*

When an attribution line follows a passage of poetry, the line may be set flush right, or it may be centered on the longest line in the quotation, or it may be indented a standard distance from the right margin.

> If this belief from heaven be sent,
> If such be Nature's holy plan,
> Have I not reason to lament
> What Man has made of Man?
> —William Wordsworth,
> "Lines Written in Early Spring"

> The sun descending in the west,
> The evening star does shine;
> The birds are silent in their nest,
> And I must seek for mine.
> —William Blake, "Night"

> Happy the man whose wish and care
> A few paternal acres bound,
> Content to breathe his native air
> In his own ground.
> —Alexander Pope, "Ode on Solitude"

Chapter 9

Copyediting and Proofreading

CONTENTS

This chapter describes the basic editorial steps that writers, editors, and proofreaders go through in order to produce accurate, readable, and attractive written or printed materials. For people involved with writing that is not intended for publication, some of the steps described in this chapter, such as those having to do with giving instructions to typesetters and handling page proofs, will not be necessary. However, for anyone who is writing for publication, this chapter should serve as a basic introduction to the range of activities often referred to as *editorial production,* or simply *production.*

The term *production* refers to the processes by which a publication is produced: from the completion of the manuscript to the making of the plates from which the pages will be printed. During production, the author's copy is edited to increase its accuracy and readability and is marked up in such a way that it can be readily typeset. The typeset copy is proofread, fitted on pages, and reproduced as film negatives. The negatives are used to make the printing plates, which lay down ink on paper on a printing press.

Depending upon the nature of the project, editorial production may be handled by a large staff of specialists or by a single person. In this chapter, the tasks are somewhat arbitrarily allocated to an *editor* (who has overall charge of getting the author's manuscript into copy that the typesetter can interpret) and a *proofreader* (who checks any newly typeset proofs against the copy from which type was set).

To an ever-increasing degree, many of the production steps described in this chapter are handled electronically, through the use of word processors, desktop-publishing systems, and computerized typesetting systems. The range of possibilities that an author or editor may encounter in terms of kinds of equipment, combinations of equipment, and capabilities of equipment is virtually unlimited. Rather than try to describe a range of possibilities that is subject to constant change, this chapter focuses on describing the basic steps that are used in the handling of paper copy. The point is that, with very few exceptions, no piece of electronic equipment can eliminate any of these steps; rather this equipment simply does electronically, and hence faster and usually more easily, what was once done manually. Therefore, the first step in understanding electronic editing is to understand the basic steps that have traditionally been part of the production process.

Manuscript Format

Manuscript preparation begins when the author's manuscript is typed. Copy should be typed clearly, without strikeovers, on good-quality paper that can be handled frequently without damage. Erasable paper is not recommended, because it smudges when handled. Copy should be typed on one side of the page only, because inserts written on the back of the page are easily overlooked.

Authors who are submitting a manuscript that is actually a printout from a word processor should keep in mind that some publishers will not accept manuscripts printed by a dot-matrix printer. All pages of the manuscript should be of the same size, preferably a standard size such as 8½ by 11 inches. Even so-called reprint copy made from tear sheets, or photocopied matter that is being used as extracts, should be taped to paper of that size.

Double spacing is also required. Even tables, footnotes, and bibliographies are double-spaced. This interlinear space, plus margins of at least one inch at top and bottom as well as both sides, allow the copy editor to mark corrections and specifications legibly.

The editor may also require the author to have the pages typed with the same number of lines on each full page and with a prescribed typewriter width setting, and to have all typing done on either a pica or elite machine. These considerations make it easier for the editor to estimate the length of the manuscript.

The author may also be asked to submit a second copy of the manuscript, which is filed for reference or which is used during production. Two people may work on copy simultaneously to save time; for example, one may verify the content while another copyedits. But this division of labor can be disadvantageous, because there can be only one master copy and eventually the marks from one copy will have to be carried to the other.

Copyediting the Manuscript

Copyediting is important because it is usually the last full reading of a manuscript before it is set in type. Revisions in manuscript are cheap; they take but a moment of the author's or editor's time. But mistakes in typeset copy are expensive to correct. Thus, the more closely the manuscript is read, the less expensive the project will be. Typesetters, also referred to as *compositors,* are supposed to "follow copy," mistakes and all; and although many will automatically correct obvious typing errors, they should never be expected to do so.

Basic Tasks

Specific duties of the copy editor can include any or all of the tasks described in the following paragraphs.

1. *Style the manuscript.* The changes that a copy editor makes are usually "mechanical" or stylistic—changes in punctuation, the use of capital letters, abbreviations, numbers, hyphens, etc.— so that the style of the text adheres to the particular style chosen by the publisher or by the editor. Consistency is a major goal. There are so many variations of style in standard use that inconsistencies appear even in the best writing. Removing these inconsistencies so that they do not distract the reader from the writer's purpose is usually the copy editor's principal job.

2. *Rewrite parts of the manuscript only when necessary.* Rewriting the author's prose where its intention is unclear or its style awkward is a responsibility that is handled judiciously. It is all too easy to change the author's meaning inadvertently. A query to the author may be preferable to an editor's attempt to rewrite on the basis of possibly imperfect understanding.

3. *Rearrange the content as needed.* Words, sentences, paragraphs, or whole sections may have to be transposed and sequences renumbered. Certain text matter might be better handled as a note or in an appendix, and vice versa. It is often best to consult with the author before undertaking these kinds of changes.

4. *Verify the data.* Fact-checking is an important part of the production process; some publishers employ people who do nothing but check facts. Quotations should be verified and revised as necessary to match their sources. Bibliographical references should be checked. Dates and the spelling of proper names should be looked up in reference books.

5. *Look for trademarks.* Brand names like Xerox and Vaseline should be spelled and capitalized precisely. Where appropriate, generic names can be substituted for these brand names.

6. *Look for examples of sexual bias.* Rewrite the copy to remove such bias if you have permission to do so from the publisher or author.

7. *Query the author.* Ask for clarification or for approval of revisions you have made.

8. *Make a style sheet.* For suggestions on how to prepare and maintain a style sheet, see pages 256–260 below.

9. *Typemark the manuscript.* Add all of the marks and notations that the compositor will need in order to typeset the text in accordance with agreed-upon specifications.

10. *Add, delete, or otherwise revise headings.* Headings should be edited so that they accurately describe the material that follows them and so that their styling is consistent.

11. *Check all cross-references.* Verify the author's cross-references and add new ones if necessary. Phrase the cross-references according to the suggestions on pages 272–273.

12. *Examine the table of contents.* The headings there should match those on the manuscript.

13. *Check all sequences.* All numerical lists, all alphabetically arranged items such as bibliographies and glossaries, as well as all sequences of table or figure numbers must be in order.

14. *Check for possible instances of copyright violation, libel, or other potential legal problems.* Ensure that the author has obtained permission to reproduce copyrighted materials.

15. *Renumber the pages if needed.* If numerous additions have been made on separate sheets, the pages should be renumbered.

16. *Create and typemark running heads.* Running heads are the short phrases that appear at the top of the page in most books. In

some books the running head on the left hand page (often referred to as the *verso* page) is simply the title of the book or a
shortened form of the title. In such books, the running head
on the right-hand page (often called the *recto* page) is usually
the chapter title or a shortened form of it. In books in which
the chapters have numerous subdivisions, the running head
on the verso page is the chapter title; the running head on the
recto page is the subheading within the chapter that covers
the contents of the recto page.

17. *Make a list of special characters in the copy.* This list should include the number of the manuscript page on which each character first appears. Two copies of this list are needed, one for
the typesetter and one for the files.

Because of these various duties, the copy editor usually reads
a manuscript twice—more if it is complex or poorly written—at
least once for content and again for details such as errors in punctuation and for the verification of such things as the spelling of
proper names. It is usually more efficient to copyedit similar
things—tables, footnotes, captions, and the like—together. In this
way the editor will be more likely to notice inconsistencies and will
be more alert for ways to style similar items consistently. In most
cases the editor corrects the errors, but sometimes a query to the
author is in order.

In some publishing houses, the edited manuscript is sent to
the author for approval before being typeset. The author is usually instructed to make his or her revisions with a colored pencil
or pen. The author is sent either the master manuscript or a photocopy of it. If the author is sent the master manuscript, a photocopy of it should be made first, in case it is lost in transit. If a
photocopy is sent, any revisions made by the author on the photocopy will have to be carefully copied, or *carried,* to the master
manuscript.

How to Mark a Manuscript

There are certain conventions, symbols, and codes used and understood by editors and typesetters. Most of these are described
and illustrated in this chapter, beginning on page 262. In addition, special instructions have to be written in from time to time,
and these should be concise, precise, and legible.

Conciseness is essential because of the limited space on which
the copy editor works—margins and interlinear spaces. Corrections are made on the manuscript as close to the normal reading
order as possible, because the compositor reads the manuscript
through in sequence and must be allowed to find additions and
revisions without having to search for them. Normally, the right
margin is reserved for notations concerning revisions, the left

margin for notations concerning typography. However, a heavily revised manuscript may require revisions to be marked in both margins in addition to the space between the lines.

All instructions to the compositor are circled to distinguish them from actual revisions. Special notes often begin with the abbreviation "Comp:" to call attention to them. Margin notes should not be written so close to the edge of the paper that they will fail to duplicate in a photocopier.

Should the editor use pen or pencil? Beginners understandably prefer pencil, but a bright-colored, fine-point pen is preferable, because it is easier for the compositor to read and it does not smudge. Colored pens and pencils are necessary if more than one person handles the copy; each should mark the copy with a color that identifies that person. To ensure neatness, the editor's mistakes should not be crossed out but rather whited out or erased with ink eraser or strips of white tape. Mistakes made by the author, however, should never be erased but only crossed out; the author's original should always be visible behind the deletion marks.

Additions to the Text

Brief additions to the text may be written in between the lines of the manuscript or in the margins, as explained later in this section. Lengthy additions, however, should be typed on a separate page of the same size as the manuscript—never on a slip of paper stapled or taped to the manuscript page. The insertion is typed double space and to the same width as the rest of the manuscript copy. It should be clearly identified, too. A typical identification is a note at the top of the page: "Insert 24A. Insert as shown on msp 24." Then, on manuscript page 24, a caret is drawn at the point of insertion, and this instruction is written in the margin: "Insert 24A." Both instructions are circled to ensure that they are not mistakenly set in type.

To ensure that the compositor knows whether the insert should be run in or set as a separate paragraph, the identification and the instructions may be more explicit; for example, "Insert 24A; insert as shown on msp 24; run in" and "Run in insert 24A here"; or the instructions could tell the compositor to "set as new paragraph." Several brief inserts can be typed on one extra page if they are all to be inserted on the same manuscript page and if each is clearly identified as Insert A, Insert B, and so forth. However, this method of inserting additions is advisable only if the number of such inserts is small and manageable.

An alternative, which results in copy much easier for the typesetter to handle, is the cut-and-paste method. Additions are typed on separate pages as described above, and the pieces of copy are cut and pasted or taped in proper sequence on pages of

the same size as the rest of the manuscript. This met...
tra pages to the manuscript, which will have to be repag...

Special care must be taken to insert the additions pr...
and also to revise punctuation. All too often copy editors, conce...
trating on the content of the addition, fail to position it properly
in the copy.

Pagination

Manuscript page numbers are checked so that the compositor is
not left to wonder about a missing or repeated page number.
Page numbers should be complete, in sequence, and positioned
near the upper right corner, where they will be readily seen by all
who handle the manuscript.

Any pages inserted after the typing of the manuscript should
be identified with a letter following the number of the preceding
page. Pages 4a and 4b would thus fall between pages 4 and 5. In
addition, on the bottom of the preceding page, the instruction
"Go to pages 4a and 4b" or "Page 4a follows" should be written
(and circled) so the compositor will know what to expect. For
added clarity, one may also write at the top of page 4a, "follows
page 4." If the manuscript fills up with numerous *a* and *b* pages,
one should renumber the manuscript entirely, taking care to delete any notations such as "Page 4a follows."

Indicating deleted pages is simpler. If pages 15 and 16 are
deleted, for example, one simply adds a hyphen plus 16 to the
number on page 14 so that it reads: 14-16. This tells the compositor to expect page 17 to follow page 14.

Special Symbols

Any symbol that does not appear on a typewriter keyboard should
be *called for* in the margin of the copy the first time that it appears
on a page. For example, if the author has written > in a table, the
copy editor calls attention to and clarifies the symbol by writing
and circling "greater than" in the margin. Similarly, any odd spellings or stylings that are intentional but that the compositor might
misread or be tempted to "correct" should also be noted: either
by placing stet points (usually in the form of four or more dots
written in below the word or words) or by writing a note in the
margin to "follow copy." When there might be confusion between
a zero and a capital *O*, or between the numeral 1 and the letter *l*,
the copy editor should write in the margins *zero, Arabic 1, cap oh*,
or *ell*.

Editors should know the names of special symbols, including
the Greek alphabet, diacritics, and basic mathematical symbols, so
that they can call for them by name in the margin when the symbols appear in the text. Also, on going through a manuscript for
the first time, the copy editor makes a list of all these uncommon

mbols. Often the author is asked to supply this list instead. This list, which consists of a drawing of the symbol, its name, the size and face of type desired, and the manuscript page on which it first appears, is given to the compositor. It is sent even before the manuscript is sent, because the compositor may not have these symbols in the particular font chosen and may have to order them specially or arrange to set them in a different size of type that is already on hand in the shop.

The Style Sheet

Copy editors work with a style sheet. There are two basic kinds. One, representing the publisher's house style, is a predetermined list of styling decisions which the publisher may give to the editor along with the manuscript. Some publishers even issue their own full-fledged style manuals. The other kind of style sheet is created by the copy editor while reading the manuscript. On these blank pages the editor keeps track of how to handle all words and phrases that have alternate forms. In addition, note is made of formatting and typography decisions. The form that is recorded on the style sheet represents the final decision of the editor, whether it is based on the author's original styling or the editor's preference or the publisher's style sheet.

Everything that might have an alternate form is written on the style sheet because inconsistencies may appear unexpectedly on later pages, forcing the editor to go back to look for the earlier form. Throughout the readings of the manuscript, the editor will both develop the style sheet and consult it. Until the final reading is finished, the style sheet is not finished. Words that have alternate spellings (*acknowledgement* or *acknowledgment*) or alternate forms of capitalization or hyphenation are automatically included. Words that are often but not always italicized (e.g. or *e.g.*) or that may or may not have diacritical marks (*fiance* or *fiancé*) are included. When the author spells a word inconsistently, the copy editor usually chooses the form that appears most frequently on the copy, but the editor always feels free to correct nonstandard words and phrases.

To make a style sheet, the editor divides a few blank pages into categories such as Numbers and Dates, Footnotes, Abbreviations, Headings, and so forth. Additional pages are assembled on which individual words and phrases will be listed in approximate alphabetical order. Examples of problematical stylings are listed on these pages as the manuscript is read. The editor may wish to add manuscript page numbers to certain items on the chance that he or she will need to go back and make styling changes on the basis of stylings encountered later in the text.

All variations on one styling decision need not be listed; a single notation may indicate that similar cases are to be handled in

ABCD	EFGHIJ	KLMNO

benefitted (4)
Atlantic coast (5)
anticyclonic (5)
crosswind (6)
buildup (n) (8)
advisor (23)
acknowledgment (27)
data base (28)
airflow (36)
bird cage (41)
air speed (42)
	headwind (6)
	flood plain (7)
	funneling (8)
	field data
	   sheet (43)
	inter=individual
	   spacing (44)
	interspecific (46)
		mid=1950s (6)
		Nearctic zone (7)
		non=breeding (12)
		midday (13)
		midpoint (24)
		Midwest (25)
		M.S. thesis (38)
		non=motorized
		   glider (42)
		ms. (manuscript)(47)

PQRST	UVWXYZ	Numbers
re=enter (3) take=off (6) sizeable (7) setup (8) shoreline (15) reappear (27) subadult (42) tail feather (43) postdoctoral (47) prefrontal (50)	Wrangel $\frac{1}{N}$ St. Elias National Park (7)	one fourth (n) ten, 11 1,000 1980s $1970\frac{1}{N}77$ 2d, 3d 6° C 23 July 1968

	Abbreviations
	mph (5)
	P.O. Box (7)
	EST (12)
	e.g. (22)
	WSW (tables) (23)
	St. Louis (but Fort
	   Worth) (25,27)
	Spell out state and
	nation names except
	in addresses (MA, CT)
	and tables (Mass.,
	Conn.)
		Capitals
		the Cooper River delta
		the east coast
		New York state
		among + <u>between</u> l.c.
		  in titles
		seasons of year l.c.

Figure 9.1. An editor's style sheet

the same manner. For example, the notation "west-northwest (text)—WNW (tables)" tells the reader that other directions are to be styled in the same way.

The notations should also be brief. A single word, "résumé," in the alphabetical listing of particular words and phrases indicates that all instances of that word include the acute accent marks. Similarly, instead of writing the sentence "Decades have no apostrophe before the final *s*," the simple term "1980s" could be listed in the Numbers section. This means that all such forms— *1970s*, etc.—are styled in the same way, without the optional apostrophe. Also, a single sample number like "5,200" on the style sheet can indicate that all four-digit numbers use the optional comma.

When the style sheet is finished—after the last reading of the copy—it is put in final alphabetical order and typed. At this point the entries are checked for clarity, and further descriptive details, such as the abbreviations for parts of speech, are added where appropriate. From now on, the style sheet may be copied and used by the compositor, the author, and the proofreader.

The following alphabetically ordered listing contains suggestions about the kinds of things that may be included on a style sheet.

Abbreviations Every abbreviation on the copy should be taken note of, checked in a dictionary for accuracy, and written in its desired form on the style sheet. Attention should be paid to the use of capital letters (some abbreviations are traditionally set in small capitals), punctuation, and spacing. See Chapter 4 for a full discussion of abbreviation styling.

Bibliography Sample listings should be recorded in this section that represent all variations encountered in the copy. The bibliographic form chosen should be one of the standard forms discussed in Chapter 7, "Notes and Bibliographies."

Capitalization The capitalization of individual words is indicated by putting those words in the main alphabetical listing in either a capitalized or lowercase form.

Cross-references The style sheet should specify the styling of cross-references. Will they refer to page numbers or to chapter titles, for example? Will the word *page* be abbreviated?

Dates The chosen styling may be indicated with one or two examples, as follows: "26 September 1972" or "September 26, 1972"; "September 1972" or "September, 1972." If abbreviations of months are acceptable in certain instances, those instances should be specified. For example, "Sept. 26, Sept. 1972 (tables only)."

Definitions Some books set off definitions (or sometimes words that are followed by glosses) within running text by printing them in italic or boldface type. The style sheet should tell how to handle these.

Footnotes The style sheet contains samples of footnotes in every variation. It shows such choices as whether *ibid.* is italic or roman and how to style footnote reference symbols.

Foreign words The editor decides if foreign words will be generally italicized or not. Specific words are written on the main alphabetical list, either underlined to indicate italics or typed regularly (for emphasis, with the word *roman* in parentheses next to them).

Hyphenation of compound words Compound words will comprise a good part of the main alphabetical section of the style sheet, since many compounds have open, hyphenated, and closed-up forms. It is sometimes helpful to distinguish between a phrase used as a compound noun and an identical phrase used an an adjective. The distinction may be made simply by writing the initial for the part of speech next to the appropriate term:

> low pressure (n)
> low-pressure system

Lists The copy editor often has to choose whether items in lists are numbered or lettered, whether the numbers are enclosed in parentheses, and whether they are set roman or italic. A different set of rules has to be devised for displayed lists (that is, lists set off from the rest of the text, with each new item beginning a new line). The style sheet states whether items in displayed lists are listed by number or letter, what punctuation and spacing appears around each letter or number, and whether and how far each item is indented.

Numbers The style sheet shows the cutoff point for numbers appearing as numerals or as words. This can be done by writing, in the section on numbers, a shorthand notation such as the following: ten, 11. This reminds the editor that all numbers up to and including ten are spelled out, while all numbers beyond ten are expressed in digits. A rule can also be stated as a sentence, for example: "All numbers are digits except when they begin a sentence."

If the copy contains fractions within the text, the style sheet states whether they are to be spelled out or set as fractions; and, if set as fractions, whether they are solidus fractions (as 3/4) or as case or piece fractions (as ¾ or $\frac{3}{4}$) that fit on a line of text. More complex types of fractions are usually set on their own separate lines, because they do not fit easily on a line of text. A style sheet guide to fractions might be written this way: "one-half, one-fourth, three-fourths (in running text). All fractions with units smaller than tenths in running text set solidus."

Other questions to resolve and record on the style sheet might include the styling of ordinals (second, 2nd, or 2d) and the handling of inclusive figures and dates. For example, should the copy read 1978–80 or 1978–1980? 395–97 or 395–397? How about dollar figures: five cents or 5¢? two million dollars or $2 million? These and many other options are discussed in Chapter 5, "The Treatment of Numbers."

Punctuation The style sheet records all stylings for which there are alternatives. If it is decided to place a comma before the *and* at the end of a series, write "series comma." If it is decided to capitalize a full sentence following a colon, the following might be written: ": Full sentence, : phrase" to show that a phrase following a colon is lowercased.

Spelling One source—a good general dictionary—should be chosen for the checking of spelling. For proper names, an encyclopedia or biographical or geographical dictionary is usually the best source to use. All proper nouns are recorded on the style sheet.

Tables The style sheet states such things as how column heads are to be capitalized, whether they should be set in bold, italic, or roman type, and whether they are centered over the column or aligned in another way. Consistency in the use of rules and the styling and position of table numbers, titles, captions, and source notes is important, and the style sheet will probably describe these specifications in detail.

Copyright and Acknowledgment of Sources

One of an editor's most important responsibilities is to remain alert to the possibility of copyright violations, libel, and other invasions of a person's right to privacy. These should be brought to the author's attention. All too frequently an editor finds that an author has been careless in quoting or acknowledging an original source. In those cases the author may be tactfully queried, "Author: please supply source."

Interpretations of the 1978 U.S. copyright law have not been fully standardized, but in general an editor should know that all printed material in the *public domain* can be reproduced without permission, though the source should always be acknowledged. Material in the public domain includes, but is not limited to, works published before the twentieth century and also public records and federal or state government publications. In addition, the copyright law allows *fair use* of small amounts of copyrighted material for the purposes of criticism and comment in scholarship.

While reading a manuscript, the editor should keep a list of every item that is credited or that might need to be credited to a source. The entries on this list would include the following information, which should be requested from the author if not available:

1. Title and author of the source

2. Year of publication

3. Name of publisher and copyright holder (These may be different.)

4. Page on which the source originally appeared

5. Whether permission to reprint is needed and has been obtained

6. Fee required, if any

7. Name and address of the person representing the copyright holder

8. Whether the author has permission to adapt the original if requested

Some of this information may be found in a credit line or source note supplied by the author. But much of it will be found in a copy of the permissions correspondence that the publisher usually asks the author to submit along with the manuscript.

Permission to reprint It is important to begin the process of obtaining permission to reprint early. Many publishers are notoriously slow to respond to such requests and may have to be prodded by follow-up letters. The letter of request should supply full information about the source to be reproduced: title, author, year of publication and copyright; an exact description of the part to be quoted or reprinted, including page number or figure or table number and the total number of lines or pages involved. In addition, the copyright holder needs to know about the work in which the source will be reproduced: name of author and publisher, proposed title, approximate date of publication, type of publication, the number of copies to be printed, and the market. The letter should also tell the copyright holder whether the material is to be adapted in any way, as is common with reprinted illustrations and tables, and show precisely how it will be changed.

A letter of approval from the copyright holder will specify

certain conditions which must be strictly adhered to. The conditions might include a fee, the number of copies to be sent to the copyright holder, or the precise wording and position of the credit line.

All material taken from another source, with or without permission, should be acknowledged—in running text, in footnotes, or on special acknowledgment pages. If the copyright holders permit, credit lines may be grouped together on a single page headed "Acknowledgments" or on the copyright page of the book (which is usually on the back of the title page), under a heading such as "Grateful acknowledgment is made for the use of the following material."

Copyediting Marks

The following section describes the use of copyediting marks to indicate certain kinds of elements in and changes to a text. Many of these uses are illustrated in the example of a copyedited passage on page 263. The marks themselves are the same as the proofreaders' marks listed on page 281.

Additions to the text There are several ways to add passages to a manuscript that is already typed, depending upon the length of the addition and how easily it can be marked for insertion. The symbol commonly used to indicate an addition is a caret placed at the point of insertion; the addition is written over the caret and above the line.

If a character is added in mid-word, only a caret is needed below the inserted character. However, if a character is added to the beginning or end of a word, a close-up sign should be added to the character above the caret to ensure that the typesetter knows that the character should be set closed-up. When a word or phrase is crossed out, the replacement word or phrase may be simply written above the deleted passage, without a caret to point to it. Any large group of added words should be enclosed in a brace so that the typesetter can readily find the beginning and ending of the new phrase.

A very large insertion that will not fit easily between the lines may be written in the margin, with a line drawn from the words to a caret that marks the point of insertion. Any additions within the margin must be written horizontally. The typesetter must never be expected to turn the page in order to read any passage. If the margin is crowded with other notations, the editor must write the insertion so that it is readily seen as a single passage. This may be accomplished by enclosing it partly in a box or brace or by connecting the lines with connecting arrows.

Any insertion that is too long to fit in the margin should be typed on a separate sheet, as explained on page 254.

A copy editor must have an easy familiarity with the
conventions of the English language, a fairly wide general
knowledge, the ability to use reference books, and a knowledge of the basics of book production, including typography.
Familiarity with house style is also required. In addition,
the editor must be able to read extremely closely, ~~to be
alert for~~ spot details, and remember them so thoroughly that he
or she will ~~notice~~ the smallest inconsistency. A copy editor
must also learn the conventional symbols used to mark up a
manuscript, as ~~and be able to write precise and unambiguous
instructions to the compositor.~~

[margin note: the specific styling conventions preferred by a particular publisher]

Copy editing involves not only reading the copy carefully
and making needed revisions, but also ~~it involves~~ making those revisions
in such a way as to make them ~~totally~~ unambiguous to the type-
setter. When revisions are required, the editor must be able to make ~~and making~~ them with an eye to how they fit with the
rest of the copy.

Does the copy editor rewrite copy? Not unless specifically
instructed to do so. Senior editors, with authority from the
publisher or author, often rewrite or reorganize the material
to better achieve the author's purpose, or they suggest these
revisions to the author. However, most copy editors have to resist
the temptation to rewrite a manuscript in their own style. Their
first duty is to the author. Revisions are made only to correct
factual or stylistic errors, to make the author's meaning clearer,
or to make the material consistent.

Figure 9.2. A copyedited page

Deletions There are three ways to delete material in a manuscript. One is for the editor to simply draw a heavy line through the unwanted copy. The line must be heavy and confident, drawn straight through the copy so that it cannot be mistaken for an underscore. The editor must also take care to begin and end the crossout bar precisely so that no characters or punctuation marks are missed and also so that extra characters are not mistakenly deleted.

The second method is to use the delete sign shown on page 281. This symbol may be used to delete a single character or, when it is appended to a heavy line, to delete larger amounts of copy. The symbol may also be used when the editor wishes to cut a large section such as a whole paragraph. Rather than drawing bars through every line in the paragraph, the editor draws a box around the paragraph, makes a large X within the box, and appends a delete sign to its side in the margin. The advantage of this method is that it makes it instantly clear to the compositor that the whole section can be skipped.

A single character may also be crossed out with a vertical line without an attached delete sign loop. This is done mostly when the delete sign might interfere with an accompanying mark such as a close-up sign.

To delete an underscore, one obviously cannot use a crossout line. Instead, the editor adds a delete mark to the end of the underscore. It is more difficult to delete only part of an underscore, but it can be done. Divide the underscore with vertical lines and place delete marks only on the appropriate sections of the line. If the copy is crowded, it may be preferable to write *ital* or *rom* in the margin, circle the pertinent sections of the underscored material, and draw an arrow between those sections and the margin notation.

Guide to Western Birds, vol. 2, p. 57.

Guide to Western Birds, vol. 2, p. 57. ⟵ rom

The editor's job is to make the compositor's job easy. Thus, to prevent the compositor's having to search the copy to see where deletions begin and end, the editor should add close-up signs, run-in signs, or arrows to guide the compositor from one part of the copy to another. This is especially important when the copy is heavily marked up. The editor should also help by rewriting single words and punctuation marks in their new positions instead of expecting the compositor to search for small pieces of copy in a maze of deletions. One should always rewrite punctuation marks so that they appear immediately after the word they follow.

Close-up A close-up sign indicates a deletion of space. It is used to turn two or more separate words into a single word. Used at the end of a line, it tells the compositor to join this word to the first word of the following line. The symbol is frequently combined with the deletion of a hyphen to instruct the typesetter to set a closed-up word rather than two separate words or one hyphenated word.

stone⁀walled   water⁀fall

A large close-up sign is used in combination with a crossout bar to guide the compositor from the beginning of a deletion to its end. The close-up sign includes both a bottom and a top arc, but one of these alone suffices, especially if there are other markings on the copy that may interfere.

Capitals, small capitals, and lowercase letters Capital letters are marked by three underscores. These are drawn below lowercase letters to indicate a change to capitals, or below capital letters when needed for clarity. Clearly typed capital letters should be left alone, but any handwritten capitals that might be mistaken for lowercase should be reinforced with triple underscoring.

The lowercase symbol, a slash mark through a letter going down from right to left, is used to change a typewritten capital letter and also to ensure that a handwritten lowercase letter is not mistaken for a capital. To change a lengthy phrase to lowercase when it is typed all in capitals, the editor need only slash the first letter of each word. To ensure that the compositor sees the mark, the top of the slash can be extended as a horizontal line across the top of all the other letters in the word.

Small capitals look like capital letters but have less height. They are frequently used to set certain abbreviations, such as A.D. and B.C. Their chief use, however, is in headings and captions, where they are often set with initial capital letters. To call for small capitals, the editor draws a double underscore below typewritten capital or lowercase letters. A combination of three and two underscores is drawn to indicate a combination of capitals and small capitals.

In addition to the symbols, editors use abbreviations such as *cap, lc, sm caps,* and *cap/sc* to call for specific styles of capitalization when writing in margins of copy.

Space The space symbol instructs the typesetter to insert a *word space,* which is the amount of spacing that appears between each adjacent pair of words on a particular line. To separate two words that were inadvertently closed up on the copy, the editor draws a vertical line between them. It is not necessary to add the space symbol above the line, but it may be added. Sometimes the editor instructs the compositor to add a *thin space,* which is smaller than a word space and which is used on either side of operational signs in mathematics and in other special cases. Usually a vertical line is drawn where the space is desired and a note circled in the margin, "Insert thin #." In certain circumstances, the editor may ask the compositor to insert thin spaces between the letters of all the words in an all-capitalized heading and extra word space between the words of the heading. This process is called *letterspacing.* To achieve it, the editor writes in the margin, "Comp: letterspace this heading." Occasionally an editor or proofreader calls for a *hair space,* which is smaller than a regular thin space. A hair space, barely obvious, is often inserted between two characters that might cause confusion when closed up entirely, as a single quotation mark set next to a double quotation mark. *Em spaces* and *en spaces* are discussed on page 272.

Italic and roman type   Italic type is indicated by a single underscore. If it is necessary to mark the same copy for capital letters, four separate underscores are drawn. For lengthy italic copy, it is neater to write and circle *ital* in the margin and circle or point out the passage so that the compositor can see clearly where it begins and ends. Roman type is not ordinarily marked with special notations. However, the editor should write *rom* in the margin to mark a change from a large block of italic type such as an extract.

When one is marking already-printed copy, such as a tear sheet taped to a copy page, there is no need to underscore words that are already italicized. If any italic copy is to be changed to roman, however, one should underscore or circle the italicized word and write *rom* in the margin directly opposite the word.

Boldface   Boldface is a dark, heavy type used sometimes for emphasis and frequently for headings. Design specifications usually determine in advance what words will be set bold, but the editor reminds the compositor by marking the copy. To tell the compositor to set a word or passage in boldface type, the editor draws a wavy underscore below the relevant copy, including its punctuation. If the copy is more than a line long, the abbreviation *bf* may be circled in the margin and the copy clearly pointed out with a brace and an arrow.

To correct copy already marked for boldface that should not be so marked, the editor circles the affected words and in the margin writes *lf* (lightface). This abbreviation is written carefully because a handwritten *lf* can easily be mistaken for a *bf.*

Boldface italic type (abbreviated *bold ital*) is indicated by a straight underscore with a wavy underscore below it. Since not every font has this rarely used typeface, however, one should check with the typesetter first before designing a page that requires the use of bold italic letters or numbers.

Punctuation marks An editor may add or delete marks of punctuation or change them to different marks of punctuation.

Period The copy editor's mark to denote a period, a point enclosed in a small circle, is used only when needed for legibility—when the compositor might miss the period because it is handwritten or otherwise obscured—and also when changing a comma to a period. To make this change, the editor circles the typed comma; the typesetter will know that it has become a period.

Comma Legible commas need no further markup. Commas that are not clear—those inserted next to a deletion, for example—are flagged by a caret drawn over the comma.

Semicolon The semicolon also is signaled by the placing of a caret over it whenever it is felt that it might not be legible. The editor can also change a comma to a semicolon by adding a point over the comma and a caret over the point. To change a semicolon to a comma, the editor simply draws a caret over the comma in such a way that it obscures the point of the semicolon. To change a colon to a semicolon, a tail is drawn on the lower point and a caret drawn over the newly made semicolon.

Colon A small circle or oval is drawn around a colon if it needs clarification, or if it has been changed from a period by drawing in the second point. A semicolon can be changed to a colon by superimposing two heavy dots over the semicolon so that the tail of the lower part of the semicolon is obscured.

Parentheses Parentheses should be inserted carefully. They should be slightly oversize but should still look like parentheses. Some copy editors draw one or two tiny horizontal slashes through each handwritten parenthesis to ensure its identity. Parentheses are set in the same type as the copy surrounding them. Thus, if the material within parentheses is italicized and the surrounding copy is roman, the parentheses would also be set roman and thus would not be underscored.

Brackets Brackets should always be drawn in by the editor unless the brackets on the copy were produced by an authentic bracket key on the typewriter. If the typist made brackets from a combination of slashes and underscores, the editor draws over them so that they look like square brackets.

Ellipsis points Ellipsis points, except for those used as periods following a sentence, should be spaced. In the margin, the editor may call for the insertion of thin spaces between the points if they are typed closed up on the copy. Ellipsis points in mathematical copy are often raised off of the base line instead of being positioned on it. To mark these for typesetting, the editor places a caret above and an inverted caret below each point or writes "center points" in the margin.

Quotation marks An inverted caret flags quotation marks only when they might be misread, as when they form part of a handwritten insertion. Combinations of single and double quotation marks might confuse the typesetter, so it is helpful to describe in the margin what is intended. The easiest way to do this is to write and circle "single" in the margin, with a line and arrows pointing to the single quotation marks. Typesetters usually insert a hair space between double and single quotation marks, but editors often ask for the space to ensure that it is set.

Most—but not all—typefaces distinguish between apostrophes and single quotation marks. If there is any possibility of misinterpretation, the compositor should be told which to set in a particular case.

Dashes The em dash, which is typewritten usually as two hyphens or one hyphen with a space on both sides, is marked for the typesetter with a numeral 1 over the typewritten hyphen or hyphens and a capital M below it. To call for dashes longer than one em, the editor writes a larger number over the hyphens. For example, the dash that represents the repetition of an author's name in a bibliography is marked as a three-em dash, with the numeral 3 above and a capital M below the hyphen.

In print, the em dash is usually closed up—that is, it is printed with no space on either side. It is unnecessary for the editor to add close-up marks to an em dash unless the hyphens in the copy are spaced.

The en dash is represented in typewritten copy by a hyphen. Thus, the copy must be marked to distinguish en dashes from hyphens. This is done by writing a numeral 1 above the typewritten hyphen and a capital N below it. If en dashes are not so marked, the typesetter will probably set them all as hyphens.

All handwritten copy containing dashes should be marked to identify the kind of dash desired.

Hyphen The hyphen, the shortest dash, is used to divide words at the end of a line and to form some compound words. The double hyphen is an editorial mark that is made by adding a second line below a typewritten or handwritten hyphen. The double hyphen is used by editors to make it clear that a hyphen is being asked for. Any hyphen within a handwritten insertion should be doubled.

Editors also use the double hyphen when the hyphen within a compound word corresponds with a word break at the end of a line. They mark the double hyphen to ensure that the compositor will not drop the hyphen within the compound when the line breaks differently. Conversely, any end-of-line hyphen that denotes a syllabic break in a word and that might mistakenly be retained by the compositor should be marked for deletion with a vertical line and a close-up mark to show that it connects with the first word of the next line. If there is an end-of-line hyphen to be deleted without closing up the word, the hyphen is crossed with a vertical line and a space symbol is added to indicate that the compound should not be closed.

Some editors mark all end-of-line hyphens for retention or deletion, but usually it is necessary only to mark those hyphens that might be mistakenly deleted or retained because they occur in words that could reasonably be spelled with or without the hyphen.

A handwritten double hyphen is also used to tell a typesetter to insert a hyphen.

Transposition sign The transposition sign—a line curving over one element and under another—is used to indicate transposition of characters, words, phrases, or sentences. Often the transposition symbol on the copy is reinforced by the abbreviation *tr* written and circled in the margin.

A variation of the symbol is used to indicate transposition of more than two elements. The copy editor's marks in the example below, for instance, tell the typesetter to leave the middle word and transpose the other two.

aft and fore

When the material to be transposed is typed on more than one line, the conventional symbol is unwieldy. In these cases, the editor usually circles one of the elements and shows its new position with a line and a caret or arrow. Very complicated transpositions should probably be rewritten by the editor, at least in part, so as not to force the compositor to follow a series of complex arrows and lines.

To delete punctuation during a transposition, one may simply draw the curved line in such a way that it covers and obscures the punctuation mark. All transpositions must be marked with great care and double-checked because it is easy to make a mistake. Punctuation marks are often overlooked in this kind of editing; they frequently have to be rewritten.

Run in The run-in sign—a line with curved ends that leads the reader's eye from one part of the copy to another—is used to connect copy typed on two separate lines so that the compositor will automatically run one right after the other.

Stet *Stet,* a Latin word meaning "let it stand," is used to restore words mistakenly crossed out on the copy. The editor places a series of heavy dots below the deleted material and writes *stet* in the margin to ensure that the compositor notices the dots. Or, if the crossout bar has obscured the original, the editor may prefer to erase the crossout bar and place stet points below the word without a note in the margin.

Spell-out sign To indicate to the compositor that a number is to be spelled out or an abbreviation to be spelled in full, the editor simply circles the short form on the copy. Sometimes *sp* is also written and circled in the margin. However, this can be done only when the intended change is unambiguous. The numeral 3, for example, would pose no problem when circled on the copy; the compositor will set *three.* But what about the circled fraction 1/2? Will the compositor know whether to set *one half* or *one-half?* It is the same with abbreviations. When the abbreviation in *Springfield, Vt.,* is circled, the compositor will unhesitatingly substitute *Vermont.* But the typesetter cannot be expected to know what you want when you circle obscure or ambiguous abbreviations such as *pt.* Often it is better for the editor to cross out the abbreviation and write its replacement above the line. Alternatively, the abbreviation may be circled on the copy and the full word written in the margin if interlinear additions are already crowding the copy.

The spell-out sign may also be used to indicate the reverse, but only in circumstances where the author's intention is absolutely clear. The word *ten,* circled on the copy, would thus automatically tell the compositor to set the numeral 10.

Alignment Proper alignment is usually more of a concern for proofreaders than for editors, but an editor may have to instruct the typesetter concerning alignment of tables and other columns or lists. Usually general instructions are written on the page, such as "Align all figure columns right," but alignment symbols may also be drawn on the copy. To indicate vertical alignment, for example, a pair of vertical parallel lines is drawn against the sides of the two or more lines of copy that should be aligned.

Diacritics and other special symbols Authors frequently fail to add diacritical marks to foreign words because their keyboards do not include these marks. The editor must add these by hand, after checking the spelling of the word in an appropriate dictionary. It also helps the compositor either to write and circle in the margin, next to the line, the name of the diacritic or to rewrite the word in the margin with diacritics made obvious. Some commonly used diacritics and their names are listed here:

´	(é)	acute accent	˘	(ŭ)	breve
`	(è)	grave accent	ˇ	(č)	haček
^	(ô)	circumflex	¨	(oö)	diaeresis
~	(ñ)	tilde	˛	(ç)	cedilla
¯	(ō)	macron			

Typists often use the typewriter's apostrophe to indicate a number of similar symbols that are not found on the keyboard but that are distinguished in a printer's type font: the prime sign, the minute sign, and the symbols for feet, as well as acute and grave accents. The editor names the symbol in the margin, circles the notation, and draws an arrow to the copy to identify it for the compositor.

Subscript and superscript The editor places a caret over any subscripts in handwritten copy or copy that is hard to read. An inverted caret is placed below any superscript (as footnote numbers) in handwritten copy or other copy where these marks might be misread.

Indention and paragraphs Manuscript copy is marked to tell the compositor whether lines should be set flush left, indented on the left, or indented on both sides, as well as the specific amount of indention measured in ems. Most publications contain paragraphs whose first lines are indented and whose remaining lines are flush left. Some kinds of copy require reverse, or hanging, indention, in which the first line of a paragraph is flush left and the others indented. These flush-and-hang paragraphs are used in bibliographies and other alphabetical listings where it is important for the first word of the paragraph to catch the reader's eye.

When paragraph divisions are clear in the manuscript, the editor does not need to mark them further. However, when the starting point of a paragraph is obscure, or when the editor wants to put a new paragraph break in mid-line, the paragraph symbol should be added next to the first word of the new paragraph. If the paragraph break does not occur at the beginning of the line, a line-break symbol, illustrated below, may be inserted to mark the point where the new paragraph begins. The line-break symbol is also used frequently in math copy. Any time that this sign is used, the editor must see to it that the compositor understands—either from the general design specifications or from a particular instruction—whether the new line will be indented or flush left.

Last line of one paragraph. ⌐ The first line of the next.

If an editor wants to change an indented paragraph so that it is set against the left margin, as often occurs with new paragraphs that follow an illustration or other display, the move-left symbol is used. For added clarity, the symbol can be reinforced with the abbreviation *fl l* circled in the margin.

When the editor needs to mark a specific amount of indention for an item not covered by the general design specification, *em quads* are used. These symbols are placed just to the side of the line to be indented; they tell the typesetter how much indention to use. The em quad, a small square, indicates one em of space. (An em space, like an em dash, is approximately as wide as a capital M in type.) A number written within the quad indicates a multiple of an em space, so that an em quad enclosing the numeral 3 tells the compositor to set a three-em space. Alternatively, the editor may draw in multiple quads, one for each space requested. Spaces larger than two ems are usually measured in picas but may also be measured in ems.

An en space, which is half as wide as an em space, is symbolized by an em quad with a diagonal line drawn through it and is used mainly to indicate the amount of space between the period that follows a numeral and the first item on a numbered list. It is rarely used to indicate indention.

Em and en quads are usually drawn only at the beginning of an indented section to familiarize the compositor with the desired format. They do not need to be used opposite every indented line.

Special Text Elements

In addition to the running text of which most prose pieces are principally composed, there are special text elements with which authors and editors must be concerned. This section describes marking and styling considerations related to cross-references, lists, headings, notes, and bibliographies.

Cross-References

While reading the manuscript, the copy editor inserts needed cross-references where there are none and checks those already in the manuscript. Cross-references should be rephrased if necessary so that they are accurate and stylistically consistent. Styling directions should be included on the editor's style sheet, and they should address such matters as whether the words *chapter* and *section* are capitalized and whether the word *page* is abbreviated. Page numbers are always given in digits, while chapter and section numbers may be spelled out if desired.

Where the author refers to another page of the manuscript, the editor changes the number to 000 so that the manuscript page number will not be typeset. 000 alerts the proofreader, editor, and compositor to the fact that, later on when pages are made up, the appropriate cross-reference page numbers will have to be added. The editor may also wish to write *X-R* in the margin (circled, of course) to ensure that every 000 is found and changed to the proper page number. In addition, the original manuscript page number is usually written in the margin of the copy to facilitate finding the new position of the original cross-reference. The proofreader is responsible for carrying all of these notations to the margins of the galleys.

To save time and expense, the editor may simply choose to phrase all cross-references so that they refer to chapter or section numbers or titles, thus avoiding any mention of page numbers.

Lists

If the copy contains more than one list, specifications need to be established about how to set up lists so that they are styled consistently. The specifications would state whether lists are to be indented like paragraphs or flush left, and they would specify how much space to put around the introductory letters or numbers and above and below lists, how to indent runover lines, and whether extra leading is required between the items on a list when some of the items have runover lines. Lists may be numbered or unnumbered; unnumbered items may or may not be flagged by bullets. If the specifications supplying this detailed information have already been provided, the copy editor needs only to note in the margin, "Set as list; see specs."

The editor checks all lists for alignment. Columns of numbers should align at the right and along periods or decimal points. If a numbered list contains more than nine items, the editor writes an instruction in the margin, "Clear for ten." This tells the compositor not to set numbers one through nine flush left but to leave enough space so that number nine will align over the zero in ten.

Lists with runover lines should be marked to look as even as possible when set. Runovers are usually set flush below the first word of the item, not below the number or letter that identifies the item.

Headings

Any long piece of nonfiction benefits from the addition of headings to mark the major divisions. Headings help the reader understand the material, and they facilitate finding certain passages.

The editor examines each heading to see that it accurately and concisely summarizes the material below it. The editor also compares headings and subheadings, making sure that typeface, style, and position are consistent for all headings and subheadings of the same level throughout the book.

Headings are usually nouns or concise noun phrases, though newspaper and magazine headings, which often describe actions, may use a phrase or sentence with a verb as a heading.

Notes

For the formatting of notes and reference lists, the editor should be familiar with the various stylings that are discussed in Chapter 7, "Notes and Bibliographies," and should recognize the styling that the author has chosen.

A major decision is whether notes will be set as footnotes or endnotes. If the author has typed reference information as footnotes, and endnotes are required by the publisher, the editor must (1) mark in the margin next to each footnote or set of footnotes: "Set all footnotes together at end of chapter" (or article or book), (2) renumber the notes if necessary so that all the notes in a chapter are numbered sequentially, and (3) at the end of the chapter (or article or book) create a new head called Notes and write the notation, "Insert footnotes 1–00 here."

Likewise, if the author has typed endnotes when footnotes are desired instead, the editor (1) writes a notation such as the following in the margins of the manuscript pages at the points where each note corresponds to the text: "Footnote 7 here from msp 90," and (2) in the margin opposite each endnote writes the appropriate manuscript page number, as "Take footnote 7 to msp 12."

Part of the editor's job is to consider the appropriateness of the footnotes and to transfer material from the notes to the text or vice versa where needed. The author's permission is desirable for this type of change. Finally, the editor checks the position of all reference symbols in the text and removes them from improper positions such as chapter titles. Footnote symbols in mathematical copy and numerical tables are examined closely, because a footnote number or letter in those contexts might be mistaken for an exponent or other symbol. A different system may be used to denote the references, as described on page 211 in Chapter 7, "Notes and Bibliographies." Alternatively, the symbol may be moved to a word instead of a figure.

Bibliography

In copyediting bibliographies and other reference lists, the editor will have to (1) check alphabetical order, (2) compare footnote and bibliography references to see that they correspond, and (3) add entries that the author has overlooked, especially those mentioned in the text. In general, the editor sees to it that the copy consistently follows whatever styling the author has chosen.

Some of the minor changes that an editor is allowed to make in the content of the bibliography are the following:

1. Publishers' names are frequently shortened in bibliographies. For example, instead of *John Wiley and Sons,* the short form *Wiley* or *John Wiley* may be used if it is used consistently.

2. Books are often published under the old name of the current publisher, and mergers sometimes affect the publisher currently handling a book published under an obsolete name. It may be helpful to the reader to use the current publisher's name, since one purpose of a bibliography is to direct readers to sources they might wish to search.

3. Long journal titles may be subjected to a standard abbreviated form. Such forms are commonly used in scientific reference lists.

4. As described on page 227 in Chapter 7, "Notes and Bibliographies," a long dash replaces the name of an author used more than once in a bibliography. This dash is usually a three-em dash and is followed by a period and a space.

Sometimes an editor is required to style an annotated bibliography. The descriptive part of this kind of bibliography is sometimes set in italic type or in smaller type. It may be run in with the entry or set as a separate paragraph. As a separate paragraph, it may be set with all lines equally indented, or it may use the hanging-indention format, with its first line indented and all runover lines further indented.

Galley Proofs

A manuscript that is sent to the typesetter usually returns to the publisher in the form of *galley proofs* or *galleys*—long sheets of paper on which are printed text and headings set the full width of the type page. This stage of production is sometimes omitted. For example, a neatly typewritten manuscript with a very simple format may be returned to the publisher as page proofs without the intermediary galleys. In most cases, however, galley proofs provide a useful transitional tool.

Not all copy is included on the galleys. Page numbers, of course, cannot be set until later. Illustrations are handled separately. Other types of copy such as footnotes, tables, and sometimes running heads are set on the galleys, but not necessarily in proper position; their final position will be known only when the material is fitted onto pages. Footnotes may be set together on a separate galley, or they may be set directly below the line which contains the footnote reference symbol and separated from the

```
3        06-06-91 14:49:08   PM  885$$$$$85
4    Merriam-Webster Inc.   Trade Paperback Writer's Guide
5    —Lisa—O.K.
6
```

7   Chapter 9

8 Copyediting and
9 Proofreading
10

11 CONTENTS
12

18
19
20 This chapter describes the basic editorial steps that writers, edi-
21 tors, and proofreaders go through in order to produce accurate,
22 readable, and attractive written or printed materials. For people
23 involved with writing that is not intended for publication, some of
24 the steps described in this chapter, such as those having to do with
25 giving instructions to typesetters and handling page proofs, will
26 not be necessary. However, for anyone who is writing for publica-
27 tion, this chapter should serve as a basic introduction to the range
28 of activities often referred to as *editorial production*, or simply *pro-*
29 *duction.*
30   The term *production* refers to the processes by which a publi-
31 cation is produced: from the completion of the manuscript to the
32 making of the plates from which the pages will be printed. During
33 production, the author's copy is edited to increase its accuracy and
34 readability and is marked up in such a way that it can be readily
35 typeset. The typeset copy is proofread, fitted on pages, and repro-
36 duced as film negatives. The negatives are used to make the print-
37 ing plates, which lay down ink on paper on a printing press.
38   Depending upon the nature of the project, editorial produc-
39 tion may be handled by a large staff of specialists or by a single
40 person. In this chapter, the tasks are somewhat arbitrarily allo-
41 cated to an *editor* (who has overall charge of getting the author's
42 manuscript into copy that the typesetter can interpret) and a *proof-*
43 *reader* (who checks any newly typeset proofs against the copy from
44 which type was set).
45   To an ever-increasing degree, many of the production steps
46 described in this chapter are handled electronically, through the
47 use of word processors, desktop-publishing systems, and compu-
48 terized typesetting systems. The range of possibilities that an au-
49 thor or editor may encounter in terms of kinds of equipment,
50 combinations of equipment, and capabilities of equipment is virtu-
51 ally unlimited. Rather than try to describe a range of possibilities
52 that is subject to constant change, this chapter focuses on describ-
53 ing the basic steps that are used in the handling of paper copy.
54 The point is that, with very few exceptions, no piece of electronic
55 equipment can eliminate any of these steps; rather this equipment
56 simply does electronically, and hence faster and usually more eas-
57 ily, what was once done manually. Therefore, the first step in un-
58 derstanding electronic editing is to understand the basic steps that
59 have traditionally been part of the production process.

60
61 ## Manuscript Format
62
63 Manuscript preparation begins when the author's manuscript is
64 typed. Copy should be typed clearly, without strikeovers, on good-
65 quality paper that can be handled frequently without damage.
66 Erasable paper is not recommended, because it smudges when
67 handled. Copy should be typed on one side of the page only, be-
68 cause inserts written on the back of the page are easily over-
69 looked.

Figure 9.3.   A galley proof

text by lines of space. Indexes are not ordinarily set in galleys at all. To save time, an index is typeset directly in page format.

Galleys are usually returned in groupings so that the publisher can proofread the galleys while the compositor continues to typeset another grouping. The compositor sends two copies or more of each galley proof. One of these is designated the master proof or master galley; that is the one that will be returned to the compositor with all corrections neatly marked on it. Another may be sent to the author for final corrections, or it may be handled by the production department at the publisher's office. A division of labor there might include a proofreader who compares the galley with the manuscript and an editor who measures the typeset material to see if it is running long or short or who marks the galley to show where footnotes should be positioned. Whenever more than one person works on a galley proof, it is essential that each use an identifiable color of pencil or pen. And the editor or proofreader must take special care, before the master proof is returned to the compositor, that all revisions and instructions from all people who handled the proofs are properly transferred, or *carried,* to the master galley.

Like any proofs, galleys will have physical flaws, such as light or blurry type, which should not concern the proofreader. Most galley proofs that are received in publisher's offices today are not real proofs but photocopies of the compositor's proofs, and the photocopy process may further distort the printed image.

At the top of each galley will be a series of identification codes which should not concern the proofreader. The galley number, however, will be included in the codes, and the proofreader may need to refer to this number when communicating with the compositor or the editor.

Revisions at this stage of production should be kept to a minimum because it is expensive to make changes in galleys. The resetting of lines in most composition systems means that the new line must be recomposed and spliced in with the original typesetting from which the galley proof was made. For this reason, a proofreader is usually told to "read proof" only—that is, to compare the galley proof with the manuscript copy and mark the necessary corrections on the galley, and not to make other revisions. Any other revisions that are considered necessary by the editor or proofreader at this stage are usually made in such a way as to minimize the number of lines that have to be reset and thus to minimize the cost of revision.

Revisions by the Author

A set of galley proofs is often sent to the author along with a request to read it through and verify such things as the spellings of proper names, the accuracy of mathematical material and tabular data, content of bibliography and footnote items—things easily missed by a copy editor. The edited manuscript should be included with the galleys to make comparison and checking easier. Authors should always be asked to keep corrections to a minimum; they should be advised how expensive revisions are, especially if the cost of revision will be charged to them.

Galleys are usually sent to the author after the proofreader has read proof. The proofreader's corrections are carried to the author's copy so that the author can concentrate on substantive matters. It is not advisable to have authors write directly on the master galley; their comments may run long and take up margin space that is needed for instructions to the typesetter. It is better for the editor to carry the author's corrections to the master galley in a form that the typesetter can quickly comprehend.

The proofreader's queries to the author are usually written in the margin, preceded by *Au:* or *Qu:* or a question mark, and circled. The common procedure is for the proofreader to make the correction, then ask for confirmation in the margin, as *Au: ?* The author is then instructed in a cover letter to cross out the question mark (or the word *query*) and let the correction stand if it is acceptable. If the proofreader's suggested change is not acceptable, the author is instructed to cross out the whole query, including the suggested change, in the margin and then to add either "OK as set" or an alternate revision. The abbreviation *OK* by itself should be avoided in the query because the typesetter may not be able to figure whether it is the original or the revision that is "OK."

The author should be instructed not to erase any marks that are written on the galleys. A large X drawn over a notation will indicate that it is unacceptable without obliterating it.

Proofreading the Galley

The main job of a proofreader is to *read proof,* or to compare copy with proof, by reading small sections of copy first, then the corresponding sections of proof, character by character, and to mark the galley proofs so that they follow the copy and its typesetting instructions. A small ruler or an index card can be used to help the eyes focus on one line at a time. In a second reading, the proofreader concentrates on the sense of the material and prepares queries for the author or editor. Proofreaders do not show concern for literary style. Their job is to correct typographical errors, correct obvious errors that were missed by the copy editor, and to point out to the editor or author any other problems in the galley proofs.

It used to be that proofreaders spent time examining lines for evidence of broken letters or letters set slightly out of alignment. With today's typesetting equipment, however, these printing errors are rare.

The correction marks used by proofreaders are listed on page 281. Copy editors use these symbols as well, but there is a major difference in how the symbols are used. Unlike the copy editor's revisions, all proofreader's marks occur in the margin opposite the affected line, with only a corresponding caret or deletion line in the text to show where the correction should be made. When two or more corrections occur in a line, diagonal marks are used to separate the symbols in the margin. The symbols are written in the same sequence as the errors in the line, reading from left to right. Proofreading symbols are usually written in the right margin, but the left margin may also be used. Sometimes there is not enough room in the margin to indicate a large number of revisions; in these cases the symbols or instructions may be written elsewhere in the margin, but a guideline must be drawn that clearly connects the symbol or instruction with the point in the line that it refers to.

One reason for placing all proofreading marks in the margin is that typeset lines are single-spaced, and there is simply no room for the interlinear marks used by copy editors. But the main reason is that compositors look for proofreading marks only in the margins. When they set text from manuscript copy, they read everything in sequence and can easily follow revisions written above the line. But when they revise a galley that has already been typeset, there is no need for them to reread the whole text, and if a proofreader inserts a mark in the text without a corresponding symbol in the margin to alert the typesetter, that mark may not even be seen.

Proofreaders' Marks

The following paragraphs describe the use of the marks listed on page 281.

Delete Cross out the line or part of the line (use a diagonal to delete a single letter), then place a delete sign in the margin. Place the delete sign within a close-up sign only when letters are deleted from the middle of a word. The delete sign is not used when a substitution is written in the margin to replace a part of the line that has been crossed out. A large section of type such as a paragraph may be deleted neatly by outlining the whole section, placing large X's over the text, and writing a single delete sign in the margin.

Close-up sign Place this sign at the appropriate point in the text and repeat it in the margin.

Caret Use this to point out the exact place in the text where something needs to be inserted. Write the insert in the margin.

Space sign Place a vertical mark on the line to show where space should be added. Write the space symbol in the margin. This symbol may also be used to instruct the typesetter to add space between lines, or as shorthand for the word *space* in any instructions to the typesetter.

Equal space Place carets or vertical lines in the text and the notation *eq.* # in the margin to ask for even spacing between words in a particular line.

Transpose Use the curving line within the lines of text, and add the circled notation *tr* in the margin.

Move left or move right Place the appropriate mark in the text and in the margin in order to instruct the typesetter to move a section of type left or right.

Center Enclose the word or phrase to be centered within a move-right mark on the left and a move-left mark on the right. Repeat the symbol in the margin or write and circle "center." Sometimes the instruction needs to be more specific, as "Center below heading of column 1."

Stet Place dots below the inadvertently deleted material in the text and write *stet* in the margin. Or, if deleting a proofreading notation in the margin, simply cross out the notation.

Align Use in the text to show where type should be aligned. In the margin, repeat the symbol, write the word, "align," or give specific instructions about what is to be aligned, such as "Align column heads."

Imperfect character Use in the margin to denote a broken or otherwise imperfectly printed character; circle the character in the line.

Indent or insert one em space Draw the symbol in the margin. In the text, repeat the symbol or use a caret to show its location on the line. To indicate more than one em of indention, insert the number 2, 3, and so on within the symbol, or repeat the symbol for each em of indention that is being requested.

Paragraph Use in the margin to indicate a new paragraph. In the text, use either this symbol or a line-break symbol illustrated on page 271 to mark where the line should be broken to form a new paragraph. To join paragraphs that are separated in the galley, write *run in* or *no* ¶ in the margin and connect the separated paragraphs with a line.

PROOFREADERS' MARKS

ℰ or ﻭ or ꟼ   delete; take it out

⌒   close up; print as one word

ℬ̶   delete and close up

∧ or › or ⋋   caret; insert here ⟨something

insert a space

eq#   space evenly where indicated

stet   let marked text stand as set

tr   transpose; change order the

[⌊   set farther to the left

⌉ set⌊   farther to the right

=   straighten alignment

‖ ‖   straighten or align

✗   imperfect or broken character

□   indent or insert em quad space

¶   begin a new paragraph

ⓢⓟ   spell out ⟨set 5 lbs. as five pounds⟩

cap   set in capitals ⟨CAPITALS⟩

sm cap or *s.c.*   set in small capitals ⟨SMALL CAPITALS⟩

lc   set in lowercase ⟨lowercase⟩

ital   set in italic ⟨*italic*⟩

rom   set in roman ⟨roman⟩

bf   set in boldface ⟨**boldface**⟩

= or –/ or ⌢ or /ᴴ/ hyphen

$\frac{|}{N}$ or *en* or /N̲/ en dash ⟨1965–72⟩

$\frac{|}{M}$ or *em* or /M̲/ em — or long — dash

∨   superscript or superior ⟨2 as in πr^2⟩

∧   subscript or inferior ⟨2 as in H_2O⟩

⌄̂ or ⤬   centered ⟨· for a centered dot in $p \cdot q$⟩

⌐ comma

ᴠ apostrophe

⊙ period

; or ;/ semicolon

: or ⊙: colon

⌄⌄ or ᴠᴠ quotation marks

(/) parentheses

[/] brackets

Spell out Circle the typeset number or abbreviation and write this symbol in the margin. If there is any ambiguity, however, write the spelled-out form in the margin instead.

Capital letter Draw three lines under lowercase type in the text; write *cap* or *uc* in the margin.

Small capitals Draw two lines under lowercase or capitalized type in the text; write and circle *sm cap* or *sc* in the margin.

Lowercase Draw a diagonal line through the capital letter in the text; write and circle *lc* in the margin.

Italic Draw one line below that part of the text to be italicized; write and circle *ital* in the margin.

Roman Underline or circle the affected part of the text; write and circle *rom* in the margin.

Boldface Draw a wavy line below the affected text; write and circle *bf* in the margin.

Hyphen Use any of these symbols in the margin; place a caret in the text to show where the hyphen should be inserted.

En dash Use any of these symbols in the margin; place a caret in the text to show where the dash should be inserted.

Em dash Use any of these symbols in the margin; place a caret in the text to show where the dash should be inserted.

Superscript Use this symbol below a number in the margin to ask for the addition of or a change to a superior or superscript number; circle the affected number in the text. Also, use below quotation marks and apostrophes that are written in the margin.

Subscript Use this symbol above a number in the margin to ask for a change to an inferior or subscript number; circle the affected number in the text. Also, use above commas that are written in the margin.

Centered dot Draw the symbol with dot in the margin and draw the symbol above and below the dot in the text.

Change or add punctuation To change punctuation, draw a vertical line through incorrect punctuation and write the correct punctuation in the margin. To add punctuation, draw a caret at the point in the line where the punctuation should be inserted and write the punctuation in the margin. Use the symbols for punctuation marks listed in the table.

Further Preparation of Galley Proofs

In addition to reading proof from manuscript copy, the proof-reader attends to other matters while handling galley proofs. One of these jobs is seeing that the galley conforms to the design speci-fications that accompanied the manuscript. Another is preparing the galley type for positioning on pages.

The proofreader measures the width of the type page; the amount of spacing around headings, equations, enumerations, and other types of displayed copy; and the amount of indention for extracts, to ensure that design specifications were followed. After taking initial measurements on the first galleys, the proof-reader merely checks to see that the spacing around similar items matches.

Each new typographic change is also checked for conformity to specifications. After the initial measurements, similar items such as headings are simply compared to ensure that the same size and face of type was used.

Word division For the sake of consistency, a single dictionary should be chosen and consulted for the division of words at the end of a line. Specialized dictionaries should be consulted for the division of proper names. The proofreader corrects any faultily divided words, usually by inserting a line-break symbol within the word and repeating the symbol or writing "break as shown" in the margin.

Paragraph endings Printing conventions require that the last word of a paragraph not be divided at the end of the line. Also, a very short word should not occur by itself on the last line of a para-graph. To correct these visual problems an editor may be called upon to insert a word or two in the next-to-last line (preferably no earlier in the paragraph, because the fewer the number of lines revised, the less expensive the revision) so that it runs over to the last line. Or the proofreader may insert a line-break symbol that forces a word or part of a word to run over.

The last line of a paragraph should have at least an em of space following the last word to avoid the appearance of having been left unjustified in error. If the space is less than an em quad, the proofreader uses the "set farther right" symbol and instructs the typesetter to justify the line.

Headings The proofreader sees that runover lines in a heading break at a logical point. Words within headings should not be di-vided at all. Headings should also be checked for visual appeal. Those that are set all in capitals or in very large type, for example, may require the insertion of extra space between words.

Footnotes, tables, and illustrations If the specifications indicate that notes are to be set as footnotes and not as endnotes, the galleys should be checked to see where the footnotes are located. The proofreader should make a note in the margin of the galley next to the line where a footnote reference occurs, such as "Ftn 2 here." Similarly, notations in the margins of the manuscript that concern tables and illustrations are carried to the galley margins. The typesetter will see these instructions on the galleys—"Insert Fig. 3 about here" or "Ftn 2 here"—and will plan the page formats accordingly.

Lists Lists consisting of brief items that have been set in a single column but that should appear as two or more columns on pages are identified in the margin with a notation such as "set two columns in pages."

Lengthy insertions Occasionally the proofreader will have to insert lengthy material that the compositor has inadvertently omitted or will have to carry to the master proof some addition from the author. Lengthy material that does not fit at the bottom of the galley should be typed on a separate page and identified as "Insert A," "Insert B," and so on. The precise point of insertion should be marked with a caret on the galley and a note circled in the margin, such as "Insert A attached; run in." The page should be stapled or taped to the *front* of the galley so that the compositor will readily find it.

Printer's errors Frequently, but not always, the proofreader is asked to distinguish between typographic errors (typos or *printer's errors*) which result from misreading of copy or incorrect keyboarding, and *author's* (or editor's) *alterations*. This extra job requires that an additional symbol—*PE* or *AA*—be written and circled next to each correction in the galley margins. The distinction between the two types of corrections is made only for cost-allocation purposes. Examples of printer's errors include misspelled words, omission or repetition of words or of whole lines, setting the wrong type, and errors in spacing and alignment. The proofreader should never label an error with a *PE*, however, unless the copy or the instructions were absolutely clear. The typesetter may certainly be excused for misspelling a sloppily written insert that is hard to read. Author's alterations are labeled *AA* only if they are made after the copy is set in type, and the cost of making these revisions is charged to the author.

Running heads If running heads were not included with the manuscript copy and thus are not set on the galleys, the editor prepares them at this point. These heads are written on the galleys or in a cover letter to the typesetter with the instruction to "set running heads."

Carrying instructions All instructions from the editor to the type-setter, such as those concerning the position of tables and footnotes, must be carried from the manuscript to the galley proofs as long as those instructions are still pertinent. Other instructions that should be carried to galley proofs include the manuscript page on which a cross-reference can be found when the galley refers the reader to "page 000."

The editor or the proofreader at this stage also gives the typesetter instructions regarding the placement of type on the page. For example, the typesetter could be told to begin each chapter on a recto, or right-hand page; in this case, the phrase "recto page" would be written in the margin next to the chapter title. Or the typesetter could be instructed to begin a certain section on a "new page."

Estimation of length While galley proofs are in hand, the editor may wish to confirm the estimated length of the book by counting the number of pages that can be obtained from the type on the galley proofs. If the length greatly exceeds the limit, the editor may approve the deletion of whole paragraphs, while it is still relatively inexpensive.

Revised galleys Sometimes the galleys are so heavily corrected that it is necessary to request revised galleys, sometimes called *revises,* from the compositor. To reduce costs, only those galleys that are marked up heavily are sent back for revision. The purpose of this extra step is to provide a legible galley from which the compositor can make up pages, and thereby reduce the number of errors likely to be made on the page proofs.

Page Proofs

In the next stage of production, the compositor makes the revisions requested by the publisher. Then, the revised text is organized into page proofs, or *pages,* which show for the first time just what each page of the book will look like. Page proofs are usually printed on large pieces of paper that show a set of two facing pages just as the reader will see them, only with larger margins. The proofreader at this point is not concerned with such imperfections as fuzzy type or lines printed on a slant. The proofs are made cheaply, and what is sent back to the publisher is often only a photocopy of a proof.

Proofing the Pages

Again the proofreader reads proof—this time comparing the marked-up galleys and the layout instructions with the new page proofs—and ensures that all instructions to the compositor have been carried out. If so instructed, the proofreader again adds *PE* and *AA* symbols where appropriate.

Proofreading pages is essentially the same process as proof-reading galleys, but it goes faster. First, there are likely to be many fewer errors on the pages, since the original errors were presumably corrected. Second, the proofreader does not need to reread sections of material for which no corrections were requested; one can assume that this part of the typesetting was left intact. But wherever corrections were asked for on the galley, the proofreader must reread the whole paragraph in which the error occurred, paying special attention not only to the line where the correction was made but to all subsequent lines of that paragraph if they have been altered by the correction. This is essential because often, in the process of correcting one error, the typesetter introduces a different one. Even though the compositor's proofreader will already have read proof on these pages, the publisher's proofreader should carefully double-check any material that might have been reset.

Editorial Checklist

In addition to reading proof, the proofreader or editor makes a series of final checks, often using a checklist to make sure that every job is done on every page. Most editors find that the most efficient way to handle the numerous final checks is to do each job separately. The checks include making sure that all instructions to the compositor have been carried out; that page numbers (also called *folios*) are correct, as are all other sequences of numbered items in the book; that running heads are correct; that folios and running heads do not appear on any page (such as the first page of a chapter) where the specifications call for them to be omitted; and that all items on each page are properly aligned. Some additional checks that an editor should make are discussed below.

1. Look for cross-references within the text and follow up on each one to see that it refers the reader to the correct place. If the cross-reference is to the title of a chapter, be sure the wording of the title matches that of the cross-reference. If the cross-reference is to a page number which until now has probably been recorded as "page 000," insert the correct page number. If you do not know how to find the pertinent page, look at the original manuscript, where the author or editor will have written the original page number in the margin. If the cross-reference is to a passage that has not yet been set in

pages, you will have to make a note in the margin to insert the reference later. In these situations, however, it is better to avoid referring to a specific page number and instead refer to a chapter or section title. If the book has a table of contents, the page numbers are inserted at this stage.

2. Check the sequence of footnote and endnote numbers, letters, or other symbols and compare each text reference carefully with its corresponding note to be sure that they match. Footnotes must begin on the same page with their corresponding text reference symbols; however, a long footnote may run over to the following page if necessary, as long as two lines or more of the note are carried over. It is also a good idea to break such a note in mid-sentence so the reader will know that it continues on the next page.

3. Check the footnotes for conformity to design specifications and for consistency of form, including size and face of type, indention, measure of space above and below each note, etc. If necessary to save space, more than one short footnote may be set on one line. Footnotes are separated from the text either by extra space or by a short rule extending from the left margin. A footnote on the last page of a chapter is usually separated from the text in the same way. It is usually set just below the last line of text, not at the bottom of the page.

4. Look at each set of facing pages as a whole to make sure that they balance. The last line of type must align across the bottom of the two pages. If the lines are not quite in alignment, draw the double horizontal lines to indicate horizontal alignment and write in the margin, "Align bottom of page."

5. Examine the bottom of each page. For reasons of appearance, a heading should never be placed at the bottom of a page without at least two lines of text below it. To fix a mispositioned head, use the techniques described below either to add lines below the head and cut some above, or to add lines above the head in order to move it to the next page. (Remember, however, that to save costs corrections should be limited to as few pages as possible.)

6. Examine the top of each page and make revisions as necessary to avoid *widows,* which are partial lines of text (as at the end of a paragraph) that are set as the first line of a page. Either carry over one or two lines from the preceding page (which will require additional fitting on that page) or add words to the widow to fill it out. Also to be avoided at the top of a page are any short indented items, as an item on a list, by itself; a

single line of text, even a full line, above a heading; and any mark that indicates repetition, such as a ditto mark in a column or a dash at the beginning of a bibliography entry.

7. If passages of poetry are broken at the bottom of a page, try to break the lines between stanzas, or at least between sets of rhymed lines.

8. Examine the last page of all chapters. Unless new chapters are supposed to begin on the same page as the previous one, the last page should contain at least five lines of text in order to avoid an excessive amount of white space on the page.

Fitting Pages

It is expensive to make corrections on page proofs, so when changes must be made—either to correct a typographical error or for esthetic reasons or when a previous correction results in a line gained or lost—these revisions are made in places and in ways that will cause the least number of lines to be reset. As much as possible, every line added to a page must be compensated for in some way on that page—either by deleting another line or by reducing the amount of space somewhere, as above or below a table. Likewise, every line deleted from a page must be compensated for—either by adding a line of text or a line of space elsewhere on the page.

It is acceptable to print an extra line on a page, or to delete a line, thus reducing or enlarging the size of the bottom margin on that page, but each change of this sort alters the alignment of the two facing pages. Therefore, a change must be made on the opposite page. A line added to one page must be balanced by a line added to its facing page; a line cut from one must be matched by a line cut from the other.

Whenever the editor chooses to alter the bottom margin the compositor should be notified that the change is intentional. A notation at the bottom such as "1 li short OK" will suffice.

Compositors also make adjustments in an effort to make the material fit the page. Often they automatically add or delete space if they can do so without making it too obvious. But usually, to avoid widows or badly positioned headings, the compositor will deliberately set a page long (with too many lines) or short (with too few lines) and stamp *long* or *short* at the bottom of the page proof. This tells the editor to fix the situation.

The least costly way to gain lines is to extend the last line of a paragraph over to a new line by adding words (or sometimes extra word space). These additions should be made as near as possible to the end of the paragraph, because adding words in this position results in the need to reset only the last two or three lines of a paragraph rather than the whole paragraph. Similarly, when lines must be lost, the cuts should be made near the end of a paragraph.

Final Proofs

One last set of proofs comes to the publisher. In most cases, these final proofs are film proofs, also known as *blues, Ozalids, Dyluxes,* etc. They are made from the film, usually a negative, that the compositor will send to the printing plant to make printing plates from. In some cases, however, the people doing the printing make the negatives. In this case, the final proofs that the compositor provides are reproduction proofs, called *repros*. These are high-quality, camera-ready positive prints of the page, and it is from these that the negatives are made. Either kind of proof coming to the publisher should be examined carefully for scratches, stray marks, or partial opaquing of letters in the text. Repros should be handled with great care; any stray mark or scratch that gets on a repro has to be repaired, or there is a good chance that it will show up on the printed page.

Index